The Principle of Harm-Minimisation

A Naturalistic Metaphysic of Morality

by

PETER R. HOTCHIN

Contents

Preface

The world we inhabit is complex, not least because of our being part of it. Our various roles and interactions make matters very involved indeed. We may sometimes wish that things were simpler than they are, but the fact that they are not, and possibly never will be for as long as we are around, helps make life interesting. No doubt part of the complexity can be attributed to the differences in the beliefs that people harbour with respect to moral right and wrong; but that may be something we would be better off without. Our beliefs influence our interactions with others, often producing effects that would generally be described as ill-effects. If a way could be found of consolidating our beliefs around a universally acceptable moral principle our well-being and prospects for survival as a species could be enhanced. Presumably, these would be desirable outcomes.

A principle that would seem worthy of universalisation is the subject of this book. It will be referred to as The Principle of Harm-Minimisation, or PHM for short. In fact, if what I have to say is found to be reasonable, it might be concluded that universalisation of the principle has already proceeded a fair way down the track. For the PHM will be found to sit comfortably beside the quality of humaneness, and part of my argument is that humankind is generally more disposed to humaneness than towards its opposite. Implicitly or otherwise, therefore, the PHM may well have already found widespread acceptance, even adherence. But it will nevertheless be useful to state explicitly what it involves: even if only to promote its further adoption, but also to strengthen our grasp of what it entails. Universal adherence to a particular moral principle would admittedly result in our interactions being less varied in kind, perhaps with a commensurate loss of interest, at least for some people. For one thing, suffering in the world could diminish, leaving whatever inclination we might feel towards *schadenfreude*, or malice, with fewer objects to latch onto. But that would be no great loss.

Part I of the book dissects the phraseology employed in the principle, explaining and discussing its various elements. Part II examines the naturalistic ground in which the principle is embedded. That ground consists of *order*: the PHM can be looked upon as the product of an order-based theory of morality, a theory that was the subject of my PhD thesis with Deakin University, Australia. Much of Part II is based on the thesis.

The grounding of morality in order will occur via the concept of *needs*. Order and needs are pivotal features of life and experience. Moreover, the features to which they refer are arguably closely related to one another, since orderliness within our lives depends on the satisfaction of certain needs. Sufficient food and shelter enable us to maintain the orderliness of our bodies; esteem and love help to keep our social and psychological lives on an even keel; and intellectual and aesthetic experiences are important sources of understanding and accomplishment, both of which contribute to psychological balance.

I will argue that the two concepts, order and needs, are intimately connected to something else that is central to human life, namely morality. A fairly extensive body of work already exists on the relationship between needs and morality. I will propose that all of our basic needs can be traced to the need for a particular kind of order, thereby establishing a link between morality and order. The link will be referred to as *homosapient order*; as the term suggests, it is a kind of order that pertains exclusively to our species, *Homo sapiens*.

PART I:
Morality and the
Minimisation of Harm

Chapter 1: The Principle of Harm-Minimisation

There is no difference between injuring people and wronging them (Socrates).[1]

Moral Right and Wrong

Around the middle of the twentieth century the philosopher Elizabeth Anscombe (1919-2001) had become critical of ethical doctrines that have no reference to the good. Anscombe was concerned that the notions of moral duty and obligation had been rendered anchorless because of an attenuation in our understanding of what the good consists in. Bereft of an anchor, ethical doctrines had, in her view, lost contact with human needs and desires. Anscombe's concern was that of someone from a major school of thought known as 'virtue ethics', and her criticism was aimed at another major school of thought, that of 'deontology'. I will not have very much to say about the various streams of moral theory (there are a great many of them), but a few words on the two that have been mentioned may provide the reader with a point of reference for some of the ideas I will be employing.

Very broadly, adherents of virtue ethics prioritise the good, while deontologists focus more on the right; i.e. being good on the one hand, doing what is right on the other hand. Virtue ethics has ancient roots, for instance in Aristotle's (384-322 BCE) *Nicomachean Ethics*, which begins with the words 'Every art and every inquiry, and similarly every action and pursuit, is thought to aim at some good; and for this reason the good has been rightly declared to be that at which things aim.'[2] Good action is virtuous action. Deontology is more recent, having been initiated by the philosopher Immanuel Kant (1724-1804), with the demand that each

---

1 Plato, *Crito,* translated by Hugh Tredennick, in Edith Hamilton and Huntington Cairns (editors), *The Collected Dialogues of Plato* (Princeton: Princeton University Press, Bollingen Series LXXI, 1999 [first published 1961]), 49c.
2 Aristotle, *Nicomachean Ethics,* translated by W. D. Ross (Chicago: The University of Chicago, Great Books of the Western World, 1952), Vol. 9, I.1, 1094a.

of us be bound by and act in accordance with an internally formulated moral law. 'Deontological' derives from the Greek for 'that which is binding'. In keeping with its binding nature, the moral law consists of a set of categorical imperatives; not conditional imperatives, but imperatives that brook no exception. 'Categorical Imperative' is a complex notion with several layers of meaning, but its dominant sense is that of a self-imposed unconditional principle of conduct, or maxim, which one believes worthy of universal adoption. In another sense, each person is to be treated as an end in him- or herself, never as a means to the achievement of someone else's ends. Additionally, the maxims adopted by any one person should be such that universal adoption of them would give rise to a kingdom of ends, where everything has either value or dignity. Anything that has a value may be replaced by something that is equivalent, and is of relative worth. By contrast, that which possesses dignity is irreplaceable—dignity is said to be of intrinsic worth.

Returning now to Anscombe's criticism, and accepting that it was justified, how might 'good'—specifically 'moral good'—be defined? Unless we know what a term means, we would be hard pressed to attain an understanding of whatever reality might lie behind it. Perhaps, then, we could simply say that moral good consists in morally relevant behaviour that is not morally wrong. Some influential thinkers have indeed adopted that approach. In her book *Natural Goodness* the philosopher Philippa Foot (1920-2010) offers a negative definition of goodness, as have many others, including the Catholic scholar St Thomas Aquinas (1225-1274) and the philosopher Benedict de Spinoza (1632-1677). A good action, so the claim goes, is one that is not in any way bad.[3] To 'abstain from wrongdoing,' Spinoza wrote, 'is to do good.'[4] While 'bad' or 'wrongdoing', and by contrast 'good', assuredly mean different things to different people, the principle involved, that of defining something by comparing it with its opposite, is sufficiently common to warrant serious consideration.

Foot had many interesting things to say about the good, all revolving around the possibility of correspondence between the work done

---

3 Philippa Foot, *Natural Goodness* (Oxford: Oxford University Press, 2010 [first published 2001]), p. 76.

4 Benedict de Spinoza, *Theological-Political Treatise*, edited by Jonathan Israel, translated by Michael Silverthorne and Jonathan Israel (Cambridge, United Kingdom: Cambridge University Press, 2014 [first published 2007]), Chapter 3 Paragraph 7.

by the concept of a good human life in determining human goodness and that done by the concept of flourishing in determining goodness in plants and non-human animals.[5] Both concepts entail 'the life form' of the relevant species,[6] and the measure of goodness for any individual will consist in the extent to which the relevant life form is instantiated. A very important aspect of the human life form is what Foot referred to as 'practical rationality,' which consists in action (i.e. practice) that is informed by reason (i.e. rationality). Some thinkers tie practical rationality to self-interest, or the satisfaction of present desires,[7] but Foot's aim was to show that it issues from an individual's natural goodness and that it is therefore good in its own right. Virtue theory is in prospect here, where virtuous action is held to be guided by that which is believed to be good. Foot regarded the good that is practical rationality as a fact of human life, and it is practical rationality that guides virtuous actions such as promising and the provision of aid. It also culminates in sociable dispositions such as neighbourliness. A virtuous person can be understood as someone who habitually acts in a morally right manner, and a vicious person as someone who habitually acts in a morally wrong manner. What anyone does habitually is largely a function of personal character, which is the major topic of Chapter 7.

Let us now see if we can get somewhere towards a definition of moral badness. If I understand her correctly, on Foot's theory it would involve action that harms someone or something by working against their natural purposes. Such action would also be contrary to life form of the human species, and the natural goods that comprise it; specifically, the action would conflict with the principles of practical rationality, and therefore be opposed to virtuousness. If the term 'natural purposes' is understood to encompass, or perhaps even consist in 'satisfaction of basic needs', then the proffered notion of moral badness would pretty well reflect the essence of the theory I am promoting. It would also address Anscombe's concern in respect of ethics having lost touch with human needs and desires. By way of endorsement, avoidance of harm-doing would tie in with the fundamental principle of bioethics, *primum non*

---

5 Foot, p. 44.
6 Foot, p. 91.
7 Foot, p. 13.

nocere ('above all, do no harm'), an idea that found expression in the Hippocratic Oath, and one that was central to a formulation of business ethics by the twentieth century management guru Peter Drucker (1909–2005). It was also regarded by the palaeontologist Stephen Jay Gould (1941-2002) as the noblest imaginable principle of morality, one that we would all do well to internalise.[8] The idea is highly practicable, for instance in the following form: Before you act, try hard to think of any possible harm that may follow upon what you are proposing to do, and proceed carefully.

It may be the case that significant harm is unavoidable, or even necessary, the latter in order to prevent even greater harm from occurring. Two factors would determine the relative magnitudes of the harm done and the harm prevented—the needs involved on both sides, and the closeness of the relationship between the agent and the person or persons who would have been exposed to harm had the agent not acted. For example, injury inflicted in the course of fighting off someone who was attacking them or their family would generally be considered morally tolerable. If the agent had time to think about the consequences in such a situation, a belief in the acceptability of inflicting harm would likely be regarded as well-grounded; perhaps even to the extent of being embedded in human nature.

Morality and Human Nature

In so far as most, if not all, mature adult human beings have a conception of right and wrong, human beings can be said to be moral beings by nature. How did it come about that we are moral beings? Confucius (551-479 BCE) had an answer:'What is God-given is what we call human nature. To fulfil the law of our human nature is what we call the moral law'.[9] That seems right to me, on the proviso that 'God' in the formula is understood to be the kind of god envisaged by Spinoza—namely, nature in its entirety. Taking nature as his starting point, Spinoza succeeded in devising a naturalistic ethics—naturalistic because of his

8 Stephen Jay Gould, *The Lying Stones of Marrakech* (London:Vintage, 2001), p. 314.
9 Lin Yutang (translator and editor), *The Wisdom of Confucius* (New York:The Modern Library, 1966 [edition first published 1938]), p.104.

non-supernaturalistic interpretation of nature, and because of the empha-sis he placed on the explanatory power of causation in his deployment of the Principle of Sufficient Reason (PSR). There are many formula-tions of the PSR, including one from the philosopher Morris R. Cohen (1880–1947) that highlights the involvement of connectedness and interrelatedness, themes that will be found to be seminal to my order-based theory of morality. According to Cohen, the PSR holds that each and every thing is 'connected in definite ways with definite other things, so that its full nature is not revealed except by its position and relations within a system.'[10] Causation is of course one way of forming connec-tions between things.

In his work *Theological-Political Treatise* (1670), Spinoza wrote 'God's decrees and commandments, and consequently God's providence, are in truth nothing but Nature's order.'[11] Plainly enough, if the God in the Confucian dictum were a Spinozistic God, then the 'law of our human nature' would be situated within the same set of universal natural laws that enables us first to discover order within nature, and then to learn how order arises from the complex interactions of its many parts. I believe Spinoza may have found the dictum congenial to his own way of thinking, though whether Confucius would have accepted the proviso I have added is debatable; but his deeply humanistic cast of mind makes me think that he might have.

To repeat the question: How did it come about that we are moral beings? From a Spinozistic reading of Confucius, we have the answer: morality is something that was implanted in us by the deity that is nature. But we might then proceed to enrich that answer by injecting some Darwinian thinking into our understanding of nature. Our earliest ances-tors would surely have had some kind of concept, say, of what was 'good' to eat, and where satisfactory shelter could be found; and they would have been more or less adept at satisfying their need for such things. But their capacity for the essentials of morality such as self-restraint and altruism may have been very limited; perhaps because there was not very much call for them at the time. Nevertheless morality did eventuate, and

10 See Morris R. Cohen, 'The Metaphysics of Reason and Scientific Method' in *American Philosophical Naturalism in the Twentieth Century*, edited by John Ryder (New York: Prometheus Books, 1994), p. 250.
11 Quoted by Stephen Nadler, *A Book Forged in Hell* (Princeton: Princeton University Press, 2011), p. 34.

could be viewed as an emergent property or characteristic of the human species, one that evolved naturally from our need-satisfying behaviour. Morality could be thought of as having come into being when the ideas of right and wrong became attached to the notions of good and bad. 'Right' and 'wrong' seem to me to be more definitively moral terms than 'good' and 'bad', although the latter pair may have priority in human evolution. Good may exist in the absence of right, but the reverse could not apply: 'right' without any associated sense of 'good' would not make sense. A sense of 'ought' inheres in that of 'right', and a sense of 'ought not' in that of 'wrong'.

As well as being defined by the capacity for morality, human nature is such that we are needful creatures, that what we need are survival and well-being, and that the need for these things finds expression in the kinds of needs identified by the psychologist and philosopher Abraham Maslow (1908-70). We will be seeing a fair deal of Maslow later on, but it can be noted here that he was an admirer of Spinoza's philosophy. Maslow spoke of attaining 'religious states insofar as they are naturalistic.'[12] Such states were considered by him to be a condition of maximum human potential. They could also be said to reflect the spirit of Tao, for Maslow often invoked Taoist principles when articulating his own ideals. According to the *Tao Te Ching* (Taoism's 'bible'), Taoism's essence consists in knowledge of 'the ancient beginning,'[13] which is described as 'natural'. 'Man,' it is said, 'follows the earth. / Earth follows heaven. / Heaven follows the Tao. / Tao follows what is natural.'[14] Knowledge of the ancient beginning would surely go a long way towards enabling us to form a view on the place occupied by human beings within nature. But it is Maslow's theory of needs that will be of primary interest here.

Human beings can reasonably be said to have the same kinds of basic needs; for example, people generally like to have their minds stimulated, at least some of the time. But we have many different ways of satisfying our needs, including our need for amusement and excitement—as Cole

---

12 A. H. Maslow, *The Farther Reaches of Human Nature* (New York: Penguin, 1993 [first published 1971]), p. 124.
13 Lao Tzu, *Tao Te Ching*, translated by Gia-Fu Feng and Jane English (New York: Vintage Books, 1972), chapter 14.
14 Lao Tzu, *Tao Te Ching*, chapter 25.

Porter reminded us in one of his songs, people get their 'kicks' from all sorts of things. In the field of high intellectual endeavour, Spinoza strove for philosophical insight, with much light being contributed by psychology; Maslow similarly, though, for him, psychology was the focus and philosophy the source of supplementary light.

The means we use to satisfy our needs depend partly on our familial, social, cultural, geographical and political circumstances. Genetic inheritance is another determinant; for example, if we are born with impaired vision, the tools we use to obtain knowledge may differ from those employed by fully-sighted persons. The evolutionary biologist Theodosius Dobzhansky (1900-75) argued that people need different things to achieve optimal growth and self-realisation, and that we should therefore be speaking about human natures (plural) rather than human nature (singular).[15] Dobzhansky based his argument on what he called 'genetic conditioning', and the science of genetics unequivocally attests to the fact that the vast majority of people are genetically unique. But there is also the fact that the things needed are seen by Dobzhansky as being directed to the attainment of common goals, in this instance 'optimal growth' and 'self-realisation'; these too are needs, arguably of a more fundamental order than whatever we differentially use to satisfy them. The fundamental needs (or, as I will be referring to them, 'basic needs') are arguably shared by all of us, and are therefore indicative of a basic human nature.

To say that we are needful beings might not seem very enlightening, for it is surely the case that all organisms have needs. Minimally, and perhaps also maximally in some cases, living beings need whatever it is that enables them to keep on living. But my argument is that human beings are uniquely needful in respect of a particular kind of order, namely homosapient order. When we see later what homosapient order involves, it will become clear that in fact a great deal is being said with the claim that ours is a needful nature. In striving to satisfy our basic needs, ultimately the need for homosapient order, we engage in a rich variety of behaviours, including morally relevant behaviour.

---

15 Dobzhansky, Theodosius, in Richard Dawkins (editor), *The Oxford Book of Modern Science Writing* (Oxford University Press, 2008), p. 24.

An understanding of our needfulness is critical to an understanding of morality, not least because harm that is morally relevant invariably involves the violation of basic needs. While all of this remains to be explained, I simply wish to note here that some people generally attend to their needs by interacting with others in a humane manner, whereas others tend to act inhumanely. If we are well-disposed towards others, we would often seek to satisfy our needs in ways that differ from those used by people who are ill-disposed towards them. In particular, the actions of those who are well-disposed would tend to measure up well against the PHM, and the actions of those who are ill-disposed not so well. At least, such is my claim. Before we can begin to test the validity of that claim, the PHM needs to be spelt out. So here it is.

The PHM

In your dealings with the world, firstly strive to ensure that no living being is harmed either cruelly or carelessly. Secondly, strive to ensure that no human being is ever harmed, except to prevent unwanted harm being done or suffered by the person who is harmed. Thirdly, strive to ensure that any preventive harm administered in accordance with the second stipulation never exceeds the minimum necessary to forestall whatever unwanted harm could reasonably have been expected in the circumstances.

In Section 4 of his book *Pensées* the philosopher and mathematician Blaise Pascal (1623-62) compares two kinds of morality, one of which is said to be true and the other less so. In Pascal's words, 'true morality makes light of morality; that is to say, the morality of the judgment, which has no rules, makes light of the morality of the intellect.'[16] Morality of the judgement would seem to involve unmediated and immediate access to an understanding of what should be done (and not done), in contrast to a relatively laborious referencing of rules by morality of the intellect. Perhaps judgement-based morality could be regarded as more instinctual and less the subject of learning; vice versa for intellect-based morality. Rules are more likely to come by way of learning than by instinct (unless one is their originator). Contrary to Pascal, the PHM would seem to

16 Blaise Pascal, *Pensées*, translated by W. F. Trotter (London: J. M. Dent & Sons, 1940).

consist of a set of rules; but, if read in that manner, abiding by the rules would still require the exercise of Pascalian judgement. In fact, however, there is no conflict, for the PHM is just what its title says: a *principle*, and principles of some kind are a necessary basis for both rules and judgement, and indeed other principles.

The PHM itself rests on another principle, the one already mentioned to the effect that avoidance of wrongdoing suffices to keep one on the right side of the moral divide. In light of that foundation, the PHM can be seen to have had a long period of gestation. Its first seeds were sown more than two and half thousand years ago with the ideas that gave rise to the Hippocratic Oath, and Socrates' identification of injury with wrong (see the epigraph). The rudiments of the principle have surfaced in various guises throughout history, for example in the nineteenth century in the form of the so-called 'harm principle', which derives from John Stuart Mill's (1806-73) view that a person should be at liberty to do anything provided no harm is done to others.[17] Since harm might sometimes be unavoidable, or even desirable (for example, the life-saving amputation of a gangrenous limb), Mill's specification should perhaps be modified along the following lines: Avoid doing harm, unless by doing some kind of harm a more grievous kind of harm may be avoided. Mill himself would have accepted the modification, and the revised formulation would be getting close to the PHM.

Dissection of the PHM proceeds in the chapters that follow.

---

17 John Stuart Mill, *On Liberty*, Chapter 1, in *Utilitarianism, Liberty and Representative Government* (London: J. M. Dent & Sons, Everyman's Library, 1971).

Chapter 2: 'In Your Dealings with the World'

The world is not such that one thing has nothing to do with another, but they are connected (Aristotle, Metaphysics, XII.10, 1075a).

The Principle of Harm-minimisation opens with the phrase 'In your dealings with the world'. The terms 'your', 'dealings' and 'the world' all require amplification.

Who is 'Your'?

The answer to that might seem obvious, but it extends a little farther than you might at first think. 'Your' is addressed initially to the individual human being, but also, and just as importantly, it embraces other entities whose dealings are influenced or controlled by the individual. By 'other entities' I mean other people and anything else that is capable of acting on or interacting with the world, i.e., everything that exists.

The idea behind the phrase 'influenced or controlled' is implicit in the famous *Serenity Prayer* formulated by the theologian Reinhold Niebuhr (1892-1971). The prayer asks that we be given three things. Firstly, the courage needed to change that which should be changed, but only that which *can* be changed by us; secondly, the forbearance to abide with that which cannot be changed by us; thirdly, the wisdom to differentiate between that which can be changed and that which cannot. The prayer expresses a great truth, and would have resonated with Mahatma Gandhi (1869-1948), who enjoined us to *become* the change that we wish to see in the world. In spite of that, we may still wonder about how much responsibility anyone should be made to bear for the actions of others.

We all assuredly have some influence over the actions of some others, but just as assuredly to varying degrees. For example, what if our democratically elected government commits the country to a war that we consider unjust? How responsible should we feel; or, more strongly, how responsible in fact *are* we, each and every one of us? As soon as we begin to talk about responsibility, morality appears on the scene. To be responsible for something that we did is to bear the weight of any moral significance attaching to our action.[1] 'What we did' can be understood to include the actions of agents over which and over whom we had some control, as well as our own dealings with the world. Indeed, one's dealings with the world encompass the ways in which such control is exercised.

Dealings

The kinds of dealings I have in mind go beyond that which is done. As well as actual deeds, 'dealings' include that which is said and written. In so far as what we say and what we write are capable of inflicting harm, they must be counted. Dealings with the world that are the responsibility of someone may be morally relevant dealings. If they are morally relevant, they will be the dealings of a moral agent, and bring moral respondency into effect.

Moral Agency and Respondency

Moral dealings consist of actions by an agent that invite judgement in terms of moral right and wrong. For behaviour to be morally relevant there must be alternative courses of action from which an agent may choose, which is also a condition of freedom. The various options must be feasible for the agent—as the philosopher Daniel Dennett (b. 1942) has said, a person must have the power or ability 'to do otherwise;'[2] this can be regarded as another condition of freedom. In order for choice to be possible, alternative courses of action must first be perceived and comprehended, constituting yet another condition of freedom. Comprehension would typically entail assessment of which course would be best to adopt; community standards (i.e. norms) and personal character would often enter into the assessment.

Morally relevant behaviour always involves an agent and at least one respondent. As the term *respondent* implies, someone or some*thing* needs to be affected by the agent's behaviour (or potentially affected) before

---

1 See Raimond Gaita, *After Romulus* (Melbourne: Text Publishing, 2011), p. 87.
2 Daniel C. Dennett, *Freedom Evolves* (New York: Viking, 2003), p. 118.

the question of moral classifiability can arise. Because of their vulnerability to harm, all living beings are potential respondents. A respondent
is an entity to whom or which an agent has some kind of responsibility;
an agent, moreover, who is responsible for his or her own behaviour, by
having chosen it. Further still, a respondent is someone or something to
whom or which an agent is required to be responsive.

Respondency to harmful action by an agent exists even when those
affected are willingly caught up in it. A fatal kick to the head of an
instigator of a brawl would be morally relevant. Conversely, a masochist
who voluntarily submits to being whipped would not be participating
in morally relevant behaviour, because of the pleasure occasioned by the
physical harm; indeed, one could say that the harm satisfied a deeply felt
need. Similarly, fair fights between boxers and wrestlers are not morally
relevant: any injuries sustained are an essential (i.e. necessary, or needed)
part of their business.

Can someone be respondent to their own morally relevant behaviour? This is a difficult question, but an answer could become evident
if it were restated thus: is a harmful act that is directed towards oneself
morally wrong? Moral wrongness, of course, requires the existence of an
agent-respondent relationship. Having restated the question, we could
then apply the PHM. For example, is it possible for people to be cruel
or harmfully careless towards themselves? Or, might self-harm occur
without the harm being intended to prevent the person concerned from
either doing or suffering unwanted harm? Or, finally, is it possible for
self-harm that is administered in order to prevent unwanted harm to be
greater than that which was necessary in the circumstances? A positive
answer to any of the questions would constitute contravention of the
PHM, and therefore moral wrongness. With the exception of cruelty, a
positive answer to any or all of them seems eminently possible. Cruelty is
excepted because, as we will see in Chapter 4, it involves the subjugation
of a weaker being by a stronger one. It would make no sense to speak
of people as being at the same time both stronger and weaker than their

own selves. Cruelty aside, application of the PHM indicates that people can indeed be respondent to their own morally relevant behaviour.

Moral dealings can arise from non-action as well as action. An act that is chosen is also an act that can be refrained from. Drunkenness, for instance, is usually avoidable, and reprehensible behaviour during a state of drunkenness is deserving of sanction, provided the perpetrator is responsible for his or her condition (someone whose drink had been spiked may not be). The same applies to impulsive action. The capacity to refrain from acting impulsively is another condition of freedom—and, as the philosopher and poet Friedrich Schiller (1759-1805) would have said, it is also fundamental to dignity. Moral rectitude is non-action in so far as it arises from a consciously taken decision to avoid a course of action that would be morally wrong. However, in the same way that right can consist in wrong not done, wrong can arise from not doing something that would be right, for example refusing to donate to a deserving charity when it is within one's means to do so. Morally relevant behaviour will henceforth be understood to encompass non-action as well as action.

To sum up, morally relevant dealings are possible only when there are alternative courses of action from which a reasonably competent agent may choose within conflicted circumstances. Morally relevant actions are a particular kind of dealing with the world. Let us now look more closely at what 'with the world' might mean.

The World

'The World' was said a short while ago to consist of 'everything that exists', including oneself, other human beings, and all of non-human nature. In other words, humankind in total, non-human animals, other organisms such as toadstools and trees, plus inorganic things such as rivers and oceans. I have also said that morally relevant behaviour involves of necessity a human agent and at least one respondent to the agent's dealings with the world, i.e. his actions, including what he says and writes. Respondency is not confined to human beings: fondness and respect for animals and the environment are so widespread that any theory of

morality that failed to encompass them would be open to serious challenge. How, then, might it be possible to accommodate other beings
within the ambit of moral concern? The answer begins in this chapter
with some comments on the notion of connectedness. Animal rights and
environmental ethics are addressed in Chapter 5.

Why should we be concerned with connectedness? The answer:
Because a world composed of things that had no connection with other
things would be a world without structure, without order, and quite
possibly a world without rational beings capable of thinking about such
matters. Moral experience could not occur if people were not connected to other people and other things. The reality of our existence is such
that all of our experiences, including moral experiences, occur within
what the philosopher Dorothy Emmet (1904-2000) referred to as an
'environing field,' with which our bodies are said to be 'continuous.'[3]
'Continuous' could be replaced by 'connected' without distorting what
Emmet was driving at. Whether by means of continuousness or via connectedness, what we have in view here are relationships between things:
things in some way affecting other things. The relationships may be of
a physical or social nature. They may also be located entirely within a
particular thing, giving rise to what I will describe as 'intrapersonal' connectedness. Physical connectedness first.

Physical Connectedness

In the same vein as Aristotle's views on the interconnectedness of the
world (see the epigraph to this chapter), the philosopher Brian Ellis (b.
1929) maintains that our world is one in which connectedness between
its parts gives rise to a highly integrated and coherent structure.[4] Many
instances of connectedness could be cited in support of Ellis's contention. Atoms depend for their existence on interactions and connections
between nuclei and electrons, and the strong nuclear force that binds
them together—physical organisation at a very elemental level. The
physical orderliness that is characteristic of life also depends upon

---

3 Dorothy Emmet, *The Nature of Metaphysical Thinking* (Great Britain: Macmillan, 1966 [first published
1945]), p. 192.
4 Brian Ellis, *The Philosophy of Nature: A Guide to the New Essentialism* (Great Britain: Acumen, 2002), p.
118.

connectedness, i.e. connections between the myriad things required to form a living being, including the atoms that bond to form molecules, and the molecules that combine to form cells. At the level of genetics, physical connectedness is implicit in a metaphor of cooperativeness used by the evolutionary biologist Richard Dawkins (b. 1941) to describe the relationship between individual genes and the organism of which they are a part.[5] Genes are passed down by organisms which depend for their survival on cooperation between their constituent parts. Non-cooperation would result in the destruction of the organism before progeny and further genes could be produced.

From connections at the sub-atomic level to connections at the level of genetics—the scope could be broadened further still. We need only think of the things that are necessary to (i.e. needed by) other things for their physical existence, for example plants that are used as food by human beings. And so on *ad infinitum*. Physical order would be impossible without connectedness. And, as we will now see, social order would not be possible without social connectedness.

Social Connectedness

The idea of social connectedness (let alone the fact of it) has ancient roots—in Stoicism for instance, whose principle of *oikeiosis* lies at the heart of the matter. *Oikeiosis* consists in a sense of kinship with other human beings, giving rise to a feeling of care. Spinoza held a similar view. The human being in Spinoza's scheme of things may be looked upon as a *part* of the whole, with the 'whole' consisting of all of nature, an 'all' that Spinoza considered synonymous with the term 'god'. So much is clear from his posthumously published *The Ethics*.[6] Human beings, like all other so-called (by Spinoza) 'modes' of nature, may be presumed to participate in the characteristics of the whole, including its freedom, its knowledge and its power. As such, a human being would be partly free,

---

5 Richard Dawkins, *The Selfish Gene* (USA: Oxford University Press, 2006 [first published 1976]), p. 47.
6 See, for example, *The Ethics*, in Benedict de Spinoza, *The Ethics and Other Works*, edited and translated by Edwin Curley (Princeton: Princeton University Press, 1994), 2p11c and 4p68d(i). (Spinoza's *The Ethics* consists of five parts; the leading numeral in the referencing scheme denotes the relevant part. Within the parts there are definitions (designated 'def'), axioms ('a'), propositions ('p'), corollaries ('c'), demonstrations ('d'), and scholia ('s'); prefaces and appendixes are designated 'pref' and 'app' respectively. Numerals following the alphabetical designations are the numbers assigned in Spinoza's text to the particular axioms, definitions, propositions, etc. Thus the first reference above points to part 2, proposition number 11, corollary.)

partly knowledgeable and partly powerful (all through the possession of more or less adequate ideas). The parts/whole paradigm lends plausibility to the relevance of connectedness to morality—again in the *Ethics*, Spinoza asserts that it is to the 'common advantage of all' when people 'strive together, as far as they can, to preserve their being.'[7] 'Striving' is one of the key concepts embedded in the PHM, and in the present context implies a form of social connectedness, arguably to the point of interdependency. These are important ideas, and I will elaborate on them in the discussion of order in Part II.

In any kind of complex society most people are dependent on others for the provision of things needed to sustain life, ranging from food to love. Esteem also, which requires other people from whom recognition might be obtained.[8] Respectful recognition would usually follow from an ascription of worthiness; and worth, as the philosopher Robert Nozick (1938-2002) opined, is a matter of meaningfulness.[9] Life is made worthwhile by investing it with meaningfulness; and it becomes meaningful in virtue of being worthwhile. And connectedness is a pre-requisite of both meaning and worthwhileness. We can see this, I believe, in the fact that many of the things that combine to constitute the 'life form' of the human species necessarily involve connections between people; things such as those mentioned previously, including truth-telling, neighbourliness, and lending a helping hand. Social connectedness is implicit in all of these things—all of them entail relations between people, either directly or indirectly. Furthermore, a person's perceived worthiness would at least partly depend on how he or she connects with other things, especially with regard to the principles and projects that are adopted and followed. There is more at stake here than simply dependence upon other things—an appropriate degree of dependability is also necessary.

There is one final kind of connectedness that I want to touch on here, that which concerns the individual. Intrapersonal connectedness, as I will call it, will serve as a platform for the discussion in Part II of a kind of order that is peculiar to human beings, namely homosapient order. As

---

7 *The Ethics*, 4p18s.
8 See Frederick Beiser, *Hegel* (Great Britain: Routledge, 2006), p. 188 ff.
9 Robert Nozick, *Philosophical Explanations* (Cambridge, Massachusetts: Harvard University Press, 1994 [first published 1981]), p. 594.

I have foreshadowed, it is homosapient order that will enable us to find a means of anchoring morality in a non-religious metaphysical ground.

Intrapersonal Connectedness
Each of us is made up of many parts: physically—atoms, molecules, cells, organs, etc.; psychologically—memories, thoughts, beliefs, and so forth. For us to persevere as the beings that we are, all of these things must some-how stay connected to one another. Disconnectedness, both physical and psychological, is of course everyone's ultimate fate, but the possibility of partial disintegration until that time is ever present. Furthermore, and this is really just another aspect of the same concern, how could the parts ever cohere sufficiently to form a recognisable, enduring individual, i.e. something that is undivided, or indeed indivisible? An individual, that is, in the sense of an entity possessed of personal identity. For something to be identical with itself from one moment to the next there must be connections that explain the identity.

Identity cannot consist solely in physical sameness, since each of us changes in that regard: a hair lost yesterday, another wrinkle today. Perhaps similarity would be enough: we could remain sufficiently alike from one moment to the next to warrant believing that it is the same person throughout the successive moments. Alternatively, psychological continuity could hold the answer. Such was the case with Monty Python's Black Knight (in the 1975 movie *Monty Python and the Holy Grail*), enough of whom remained after both of his legs and his two arms had been hacked off in a battle to want to fight on (with his teeth!); of course, his head, and therefore his mind, were still intact. Physical sim-ilarity and psychological continuity are huge topics, and I will not be venturing into them here. Suffice to say that the potential for disconti-nuity, either physical or psychological, is pervasive, and therefore poses a threat to intrapersonal connectedness.

Conclusion: Connectedness and Morality
The mathematician Henri Poincaré (1854-1912) was someone who thought deeply about connectedness and how things relate to one another. According to him, 'It is not the facts but the relation of things that results in the universal harmony that is the sole objective reality . . . .

It is this harmony, this *quality* if you will, that is the sole basis for the only reality we can ever know.'[10] Poincaré's elevation of 'universal harmony' to the status of sole objective reality bears thinking about. It is a harmony that results from relations between things; relations, I believe, that could reasonably be regarded as constitutive of various kinds of connectedness. It also reflects the sum of all of our dealings with the world.

Finally, there is the relationship between connectedness and ethics to consider. Testimony to the existence of a relationship can be found in Robert Nozick's work, where ethical action is looked upon as a form of 'responsive to connection to the world,' which is said to be a form of knowledge, and which is held to enable the individual and the world to become united.[11] Which seems right to me, for it is hard to see how unity could be otherwise achieved. Mere connectivity on the part of a human being would not be enough: any inert chunk of matter could be said to be united with the world in virtue of being connected with it, simply by being part of it. No, what we need, over and above 'mere' connectivity—what our life form demands of us—is responsive connectedness. It is responsive connectedness with the world that brings responsibility (for one's dealings with it) into play, whence morality (as Raimond Gaita might have said). By such means, the 'environing field' spoken of by Dorothy Emmet becomes enriched with meaningfulness.

Perhaps one could be forgiven if at first sight all of this were viewed merely as a complicated way of saying that we tend to react to whatever is going on around us, especially if we are affected in some way by the goings on. But responsiveness goes somewhat deeper than that. Whereas reaction can be purely physical, a classical knee-jerk, responsiveness also involves thoughts and feelings—Nozick's inclusion of 'responsive connection' under the rubric 'knowledge' says as much. If the term 'general responsiveness' reminds you of what I was saying about moral respondency, yes, Nozick's 'responsiveness' would encompass moral respondency; but moral agency would be in there as well. In other words, it would embrace the entire gamut of the relationships involved in morally relevant behaviour. Finally with regard to knowledge, it is probably fair to

---

10 See Robert M. Pirsig, *Zen and the Art of Motorcycle Maintenance: An Inquiry into Values* (Great Britain: Vintage, 1999 [first published 1974]), p. 268.
11 Nozick, p. 524.

say that the more deeply we think and reflect, the greater the likelihood of our becoming aware of the interconnections that pervade the world.[12]

Connectedness with the world obviously has physical and social dimensions, and the depth reached by both of those would arguably depend on the degree of intrapersonal connectedness. Connectedness is order is healthiness. That being the case, another way of saying what has just been said is that one's psychological health has a bearing on the stability of one's social relations, and that psychological health and social stability both affect one's physical relationships with the world. A truism, almost.

The dissection of the PHM continues in the next chapter, where the notion of 'striving' is discussed.

---

12 Thoughtfulness may indeed constitute the glue that enables connections to stick; see, e.g., Nozick, p. 598.

Chapter 3: 'Strive to Ensure'

Strenuous attention to conduct is akin to compassion (Confucius).[1]

In so far as the ordinary sense of 'strive' is 'try hard', the directive 'strive to ensure' imposes a difficult task on those of us who engage in morally relevant dealings with the world; which is to say, virtually everyone. We must try hard to do whatever is necessary to bring the object of our striving into effect; where, of course, the object consists of the things that the PHM requires of us, beginning with the striving itself and ending with the minimisation of harm.

'Strive to ensure' fits in well with Confucius's 'strenuous attention to conduct' (see the epigraph), a quality that he likened to compassion. That it fits is especially evident if the Chinese master's 'attention to conduct' is understood to involve thinking about what we do, and doing what we think should be done. And it is especially significant if compassion is understood to mean something more than pity, notwithstanding the appropriateness of pity in certain circumstances. In contrast to pity, which tends to be episodic, compassion is a more or less permanent state-of-being. To describe someone as a 'compassionate person' would be common usage, but to speak of a 'pitying person' would sound strange.

As well as being consistent with Confucian thinking, 'strive to ensure' ties in with one of Spinoza's primary tenets, that of *conatus*. According to Spinoza, everything strives constantly for self-preservation and joy, and that striving constitutes *conatus*. What he meant by self-preservation is obvious enough, while joy was regarded by him as an increase in the power of acting autonomously,[2] which in turn originates in the possession of adequate ideas. It seems to me that moral striving could well be found to be necessary to both self-preservation and joy; in other words, that it is integral to *conatus*. Should that be so, moral striving could also be regarded as fundamental to human nature. I am sure Spinoza would have thought that to be the case, and he would not have been alone. A strong coincidence exists between this aspect of his thinking

---

1 Lin Yutang, *The Wisdom of Confucius*, p. 118.
2 *The Ethics*, 3p6–p12.

and some of the things that the Stoics were saying on the same subjects two thousand years before him, around the third century BCE.
According to the Stoics, happiness can be won from virtue, where virtue
was said to consist in living in accord with one's nature. Human nature
in turn was distinguished from other kinds of nature by the faculty of
reason. So what we have from the Stoics is a formula that is very close
to Spinoza's. For Spinoza, joy comes from the possession of adequate
ideas, and adequate ideas are obviously the product of reason. For the
Stoics, happiness comes from virtue, which derives from the exercise of
reason. That the same cluster of ideas happens to have emerged from two
quite different cultures widely separated in time I find quite remarkable.
The coincidence would seem to point to features of human nature that
are common to all of us, or at least the vast majority of us. Constant
striving of the kind Spinoza had in mind can be looked upon as a natural and unavoidable condition of human being-ness, and to varying
extents other kinds of being-ness as well. And while it would often occur
unconsciously—striving of some sort is always going on, whether we
like it or not—the involvement of reason in the pursuit of joy opens up
the possibility, perhaps even inevitability, of a moral dimension to our
striving.

Moral striving culminates in morally relevant dealings with the world.
Morally relevant dealings arise from relationships between particular kinds of entities, at least one of which must be a human being, i.e.
relationships between two or more people, or between one or more
human beings and other entities such as whales and rainforests. One
aspect of morally relevant dealings—respondency—was discussed in the
previous chapter. Striving is concerned with the other side of the coin,
namely agency. Agency in moral dealings is confined to human beings,
and only those human beings capable of freely choosing from the alternative courses of action available to them. Morally relevant behaviour
is the exclusive province of human beings because, as far as we know,
we are the only entities equipped with (1) the ability to envisage and
understand alternative courses of action, (2) sufficient powers of rational
choice to weigh up the consequences of pursuing the various alternatives, and (3) an inclination to choose from the alternatives on the basis

of right and wrong. As Confucius might have expressed it, it behoves us to look carefully for alternative courses of action, to give their possible consequences our proper attention, and to choose from them wisely.

Moral agency rests on freedom, which in turn stems from the rational powers of perception, comprehension and judgement. As far as we know such powers are exclusive to human beings, at least to the extent of their being morally significant; i.e., to the point of being deployable in decisions about how one should act, on the basis of right and wrong. As the Stoics and others have long proclaimed, rationality is the defining characteristic of our species; it is what differentiates humankind from other living beings. Furthermore, having been the subject of development through natural selection, human rationality is firmly situated within the natural world of cause and effect. That being so, freedom and morality can likewise be viewed as products of nature. A multiplicity of factors may bring us to a point where a choice must be made; and having been brought to that point, we exercise our freedom by choosing what to do, after weighing up as best we can the consequences of our actions. Our reason is there to do the weighing. Failure to use our reason, when it is within our power to do so, would amount to moral failure, should matters turn out badly.

Besides moral failure of the kind just mentioned, some people might not be able to make informed assessments; young children, for example, and persons suffering from severe mental impairment. If such people seem at times to be acting upon a choice from alternative courses of action, we would nevertheless generally exempt them from moral responsibility—but on what basis? When might the capacity for responsible choice kick in? A hard and fast rule would be difficult to devise, and would in any case be likely to vary depending on time and place. But some broad criteria for responsibility are conceivable. First, a person would need to have had sufficient opportunity to develop an awareness of his or her community's moral standards—young children (how young?) would be excluded on this criterion. Second, a person would need to have the capacity for developing such awareness—the young would again be excluded, as would the insane. Both conditions would have to be met before moral responsibility becomes applicable.

The need for an effect on a respondent would seem to disqualify unsuccessful attempts at reprehensible action from moral judgement, for example where an assassin's bullet misses the target. This raises the question of the moral significance of an agent's intentions. Some ethicists maintain that no wrong will have been done if whatever happened was not intended.[3] Similarly for right. For example, Kant believed that the will is the only thing that can be unqualifiedly good. Kant's near contemporary David Hume (1711-76) seems to have been of the same mind when he proclaimed: 'By the intention we judge of the actions, and according as that is good or bad, they become causes of love or hatred.'[4] Choosing, will and intention are all intermingled. We might say that our will is such that we choose well in all circumstances, and that our intention is that we do precisely that. Or, we could say that our underlying intention is to do a certain thing, whereupon we set about choosing how best to bring it about. Whichever the case, as well as striving to choose well, the PHM implicitly requires that we strive to align our intentions with our well-chosen choice, and that our choice accords with our will: failure on either count would conceivably lead to the kind of harm prohibited by the principle. Since all of that striving occurs within the innermost recesses of our being, the principle in effect enjoins us to be moral in a way advocated by Confucius: the moral man, he maintained, watches carefully over his secret thoughts.

Present-day philosopher Kieran Setiya observes that intention can be understood in any of three ways: as a plan for the future, or as the purpose or goal for which action is undertaken, or as intentional action itself. Example: I am writing this with a view to having my book read by someone (plan for the future); the words I am writing are intended to recognise the complexities involved in the notion of intention (purposeful or goal-directed action); and I am intentionally writing what I am now writing (intentional action). The three aspects of intention have

---

3 See Nancy (Ann) Davis, 'Contemporary Deontology', in Peter Singer (editor), *A Companion to Ethics* (Cornwall, United Kingdom: Blackwell, 2003 [first published 1991], p. 210.
4 David Hume, *A Treatise of Human Nature* (London: Penguin Books, 1984 [first published 1739 and 1740]), 2.2.3.

attracted a great deal of philosophical attention.[5] All three are indicative of ways in which intention would normally be understood and spoken about.

'Plan for the future' intention is distinguishable from its other two aspects in virtue of the fact that plans may be unconsummated by action, whereas action is necessarily involved in both goal-directed action and intentional action. Because of the consequences entailed in action, the action-orientation of intention is certainly important; but its planned-but-not-acted-upon orientation also requires recognition. Some of our intentions might not result in action, or the action might differ from the intended action. A would-be assassin who conspires to kill may have his plan thwarted, but the conspiracy as an action would itself still be morally relevant, and would be wrong. Why would it? Murder might not have been committed, but were the person to learn of the assassin's intentions, he or she would probably still feel significantly threatened. Of course that would not be the case if the perpetrator had quietly left the scene and no-one else ever became aware of what had happened. Would his action then still be morally relevant? Who could possibly judge? Yes, it would be morally relevant, because the action violated the PHM's demand that we strive to minimise harm. As to who the judge would be, the offender himself would be one candidate: that he thought his action was wrong, or likely to have been deemed wrong by others, is revealed by his furtiveness.

Staying with the assassination attempt, should it become known, a plan that gets past the conspiracy stage and culminates in an unsuccess-ful attempt to kill would usually be condemned, though perhaps not always—that the many attempts to assassinate Hitler all proved unsuc-cessful would generally be regretted. Similarly, but conversely, an intended beneficent action that fails in its attempt would usually be praiseworthy. A person who dives into dangerous surf to rescue someone who has fallen in would deserve moral commendation, regardless of whether the rescue succeeds. Conspiratorial actions and attempted crimes are often legally punishable; for example, where I reside, the Victorian Crimes Act

5 Kieran Setiya, "Intention", *The Stanford Encyclopedia of Philosophy (Spring 2011 Edition)*, Edward N. Zalta (ed.), URL = http://plato.stanford.edu/archives/spr2011/entries/intention/ (accessed 4 November 2012).

1958 prescribes the same maximum penalty for conspiracy to murder and attempt to murder as that attracted by actual murder (Secs. 321, 321P). I will not be discussing the relationship between morality and law at any length, though there are some comments on the matter in Chapter 14.

Finally with respect to intention, I want to pursue the question of consonance between intention and outcome, and the related matter of carelessness in keeping them consonant. Either consonance or failure of consonance due to carelessness is required for moral relevance to apply. To illustrate, if I have the misfortune to be standing in the way of the assassin's bullet, then I may have saved the intended victim's life, but my action would not be morally relevant. It was purely accidental; there was no consonance between my intention (or whatever it was that brought me there) and what happened. Next, if I decide to get drunk and then unintentionally injure someone whilst driving, my action would be morally relevant. Getting drunk carelessly opened the way to slippage between intention and action; i.e., my drunkenness prevented me from maintaining consonance between intention (presumably to get home without hurting anyone) and outcome. What if the person injured happened to be the would-be assassin, thereby thwarting him in his endeavours? Again I might have saved the life of the intended victim, but the 'good' that I have brought about would not be morally relevant, because it bore no relation to my intentions. On the other hand, the injury sustained by the assassin would be morally relevant, because of my lack of care and attention. Care and attention are commensurate with striving. Our dealings with the world include our intentions, along with the effort we make to keep our actions in harmony with them. There is more on the subject of carelessness in Chapter 4.

The discussion has reached the point where rational choice emanating from freedom (itself dependent upon rationality) would seem to be sufficient to render any behaviour that is consequent upon choice morally relevant. Whenever we choose to act in accordance with a choice, our action affects someone somewhere, potentially for better or worse. That being the case, the effect may be measured in terms of moral significance. The action of the agent must either affect others in a reasonably significant way, or be likely to so affect them. The significance of an agent's behaviour may be very small, as, for example, action following a choice between chocolate ice-cream and vanilla ice-cream. Some choices and actions are clearly unimportant from a moral perspective: I think we must agree with the philosopher John Dewey (1859-1952) when he contended that 'it would be morbid to subject each act to moral scrutiny.'[6] Although the consequences of choices between ice-cream flavours would be minuscule, care is needed in determining what one dismisses as morally irrelevant. Something that seems trivial today could have far-reaching effects. On the other hand, the moral significance attached to a choice may be momentous and its momentousness may immediately be obvious; as would be the case if we murderously push someone out of a second-storey window, and he is lucky enough to have his fall broken by an awning just below, then the high probability of serious injury or death associated with the action (such was the intention) would be enough to make it morally relevant.

The conjunction of the ability to do otherwise and moral significance may be viewed in the form of a chiasmus, with ability to do otherwise/ inability to do otherwise and morally significant/morally insignificant as its axes. In the north-east quadrant of Figure 1, ability to do otherwise combined with moral significance is the region of all the morally praiseworthy or morally culpable behaviour that we have been discussing. Moving anti-clockwise, ability to do otherwise/morally insignificant behaviour involves trivial choices like those concerning the ice-cream; these should obviously be excluded from scrutiny, at least in normal circumstances.

6 See Ruth Anna Putnam, 'The Moral Life of a Pragmatist', in Owen Flanagan and Amélie Oksenberg Rorty (editors), *Identity, Character, and Morality: Essays in Moral Psychology* (Cambridge, Massachusetts: The MIT Press, 1993), p. 71.

Ability to do Otherwise

Morally Insignificant ————————————|———————————— Morally Significant

Inability to do Otherwise

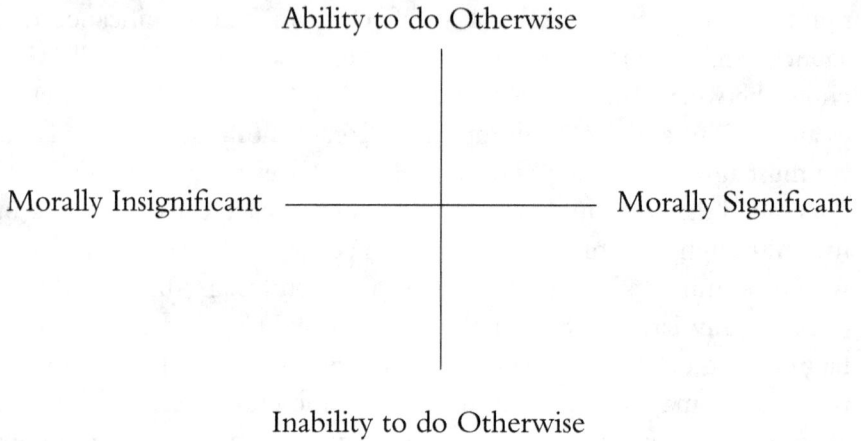

Figure 1: Moral Dealings

Next, in the south-west quadrant, inability to do otherwise/morally insignificant is the region of dealings that are constrained by the unavailability of alternative courses of action or an inability to choose on the basis of right and wrong; for example, a young child stealing an apple from his neighbour's fully-laden tree. Finally, the conjunction of inability to do otherwise with moral significance could appear oxymoronic, but betrayal of his country by a prisoner-of-war because of brain-washing might be placed here; treachery could be dimly viewed, whatever the circumstances.

This chapter has been concerned with the striving of moral agents. In the next chapter we delve further into the kinds of actions that are proscribed by the PHM. Namely harmful actions, especially those that are either cruel or careless.

Chapter 4: 'Are Never Harmed, Either Cruelly or Carelessly'

Tamas (or 'dark') action is heedless of consequences, including the hurt or wrong done to others (The Bhagavad-Gītā, Chapter 18).

The contention that harm arises from the non-satisfaction of certain kinds of needs is fundamental to the PHM. If things that are needed are not obtained then harm ensues. Why should needs be considered in the light of morality (or *vice versa*, morality in the light of needs)? The answer, we will see, comes in two parts.

Needs

First, our behaviour is largely motivated by needs, including morally relevant behaviour. Second, needs are vulnerable to insult—we suffer harm when attempts to satisfy our needs are thwarted. If other human beings are responsible for thwarting them, then moral judgement may well be invoked. Perhaps that should be qualified, by specifying that the needs involved must be basic needs. Harm that is morally relevant always involves an assault on someone's basic needs. What I mean by these terms will become clearer as we proceed, but Nelson Mandela (1918-2013) for one had no doubts about the importance of needs. In a memorandum written to himself he noted that his movement's political survival would depend on whether it could satisfactorily address the people's needs, and accommodate their aspirations. Specifically, housing, schools, unemployment and medical facilities would all require attention.[1]

Mandela's memorandum was written in 1993, when he was negotiating his way towards majority-rule in South Africa (he was elected president the following year). It is hard not to be reminded by it of the Marxist principle of justice, 'From each according to his ability, to each according to his needs,' especially given Mandela's Communist sympathies (it is unclear whether he was ever a member of the Party).

---

1 Nelson Mandela, *Conversations with Myself* (Sydney: Macmillan, 2013 [first published 2010]), p. 339.

Significantly in the note, needs are placed before aspirations (i.e. hopes), although needs and their satisfaction could well be understood as the target of our deepest aspirations. Perhaps what Mandela had in mind was the hope that the needs of his people, meaning all South Africans, would eventually be satisfied; needs in their full breadth, food, shelter and basic education as mentioned by Mandela, but also love, esteem and self-fulfilment (none of which Mandela would have considered inappropriate).

Support for the importance of needs can be drawn from another very wise man, Albert Einstein (1879-1955). According to Einstein, everything that we have ever done or thought has been directed towards the satisfaction of 'deeply felt needs' and the mitigation of pain.[2] Similarly Kant, who recognised that 'true human needs' go beyond those involving physiological survival, and include education, culture and 'various conditions essential for the development and exercise of our moral sensibility and conscience, and for the powers of reason, thought and judgement.'[3] Einstein's 'deeply felt needs' and Kant's 'true human needs' can be understood to be basic needs.

At first sight, needs might seem to be a fairly crude tool with which to craft something as intricate as a theory of morality. For one thing, it is surely the case that needs themselves constitute a theory, the substrate of which would be formed by more finely grained matters amenable to biochemical and biophysical scientific inquiry. But the upshot of an inquiry along those lines would probably be beyond the grasp of most people (me included), and if moral theory is to be of any use, then it must be intelligible to non-scientists and scientists alike. For it is surely also the case that morality is relevant to everyone. A moral theory based on needs can meet this requirement. Everyone, or nearly everyone, understands that people have need of things, first to survive, and then to live as well as possible. The concept of needs also provides us with a way of conceiving and objectifying degrees of harm. As the philosopher Thomas Hobbes (1588-1679) wrote,

seeing every man, not only by right but also by necessity of nature, is supposed to endeavour all he can to obtain that which is necessary

---

2 Albert Einstein, from *Religion and Science*, in Dawkins (editor), p. 235.
3 See John Rawls, *Lectures on the History of Moral Philosophy* (Cambridge, Massachusetts: Harvard University Press, 2000), pp. 174–175).

for his conservation, he that shall oppose himself against it for things superfluous is guilty of the war that thereupon is to follow, and therefore doth that which is contrary to the fundamental law of nature, which commandeth *to seek peace.*[4]

'Things superfluous' would no doubt be felt to be needed by those who want them, but their pursuit at the expense of someone else's more basic needs invites unbridled competition of a kind that harms, a state of affairs that Hobbes described as war. On those grounds, a theory of morality based on needs has some hope of being registrable by most people.

What we truly need as human beings are what Philippa Foot referred to as 'human necessities,' i.e. things that are generally needed for our good.[5] In keeping with a designation introduced by Elizabeth Anscombe, such things could also be called 'Aristotelian necessities.'[6] The need for homosapient order, I will argue, is one such necessity, and a very fundamental one at that. In addition to survival, such things as the cognitive powers that enable us to learn language and to understand stories were considered by Foot to be aspects of human good;[7] they are also aspects of homosapient order. In addition, Foot spoke of the importance of family ties, friendship and neighbourliness:[8] these too I regard as expressions of one of the components of the need for homosapient order, namely the need for social order.

Some of the goods referred to by Foot may be beyond the reach of some people, perhaps because of physiological incapacity or abnormality. A severe case of autism might confine its victim to a friendless world, and an intellectual disability could prevent someone from acquiring verbal skills. But an inability to attain any of the goods would not preclude anyone so afflicted from membership of the human family. Their inability, or disability, merely debars them from enjoyment of some of the goods that most human beings look upon as being necessary. For that reason it is important to note the qualifier 'generally' in Foot's description of

---

4 Thomas Hobbes, *Leviathan* (Chicago: The University of Chicago, Great Books of the Western World, 1952), Vol. 23, chapter 15.

5 Foot, p. 43.

6 Foot, p. 15.

7 Foot, p. 43.

8 Foot, p. 44.

human necessities. Many of the necessities are likely to apply whatever the affliction; and with necessities come rights (see Chapter 9).

To avoid being harmed organisms generally depend on things that are capable of insulating them from harm; so much would seem clear. It is also clear that some needs are generally the same for all people, at least in broad terms. We all need food and water, and most of us require shelter, security, love and esteem: to be deprived of any of them would entail harm. Let us call these 'basic needs'. Abraham Maslow referred to basic needs as 'instinctoid'; today, the usual descriptor would be 'genetic', or 'inherited'. Conventions and traditions are among the factors that determine how we go about satisfying our needs. These can give rise to what are generally known as 'learned needs'. For example, Hindus of certain sects will insist on vegetarian food rather than just any kind of food, while orthodox Jews will reject food that is not kosher. A people's culture will reflect their needs; possibly even determined by them.[9] That would be especially true of learned needs, whereas basic needs are trans-cultural; everyone has them, regardless of the traits characteristic of particular cultures.

Maslow's theory of needs is a theory of human motivation: it responds to the question 'why do we do what we do?' In the 1943 paper in which he first presented his theory, Maslow acknowledged that there are other determinants of behaviour besides needs, although his view was that needs predominate.[10] In the same paper Maslow drew a distinction between coping behaviour and expressive behaviour. Coping behaviour is behaviour that is need-motivated and goal-seeking, while expressive behaviour is behaviour that is indicative of an agent's character. I will later argue that expressive behaviour may also be need-motivated and goal-seeking. The two kinds of behaviour are not mutually exclusive; average behaviour, Maslow observed, is usually both.[11] Needs and personal character combine to motivate all kinds of behaviour, including morally relevant behaviour.

---

9 Mary Midgley, *Beast and Man: The Roots of Human Nature* (London, Routledge, 2002 [first published 1979]), p. 309.
10 Maslow, 'A Theory of Human Motivation', *Psychological Review* Vol. 50(4), July 1943, p. 371.
11 A Theory of Human Motivation, p. 391.

Before looking more closely at Maslow's theory of needs I want to touch on what Elizabeth Anscombe described as 'backward-looking motivation,' as evinced, for example, in acts of revenge and gratitude.[12] That we can be motivated to act by something in our past would appear to sit uneasily with Maslow's views. Needs and character are both present-time affairs: needs are felt *now*; character is a state of being that exists *now*. In making this point, I should explain that I understand Anscombe's concept to be concerned with events from the relatively distant past. A reasonable period of time would have to have elapsed between past event and present action; otherwise all motivation could be described as backward-looking, and the usefulness of Anscombe's idea would be lost. Needs-based motivation and character-based motivation invariably involve past events, since actions of all kinds are effects of antecedent causes or reasons. But the kind of motivation described by Anscombe is very common, so I will take a moment to consider whether Maslow's fundamentally duplex schema can accommodate it.

For something in one's distant past to motivate action in the present time it must have had a significant and enduring effect on the person doing the backward-looking. For that to be the case, the person's basic needs would likely have been affected in some way. In particular, if a past action was a harmful one, then by definition the backward-looking person's basic needs would have been violated. Furthermore, the backward-looking occurs from a standpoint situated in the present, a standpoint that can be described as an attitude of mind. Our attitudes of mind and the values they reflect are what our characters are about. Backward-looking a motive may be, but the looking occurs in the present and it determines action now. Backward-looking motivation can therefore be viewed as real-time motivation that arises from a combination of influences based on needs and character, as Maslow said most motivations are. That being so, Anscombe's idea can be comfortably accommodated within Maslow's needs-cum-character paradigm.

---

12 G. E. M. Anscombe, *Intention* (Cambridge, Massachusetts: Harvard University Press, 2000 [first published 1957]), Section 11.

Let us now look more closely at what Maslow had to say about needs (character will be the main topic of chapter 7).

Maslow's Hierarchy of Needs

According to Maslow, the needs (all of them basic) that motivate human behaviour can be understood in terms of a hierarchy, ranging from (at the bottom) physiological needs to (at the top) self-actualisation needs. Physiological needs include the need for food and water, while self-actualisation is primarily concerned with the need to fulfil one's potential. For Maslow, a need's position in the hierarchy reflects its motivational force, or 'prepotency'. The lower the need in the hierarchy the greater its prepotency. In general, he maintained, a need does not assume full motivational force until those below it have been satisfied.

This is how prepotency works. Imagine a person who is on the verge of starvation: he or she would be unlikely to be concerned with high intellectual pursuits, such as those engaged in by Maslow himself. George Orwell (1903-50) saw as much, a decade before Maslow. Writing on the condition of tramps Orwell remarked, 'They have nothing worthy to be called conversation, because emptiness of belly leaves no speculation in their souls.'[13] Similarly Primo Levi (1919-87), the Italian writer and scientist. In his book *If This Is a Man* (1958) Levi provides a vivid account of what life was like for people incarcerated by the Nazis at Auschwitz, as he himself was. In a subsequent volume, *The Periodic Table* (1975), he expanded on what it meant for the internees to be hungry. Levi recounts how the extreme hunger suffered by the prisoners conditioned all of their behaviour, and made him feel 'abnormal'. Their need for food dominated their minds, even to the extent of suppressing the fear of death.[14] Levi goes on to describe how he learned to steal as a means of obtaining the wherewithal to acquire food. To become a thief required him to repress the moral strictures that he had until then scrupulously followed. He stole everything, he tells us, with one exception: the bread of his

---

13 George Orwell, *Essays* (London: Penguin Books, 2000), p. 10. The quotation is from the essay 'The Spike', which was first published in 1931.
14 Primo Levi, *The Periodic Table*, translated by Raymond Rosenthal (Melbourne: Penguin Books, 2010 [first published 1975]), pp. 116-117.

companions. There are several things that are especially noteworthy about this. First, hunger is seen to have prevented Levi from feeling 'normal'; in other words, sufficient food was necessary to the attainment of a state of normality. Second, there is the deep-rooted need that guided all of his behaviour, and suppressed other motives—testimony to the hierarchical motivational force (i.e. prepotency) of the basic needs. Next, usurpation by the need for food of erstwhile moral injunctions against stealing, with the very important exception of the bread of fellow sufferers—morality survived, in the form of empathy.

Here, then, is Maslow's hierarchy:[15]

- Self-actualisation needs: self-fulfilment, normative consistency.
- Aesthetic needs: appreciation of and creation of beauty.
- Cognitive needs: knowledge, understanding.
- Esteem needs: approval, recognition.
- Belongingness needs: affiliation, love.
- Safety needs: shelter, security.
- Physiological or homeostatic needs: sleep, food, water, etc.

Maslow grouped the seven kinds of needs under two headings: the lower ones were called 'deficiency needs', and the higher ones 'meta-needs'. The dividing line was drawn between esteem and cognition.[16] Metaneeds can also be called 'being needs', in recognition of the importance that Maslow placed on the concept of being. According to him, there is a 'B-realm' and a 'D-realm', where 'B' and 'D' stand respectively for 'being' and 'deficiency'. Distinct forms of cognition, values and language are said to prevail in each of the realms. With regard to B-cognition, among the qualities listed by Maslow are detachment, unselfishness, fearlessness, humility, and 'Taoistic', and because of all those, such cognition is considered optimally receptive in respect of reality; to use Maslow's word, B-cognition is 'veridical'.[17] B-cognition is obviously values-laden, and the values with which it is invested were of great consequence for Maslow. B-values were equated by him with metaneeds.[18] Beauty, truth

---

15 Adapted from Ernest R. Hilgard, Rita L. Atkinson and Richard C. Atkinson, *Introduction to Psychology* (New York: Harcourt Brace Jovanovich, Inc., 1979 [first published 1953]), p. 316.
16 See *The Farther Reaches of Human Nature*, p. 271.
17 *The Farther Reaches of Human Nature*, pp. 123-124.
18 *The Farther Reaches of Human Nature*, pp. 294, 301.

and goodness are listed under the B-values, and the realisation of such values (i.e. when reality accords with them—whence satisfaction of the metaneeds) was regarded by Maslow as a means of human development, in the form of a step towards self-actualisation.[19] I will have more to say on these matters later, but for the time being I will refer to metaneeds as 'being needs', or 'B-needs', because of their strong association (indeed, identity) with B-values.

Intellectual achievement (a cognitive need) and aesthetic experience (an aesthetic need) were regarded by Maslow as instrumental in the attainment of self-actualisation, but also as needs in their own right. In his seminal 1943 paper, Maslow speaks of his then-unconfirmed impression that the artistic and intellectual attainments of basically satisfied people were easily distinguishable from those of basically unsatisfied people.[20] 'Basically satisfied people' are those who are best prepared for self-ac-tualisation. Maslow eventually discovered that the force of the various B-needs tends to vary among people: for example, and unsurprisingly enough, some rate aesthetic experience above intellectual achievement, whereas others reverse the order.[21] Nevertheless, while no evidence of a generalised hierarchy of prepotency among the B-needs was forthcom-ing, everyone was found by Maslow to have a hierarchy of some kind. On the whole, I think Maslow's broad 'D' and 'B' classifications make sense. Hunger and danger would commonly be thought of in terms of an absence of something, namely food and safety, while self-fulfilment would reasonably be seen as an elevation, or perhaps unification, of one's very being. Similarly for the intervening categories.

Although Maslow initially grouped basic needs under two heads, he later came to think that they might also be accommodated within a threefold classification—lower basic needs, higher basic needs, and meta-needs.[22] Lower basic needs are the physiological and safety needs at the bottom of his hierarchy, higher basic needs are belongingness and esteem, and the metaneeds at the top consist of aesthetic experience, intellec-tual achievement and self-actualisation. Lower basic needs are in effect

---

19 *The Farther Reaches of Human Nature*, pp. 307–309, 129.
20 A Theory of Human Motivation, p. 383 (footnote).
21 *The Farther Reaches of Human Nature*, pp. 312–313.
22 *The Farther Reaches of Human Nature*, p. 318.

subsistence needs: food and shelter are needed in order for us to subsist, i.e. they help make physiological survival possible. Maslow's higher basic needs are 'social needs': their satisfaction depends on particular kinds of relationships with other people. Metaneeds correspond to the being needs of the original two-tiered taxonomy. In grouping needs along these lines Maslow could be seen to have been simulating (probably unconsciously) the tripartite psychology of Plato (c. 427 – c. 347 BCE), according to which the human soul consists of an appetitive part, a spirited part, and a rational part. Many if not most of our modern ideas and theories have ancient roots, especially those concerning human nature.

Alternative Classifications of Needs

Various ways of describing and classifying needs have been proposed by other theorists besides Maslow. For instance, the philosopher David Braybrooke (1924-2013) referred to basic needs as 'course-of-life needs' and distinguished them from 'adventitious' needs and preferences. According to Braybrooke, the need for something can be considered basic if it is essential either to living or to normal functioning. Such needs, he maintained, are crucial to social policy, which was his chief interest.[23] Braybrooke also spoke of 'derived needs', which result from conceptions that erstwhile irremediable deficiencies are presently being made remediable by social, scientific, and technological advances. Example (mine): those infected with HIV in reasonably affluent societies may now be said derivatively to 'need' AZT or something similar; in less affluent societies, or in days gone by, the need would simply not have existed, either because of the drug's unavailability or because of its prohibitive cost. As Braybrooke pointed out, continuing social advancement will likely give rise to an expansion in derived needs.

Braybrooke also argued that derived needs may end up becoming course-of-life needs,[24] which seems right to me, at least to some extent (the qualification will be explained in a moment). For example, it is hard to see how we could get along in today's world without computers

23 David Braybrooke, *Meeting Needs* (Princeton: Princeton University Press, 1987), p. 32.
24 Braybrooke, *Meeting Needs*, p. 111.

and the Internet. Course-of-life needs that evolve from derived needs could be looked upon as quasi-basic needs. I use the qualifier 'quasi' because the relevant underlying Maslovian instinctoid need would conceivably remain unaffected; consisting, as it were, as a kind of nucleus around which satellite derived-cum-course-of-life needs orbit. In the case just mentioned, the instinctoid need could be any one of a number of those specified by Maslow (for example, belongingness, intellectual achievement), and the products of information technology would be the quasi-basic needs (e-mail, Facebook, scientific and design software, and so forth). More plausibly and perhaps more simply, satisfaction of the quasi-basic needs could be regarded as steps towards satisfying the core instinctoid needs; again, in the case at hand, the products of information technology could very clearly be viewed as tools that are used in the satisfaction of the associated instinctoid needs.

In general Braybrooke was critical of any attempt such as that made by Maslow to grade needs. All of the basic needs, Braybrooke maintained, are of equal rank.[25] It was his opinion that the Maslovian hierarchy is an overly ambitious 'conceptual innovation;' a more conservative approach, in his view, would be to ascertain what effect non-satisfaction of the various needs has on people's survival and the harm done to them.[26] Now one might be forgiven for thinking that the recommended approach would inevitably lead to a ranking of the basic needs, contrary to their putative parity; but apart from that, from a Maslovian perspective, such an approach would seem to be implicit in the distinction between deficiency needs and being needs. Survival is more likely to be threatened by the non-satisfaction of deficiency needs than the non-satisfaction of being needs, although harm of some kind would attend both.

Yet Braybrooke's hesitancy towards the ranking of needs does raise the question: if they are not to be arranged hierarchically, in some sort of order of importance or urgency, then how might they be arranged—if at all? I think there is one alternative worth considering, namely that of an interactive network. Needs are related to one another differently in each of the models. In the hierarchical model, they are related through

---

25 Braybrooke, *Meeting Needs*, pp. 71-72.
26 Braybrooke, *Meeting Needs*, p. 71.

Maslow's notion of prepotency: satisfaction of a relatively lower-order need 'makes room for' a relatively higher-order need to become active; i.e., to become a motivating force. That this in fact happens is supported by the evidence from Orwell and Levi, and by common sense. In the network model, needs are related in either (or both) of two ways. First, where satisfaction of one need triggers a feeling and perhaps awareness that another need remains unsatisfied, analogous to the 'making room' that occurs in the hierarchical model, but without the necessarily 'upward' movement from lower to higher; here the movement can be in any direction. The second way in which needs are related within a network is through 'satisfaction-enablement', where satisfaction of one need enables another need to be satisfied. Examples are not hard to find. Scientific discovery and hence satisfaction of the need for intellectual achievement could lead to the satisfaction of, say, someone's need for subsistence, as was the case with the twentieth century's 'green revolution', where research into agricultural production led to the development of high-yielding crops that are credited with having saved many people from starvation. Satisfaction-enablement of that kind is not necessarily at odds with hierarchical ordering. For instance, in their quest for discovery scientists could be 'driven' by a sense of communal interest, where their need for intellectual achievement is 'preceded' by a need for social bonding, and perhaps esteem. In sum, I believe the network model to be a reasonable representation of the way the various needs interact, but a place nevertheless should be retained within it for some kind of ranking in terms of importance, or urgency. The concept of prepotency should also be retained.

The discussion of needs resumes in Chapter 9, but the foregoing is enough of a platform from which to explore their relationship with harm. The relationship is straightforward: harm, I maintain, consists in the exacerbation of basic needs.

Harm

To exacerbate a need is to block or withdraw the means of satisfying it. Blocking access to the means of satisfying a basic need, or withdrawing them, results in non-trivial harm, and may therefore be morally relevant. Suffering can arise from all kinds of actions, including some that involve non-living things: for example, the destruction of sacred sites, property damage generally, despoliation of wild-life habitat, and the pollution of air and seas. More examples follow to help clarify and cement the relationship between harm and need, some from life and others from literature. Harm will be seen to come from the denial or violation of the needs of respondents, by agents acting to satisfy some kind of need of their own. We will also see how questions of moral rightness and wrongness arise from the interaction between the needs of the various parties. It is not just harm of any kind that is involved, but morally relevant, non-trivial harm.

Example 1. An agent's quest for the satisfaction of his need for aesthetic experience may serve to deny a respondent's need for esteem, for example pornographers, who see beauty where others see exploitation; those who are exploited are at risk of losing their self-respect. Another example from literature illustrates the impact of an agent's need for aesthetic experience on a respondent's need for belongingness. Oscar Wilde's eponymous anti-hero in *The Picture of Dorian Gray* (1890) is presented as a supreme aesthete, someone primarily concerned with preserving his youthfully handsome appearance while engaging in self-indulgent orgies. During Dorian's lifetime, debauchery has only a latent though cumulative effect upon him, as reflected in a magically changing portrait that he kept hidden. Others suffer more immediately and more grievously, including Lady Gwendolen, whose children are removed from her care because of her involvement with him. Satisfaction of the need for aesthetic experience may come at the cost of someone else's safety. Ancient Roman gladiatorial contests, in which lives were put at risk for the sake of spectacle, would be one such instance. Bull-fighting in the present day would be of the same kind; the construction of elaborate monuments by slave-labour would be another example. Franz Kafka's *In the Penal Settlement* (1919) could also be cited. In the story, a prisoner is condemned to death for insulting and disobeying an officer. The executioner employs a bizarre harrowing machine, which neatly inscribes the command 'be just' on the victim's body. The victim is thereby tortured to death in order to satisfy someone's perverse aesthetic taste and appease their corrupted sense of justice; there is little doubt that 'evil' would suitably describe the situation, more than mere wrong.

Example 2. Kidnapping and enslavement of someone by a person driven by a lust for power obviously impinges on the victim's need for love, and could also put his or her safety at risk. The pathology in such an instance could be egomania, or even megalomania. If not completely evil, acts of this kind would be very close to it. There can be no doubt about the evil of acts motivated by self-actualisation that impinge on the safety and survival of others. Adolph Hitler, in his quest for a Germanic empire, to be achieved at the cost of devastation of many livelihoods and societies, is an obvious example. Many dictators have been complicit in wrongs of this kind; Rafael Trujillo for instance, ruler of the Dominican Republic from 1930 to 1961, whose murderous methods and sexual predations are graphically described in Mario Vargas Llosa's novel *The Feast of the Goat* (2000). Stalin's destruction of Soviet agriculture for the sake of a political theory could also be mentioned. An arsonist who lights bushfires on a code-red day would be another case in point.

Example 3. Apart from any physical harm, paedophilia often impinges on a respondent's need for esteem, by undermining the victim's self-respect—'philia' in the term denotes merely a perverted kind of love at best: victimhood is not conducive to love. Perhaps the point could be generalised to cover all relationships involving a lover whose purpose is to exploit or otherwise harm his or her object. As Spinoza says, 'When we love a thing similar to ourselves, we endeavour, as far as we can, to bring it about that it should love us in return.'[27] Spinoza's argument relies on the proposition that our love is intended to affect the beloved pleasantly. Should that happen, the beloved will associate the pleasure he or she feels with the lover (an external cause), and love will be returned. In the absence of mutual pleasure, or joy, the relationship between lover and beloved could hardly be classed as loving.

Example 4. Agents striving for intellectual achievement may impinge on a respondent's need for esteem. Holocaust-denial belongs in this category: for the sake of propagating a hare-brained theory, respect for

---

27 *The Ethics*, 3p33.

Jewish survivors and their descendants is jeopardised. The eponymous hero of Mary Shelley's *Frankenstein* (1818) was also driven by the need for intellectual achievement. In this case, the creation of the 'monster' from inert matter comes at the expense of the created being's need for belongingness; much sought-after human sympathy was denied him. Luke Rhinehart's (a pseudonym) 'autobiographical' novel *The Dice Man* (1971) demonstrates how intellectual achievement can impinge on safety and physiological needs. The title refers to Rhinehart's decision to use the results of dice-throws to determine how he should respond when faced with alternative courses of action. Although boredom and world-weariness are given as reasons for using the dice, his initial decision resulted from an intellectual stance, the upshot of which was ironically to dispense with reason—a bit like the philosopher Ludwig Wittgenstein's (1889-1951) proposition that his *Tractatus* philosophy should be used as a ladder that can be discarded after having scaled the heights of the work. The determinations of the dice lead Rhinehart to commit various atrocities, including rape.

Example 5. In Leo Tolstoy's *Anna Karenina* (1878), the eponymous heroine falls in love with Vronsky and has a child by him. At first her husband insists that she remain with him, because of the social embarrassment that a separation would entail. Anna's need for belongingness is consequently thwarted, and she ultimately commits suicide. To cast Anna as the victim, or respondent, in this case may seem odd, since she is the one who engaged in adultery. But the calculating coldness of her husband Karenin inclines us towards sympathy for his wife. Even when Karenin temporarily relents and expresses willingness to accept the role of guilty party in divorce proceedings (to protect Anna from disgrace), he undoes his magnanimity by lauding himself for it. Karenin in this phase of the story displays the kind of pride that was condemned by the Roman emperor and philosopher Marcus Aurelius (121 – 180): 'that pride which is proud of the want of pride is the most intolerable of all.' [28] Nevertheless, Anna's behaviour could also be deemed wrong, because of the harm she inflicted whilst going about satisfying her needs. Her

---

28 Marcus Aurelius, *Meditations*, translated by George Long (Chicago: The University of Chicago, Great Books of the Western World, 1952), Vol. 12, XII.27.

attraction to Vronsky was at least partly attributable to the sexual gratification offered by their relationship, which would have presented a means
of self-actualisation. But her self-actualisation was gained at the expense
of threatening Karenin's social position. The complexities of the moral
issues contribute to the depth of the story.

Example 6. Someone's esteem may come at the expense of another
person's survival or safety. A case in point would be the theft of someone's
life-savings by a dishonest investment manager intent on preserving her
place in society. Indeed, various kinds of deception aimed at personal
gain may be placed under this head. Financial fraud such as that mentioned, intellectual fraud in the form of falsified scientific evidence, and
artistic fraud through unacknowledged use of someone else's work may
have the need for esteem as their cause, and impairment of safety as
effect. A plagiarist might attain his goal of a prestigious literary prize, to
the detriment of the financial security of legitimate contenders. To the
extent that it becomes known, dishonesty of this kind could also breed
cynicism and mistrust, thereby damaging the social fabric. In that event,
dishonesty would act as a barrier to the satisfaction of the respondent's
need for belongingness.

Example 7. Colonial invaders clearing what they deem to be *terra nul-
lius* might be afforded shelter, but only at the expense of the livelihood of
the indigenous population. A similar, but more controversial, case would
be the destruction of poppy and coca fields in Third World countries in
order to impede the flow of drugs to other nations. The poppy and coca
growers have their means of subsistence destroyed in order to mitigate
the health and economic risks posed by the drugs. Whether this is really
wrong would depend on whether the drugs are deemed to impact negatively on the physiological well-being and the safety of users. Presumably
they would, in which case the action could be regarded as being right
from one perspective and wrong from another; lives are at stake from
both of them. Determining whether an action is wrong or right can
be difficult, but thinking about it in terms of needs can at the very least
clarify the issues involved. (The PHM would decide the issue in favour
of destruction of the drug crops; see Chapter 6, 'Case Studies'.)

Exacerbation of need works against the various forms of connectedness that were discussed in Chapter 2. Relations between things break down, either physically, socially or intrapersonally. Many disconnections result from either non-moral or morally neutral causes, for example nuclear decay in the world of physics and the death of loved ones (from natural causes) in the social and psychological domains. Disconnections are happening all the time, but there is a particular cause of disconnectedness that I want to take up here: viz., destructiveness, or 'the spirit of destruction.' The concept comes from the philosopher Alexander Baumgarten (1714-62), and finds expression in acts of philistinism and vandalism, the latter regardless of whether artefacts or natural objects are targeted.[29] Artefacts are generally someone's property, and we can be harmed by having our property destroyed. We can also form attachments with natural objects, our pets for instance, and can therefore be harmed when they are harmed. But the spirit of destructiveness, destroying for the sake of destroying, is contrary to connectedness irrespective of whether human beings are themselves harmed. What, for instance, would be thought of us if we were to act like the sole occupant of an imaginary island described by the philosopher Mary Midgley (b. 1919), and destroy all of its flora and fauna shortly before we leave? We would be condemned, I suspect.[30] Such destruction could be described as having been uncaring, or care-less, and therefore a violation of the PHM. Similarly, another philosopher, John Passmore (1914-2004), charged the last surviving member of the human race with responsibility for departing without further damage to the environment. In a discussion of our obligations to non-human nature, Passmore refers to plants and non-human animals as life 'we can by our actions destroy.'[31] I will have more to say about Midgley's and Passmore's last-person scenarios in a discussion of environmental ethics in Chapter 5.

If harm via destructiveness is wrong, what kind of harm or destructiveness are we talking about? To say something along the lines of 'that which destroys without good cause' would only be begging the

---

29 John Passmore, 'Attitudes to Nature', in Robert Elliot (editor), *Environmental Ethics* (USA: Oxford University Press, 2004 [first published 1995]), p. 140.
30 Mary Midgley, 'Duties Concerning Islands', in Elliot (editor): *Environmental Ethics*, p. 98.
31 Passmore, p. 129.

question, as would 'that which destroys without care either for the thing that is destroyed or for the concatenation of things with which the thing destroyed was connected'. Some kinds of destruction are indeed necessary and inevitable, since life in all of its forms depends upon destruction—including destruction of other life forms. The destruction of cancer cells, the elimination of deadly viruses and the deactivation of weapons of mass destruction would assuredly be far removed from moral reprehensibility. Nevertheless, some destruction is clearly immoral, and we would all be better off without it.

As needful beings, we are vulnerable to harm, both physical and psychological. And from the 'humbled acknowledgement' of our own vulnerability, we are led to the recognition of the vulnerability of others. Raimond Gaita makes the point in his book, *After Romulus*.[32] The concept (and reality) of needs obviously plays a large part in Gaita's moral landscape, though not to the extent of constituting its substratum. For Gaita, the concepts (and reality) of the uniqueness and irreplaceability of each and every individual human being fulfil that role. But I think needs go rather deeper than that. In Part II I will argue that all of our basic needs stem from a fundamental need for order (in the case of human beings, our need for homosapient order), thereby enabling us to ground morality in a naturalistic principle.

Cruelty and Carelessness

Cruelty is an egregious form of harm. Most people would have a clear idea of what it involves: it is harm that is deliberately inflicted, in order to make its victim suffer. As well as that, the philosopher Judith Shklar (1928-92) perspicaciously observed that victims of cruelty tend to be weaker beings; weaker, that is, compared with their tormentors. Furthermore, besides physical pain, victims are beset with anguish and fear. Shklar regarded cruelty as the 'supreme evil.'[33] On the latter score she may well have been right: cruelty is certainly contrary to humaneness, which I

32 Gaita, p. 34.
33 See Matthew Festenstein and Simon Thompson (editors): *Richard Rorty Critical Dialogues* (Great Britain: Polity Press, 2001), p. 94.

think can be shown to be a deep-seated life form of humankind, and something that most people would subscribe to (see Chapter 7).

Cruelty's egregiousness can be made clearer by comparing it with sadism. The two are not coextensive, but they do overlap. A sadist inflicts pain primarily because of the pleasure he derives from inflicting it. A cruel person inflicts pain primarily because of his victim's suffering and humiliation; any attendant pleasure on his part is of secondary interest. Divergence might also occur in respect of the degree of pain inflicted, and the kind of victim. The sadist may obtain satisfaction from something less than the extremes of pain concomitant with cruelty, nor would his attention necessarily be directed towards a weaker being.

A multitude of beings have fallen victim to cruelty down through the ages, and it has taken many forms. Non-human animals have long been subjected to beatings and mutilation, leading to the advent of organisations like the RSPCA. And human beings continue to be bedevilled by it, for example in the form of human trafficking (itself a form of slavery). Bullying is another form of cruelty. Physical pain might not have been suffered by someone who has been bullied, but mental trauma and humiliation would almost certainly have been experienced.

Acts of cruelty often evoke powerful emotional responses in those who witness them, for example sorrow, indignation, disgust, and anger. Such emotions are unpleasant, even painful, and add weight to any reasons that might be invoked for condemning cruelty. Reasons are not hard to find, ranging from self-interest ('if they can do it to them they can do it to me') to genuine sympathy for victims. But the emotions may be needed to spur us to act against cruelty; to prevent it where we can. As Judith Shklar said, cruelty has no need of divine censure; naturalistic human feelings and beliefs provide sufficient reason to condemn it. Likewise sadism and bullying.

Cruelty is the first thing targeted by the PHM. We are enjoined to strive against its infliction on living beings, so we need to be aware of which beings might be vulnerable to it. Based on Shklar's definition, we could say that such beings are those from species whose members are normally capable of suffering physical pain, fear and anguish. I say 'normally capable' to accommodate those who have been deprived of the said capacities, for example anaesthetised patients. In such cases, cruelty would consist in acts that could reasonably be expected to cause pain or fear or anguish if the individual were not incapacitated.

Carelessness was the other matter set down for discussion in this section. It may seem strange to bracket carelessness with cruelty, but they happen to be fairly close cousins. Common to both of them is a deep-seated indifference towards the suffering of their victims. Carelessness entails inattentiveness to the consequences of one's actions; in other words, a failure to 'strive', as discussed in the previous chapter. Lack of care can amount to lack of concern for others, and is widely condemned, across many cultures. For instance, it is the 'heedlessness' referred to in the present chapter's epigraph. Hinduism's *Bhagavad-G t* delineates three qualities, or constituents, of nature: *Sattva*, *Rajas*, and *Tamas*, the first representing light, or goodness; the second signifying passionate self-absorption; and the third connoting ignorance, or dark-ness. Human nature emerges from the constituents, and our actions are said to reflect their characteristics. To act in accordance with *Sattva* is to be humble at the same time as being resolute; to act in accordance with *Rajas* is to be fundamentally selfish; and to act in accordance with *Tamas* is to be indifferent towards what might happen as a result of our actions. *Tamas* actions are careless, leading to the possibility of grievous harm. Although harm that is carelessly inflicted might not have been done with the intention of causing fear and anguish, it may nonetheless elicit them. Indeed, if we think about it, indifference itself could give rise to fright; it may also be enough to evoke sorrow and distress. If a proponent of the PHM were to address Cain's question, 'am I my brother's keeper?', the answer would be an emphatic 'yes', at least in respect of those affect-ed by his or her actions.

Cruelty and carelessness harm people by impinging on the needs in Maslow's hierarchy, by threatening physical survival, by destroying belongingness, by undermining self-respect, and so forth. Non-human beings capable of feeling pain, anguish and fear can also fall victim to cruelty, and to carelessness as well. And all living things, not just those capable of the feelings mentioned, are vulnerable to the spirit of destruc-tiveness: all of them have needs, all of them have a need for what might be called 'living order' (of which homosapient order could be regarded as a species), and can therefore suffer harm. In the next chapter we will see what a non-human animal ethics and an environmental ethics might look like, based on the PHM.

Chapter 5: Living Beings and the PHM

A thing is right when it tends to preserve the integrity, stability, and beauty of the biotic community. It is wrong when it tends otherwise (Aldo Leopold).

The expression 'living being' means simply what it says. Everything that lives, including oneself. In this chapter we will consider how the PHM applies to non-human animals and the environment. In particular, we will examine their eligibility for respondency to morally relevant behaviour by human beings. As you might expect, eligibility will be shown to hinge on the existence of needs.

Non–Human Animals

Non-human animals obviously have needs, and their needs are apparent to us largely because of the similarities between them and us, both physical and emotional. In his book *Good Natured: The Origins of Right and Wrong in Humans and Other Animals* (1996) the primatologist Frans De Waal (b. 1948) recounts many instances of sympathy and empathy among non-human animals. De Waal also finds evidence of advanced cognitive powers in some species, especially those that are genetically close to human beings, such as chimpanzees.[1] But we don't need science for knowledge of these things; we only have to open our eyes to see the similarities for ourselves, even in animals that are more genetically distant from us. My cat, for instance, has no difficulty in putting together the bundle of sense perceptions that my presence elicits in him and identifying the result as me. Furthermore, he is clearly capable of associating the assemblage of sense data with memories that please him because of what he has learned to expect from me: some food and a pat—all involving the exercise of cognitive powers, plus the activation of physiological and belongingness needs. All living things need nourishment, animals generally also possess a need for safety, and many higher animals exhibit

---

1 See also chapter 10 of Mary Midgley's *Beast and Man*.

a need for belongingness; for example cattle and sheep in their herding behaviour, gorillas and other primates in their tribalism. Aesthetic needs also seem to exist in some species; for example, some female birds have been found to select their mates based on the beauty of the male's song (songsters are usually males). Charles Darwin (1809-82) went as far as claiming that birds have 'nearly the same taste for the beautiful as we have.'[2] Regardless of whether their needs are satisfied through instinct or choice, a sense of humility and tolerance could result from recognition of the needfulness of other creatures—although undeniably different, we are also in some respects the same as other life-forms. A closely comparable sentiment pervaded the ancient cult of Pythagoreanism and remains extant in Buddhism.

Because of their needfulness and consequent vulnerability to harm, non-human animals qualify for respondency to morally relevant actions by human beings. That is especially so where the actions are cruel actions. A rational agent would adhere to the injunction against cruelty for the same reasons he adheres to other norms, essentially because of his underlying humaneness. Due care would also be involved. Adherence would be consistent with his values and serve the interests of the animal. Needs are at the centre of the PHM, including the needs of human agents and the needs of non-human respondents. The pain occasioned by cruelty is contrary to the needs of the afflicted being: there is a need to avoid it, and, for anyone seeking to avoid wrong-doing, a need to avoid inflicting it. The origin of that need will be explained in Chapter 7, as part of the discussion of humaneness.

I will now examine whether the scope of moral respondency can be expanded to accommodate the rest of nature, besides human beings and non-human animals—indeed, whether the environment in its entirety might qualify. The discussion begins with a definition.

---

2 Charles Darwin, *The Descent of Man*, in *Darwin* (Chicago: The University of Chicago, Great Books of the Western World, 1952), Vol. 49, p. 451.

The Environment

Very broadly, 'environment' refers to that which surrounds, or encircles. Surrounds or encircles what? For reasons that will soon become clear (if they are not already obvious) the answer is 'humankind', and that which does the encircling is nature in all of its non-human manifestations, both living and non-living. The living environment consists of all non-human organisms: trees, grass, flowers, bees, bacteria, mosses, birds, fish, and so forth. The non-living environment includes the four ancient elements, earth, fire, water and air, in various forms such as soil, rocks, volcanoes, rivers, oceans, rain, clouds, ozone, etc.

Why place humankind in the centre of the environing circle?—simply because we are the only beings capable of moral agency. Agency on the part of the environment can immediately be ruled out: for the reasons given earlier, morally relevant action is confined to human beings, and the environment as defined is entirely non-human. Might the environment alternatively occupy the role of respondent? Which is to say, can it be morally wronged? That is more difficult to decide.

In order for the environment to be deemed capable of suffering moral wrong, one would have to be able to speak plausibly of its needs; and through its needs, its vulnerability to harm. But it would seem nonsensical to attribute needs to the non-living environment—none of the needs catalogued by Maslow are relevant to it. How, for instance, could the seas and the air possibly stand in need of safety or belongingness? Oceans and air that have become polluted might 'need' cleansing to restore their 'health', but the need and the healthiness are not felt by sea or air—rather, they constitute needs of those who use and rely on them, namely ourselves and other dependent organisms. The living environment is different: some of the Maslovian needs do indeed apply to its denizens. Minimally, all organisms need various kinds of material sustenance to survive, and some animals also require social connectedness (including the many families of creatures referred to as 'social insects'). The moral status of non-human animals has already been dealt with, and the points made a moment ago with respect to cruelty and carelessness apply to non-human animals in the environment (i.e. 'wild' ones) with

as much force as they do to animals that have been domesticated or otherwise brought into contact with human beings. But the environment as
I have defined it encompasses many things besides non-human animals.

I think a positive answer to the question of respondency might be
obtained by treating the environment holistically; that is, by regarding
it as a whole that is more than the sum of its parts. It is from this perspective that environmental needs begin to make sense. Aldo Leopold
(1887-1948), co-founder of the Wilderness Society in the U.S., can help
explain how. As seen in the epigraph to the chapter, Leopold maintained
that 'a thing is right when it tends to preserve the integrity, stability, and
beauty of the biotic community. It is wrong when it tends otherwise.'[3]
The proposition has long served as a rallying-cry for environmental ethicists. By speaking of its 'integrity', Leopold clearly regarded the biotic
community as a fundamentally interconnected entity, one that can be
viewed as an *integrated* whole, and one whose 'internal processes must
balance, else its member-species would disappear.'[4] Similarly, balance
would be required in the internal processes of the non-living segment
of the environment, else its members could also disappear, or possibly
undergo radical change, thereby affecting other members both living
and non-living. Now we know from Darwin that nearly all of the species that comprise biotic communities are destined for replacement,
that their disappearance is inevitable. We also know that Darwin was
fully aware from his geological studies that non-living features of the
Earth are subject to constant change. Unlike Darwin, however, Leopold
was concerned with shorter time-frames than those required for natural selection and many geological processes to have perceptible effects.
Within shorter time-frames, say a few centuries, survival is possible and
stability may take hold.

Leopold tied stability to conservation, which he defined as 'a state of
harmony between men and land.'[5] By 'land' he meant everything on,
over, or in the ground, which would appear to be close in connotation to the term 'biotic community'. Close, but not identical: Leopold's

---

3 Aldo Leopold, *A Sand County Almanac: with Essays on Conservation from Round River* (New York: Ballantine Books, 1970 [*A Sand County Almanac* first published 1949, *Round River* first published 1953]), p. 262.
4 Leopold, p. 191.
5 Leopold, p. 189.

definition excludes humankind from 'land', but we are clearly part of the biotic community. 'Land' nevertheless would seem to be getting close to 'environment', where the latter is understood to consist of our natural surroundings. It was probably Leopold's wish that we become more aware of nature, and humble in light of that awareness, when he asked, 'does the educated citizen know he is only a cog in an ecological mechanism?'[6]

In his argument for what he called 'conservation education,' Leopold proclaimed that the aim of such education was to address the problem of 'how to bring about a striving for harmony with land amongst a people many of whom have forgotten there is such a thing as land, amongst whom education and culture have become almost synonymous with landlessness.'[7] For harmony to take hold, education would, in his view, need to foster 'an ethical underpinning for land economics and a universal curiosity to understand the land mechanism.'[8] In the very last sentence of *A Sand County Almanac*, he talks of 'building receptivity into the still unlovely human mind.'[9] The harmony sought by Leopold was that of 'the wild and the tame in the joint interests of stability, productivity, and beauty.'[10] A sense of tolerance can be gleaned from this, and an ethos of respect. In his advocacy of land conservation, Leopold held that 'a land ethic changes the role of *Homo sapiens* from conqueror of the land-community to plain member and citizen of it. It implies respect for his fellow-members, and also respect for the community as such.'[11] Respect of that kind, I suggest, would likely be reciprocated by fellow-members. Integrity, stability, diversity and productivity can all be regarded as environmental needs. They are needed by the environment as a whole; its survival and preservation depend upon them. Because of its needfulness, the environment is vulnerable to harm, and it therefore qualifies for respondency to morally relevant behaviour.

Before moving on I want to do a little delving into the third thing about the biotic community (i.e. besides its integrity and stability) that

---

6 Leopold, p. 210.
7 Leopold, p. 210.
8 Leopold, p. 202.
9 Leopold, p. 295.
10 Leopold, p. 199.
11 Leopold, p. 240.

Leopold considered worthy of preservation—its beauty. To begin, let us simply note that the beauty of an object is a matter of aesthetic judgement, and call on Kant for assistance in determining what that involves. The first thing to note is that beauty is one of just two categories of aesthetic judgement, the other being 'the sublime'.[12] For reasons that will soon become obvious, if Leopold had been a Kantian he might have chosen to speak of the biotic community's *sublimity* as well as its beauty. Kant's ideas on the sublime are worth pursuing, because they can help explain why the biotic community and the environment (or 'land') more widely should be paid the kind of respect that Leopold says they deserve.

According to Kant, the form and content of an object deemed to be sublime differ in some important ways from those of a beautiful one. For instance, whereas 'the beautiful in nature is a question of the form of an object, and this consists in limitation, . . . the sublime is to be found in an object even devoid of form, so far as it immediately involves, or else by its presence provokes a representation of *limitlessness*, yet with a superadded thought of its totality.'[13] Immediately a puzzle confronts us. How, one might ask, could anything that strikes us as being limitless simultaneously be regarded as a totality? A totality consists of a definitive summation of parts, so there would surely be bounds around it that enable one to perceive it as such; without them, the counting of parts would be interminable and 'totality' would be impossible. In short, if something has bounds then it cannot also be limitless; the bounds are its limits. But let us grant Kant this implicit paradox, and conclude that the sublime is pervaded by a further quality, namely mysteriousness; and with that, otherness.

In fact, for Kant, it is chiefly this sense of otherness that distinguishes the sublime from natural beauty. Natural beauty comes to us, he maintains, as having been 'pre-adapted to our judgement,' whereas the sublime strikes us as being incompatible with it.[14] We can make sense of one but have trouble with the other. Natural beauty, we might infer, generally

---

12 Immanuel Kant, *The Critique of Judgement*, translated by James Creed Meredith (Chicago: The University of Chicago, Great Books of the Western World, 1952), Vol. 42 (henceforth referred to as 'Judgement'), Introduction s. vii.

13 Kant, *Judgement*, s. 23.

14 Kant, *Judgement*, s. 23.

serves as a pleasurable, calming influence, but the sublime unsettles us. Sunsets and birdsong are greeted with joy, whereas turbulent seas and rugged mountains evoke feelings bordering on fear. Furthermore (this is me talking now, not Kant), the limitlessness of the sublime can be conceived of as extending beyond the spatial dimension to the temporal. Beauty is transient, the sublime endures. The pleasure of the first can therefore be accompanied by wistfulness, and the disquiet of the second by a sense of grandeur—grandeur that demands respect from us, perhaps even *awe*. A sense of *largeness* (in relation to one's own being) would seem to be involved; and the environment, as that which surrounds, must of necessity be larger than whatever it surrounds. In which case, the environment would be an appropriate object of appraisal under the aspect of sublimity.

Further on the subject of respect, Kant maintained that the sublime prepares us 'to esteem something highly even in opposition to our (sensible) interest.'[15] Now to esteem something even when it is opposed to our own interest would conceivably open the way to recognition of the needs of the object; whence acknowledgement of moral respondency. If we esteem something we could hardly be indifferent to its interests; rather, we may well seek to serve them, and in so doing help satisfy the object's needs. In regard to the environment, that would mean acting in ways that promote its integrity, stability, diversity, and productivity. With tolerance and humility, respect could develop from the cooperative effort that is required for sustained ecological balance and survival. When Kant defined respect as 'the conception of worth which thwarts my self-love'[16] he was clearly pointing in that direction.

The Wide Reach of the PHM

Non-human animals are morally significant, partly through participation in the environment, but also because of their vulnerability to cruelty and carelessness. And while the rest of the environment might not

---

15 Kant, *Judgement*, General Remark following s. 29.
16 Immanuel Kant, *Introduction to the Metaphysics of Morals*, translated by W. Hastie (Chicago: The University of Chicago, Great Books of the Western World, 1952), Vol. 42 (henceforth referred to as 'Morals'), note 2, p. 259.

be susceptible to cruelty, it can certainly suffer from the carelessness of human beings. Because of the role it plays in the satisfaction of human needs, the environment in general is morally significant. It can also be considered worthy of respect, partly because of the feelings that attend a sense of the sublime. The needs of animals and the environment are analogous to human needs, sufficiently so, I believe, for them to qualify for respondency in morally relevant situations. Moreover, through realisation of the connectedness of the world, their needs can become our needs. Thoughtfulness and tolerance are the underpinning principles. The same principles are of course applicable to actions directed at human beings.

Chapter 6: Human Beings and Moral Harm

The nature of justice is a pledge of reciprocal usefulness, [i.e.,] neither to harm one another nor be harmed (Epicurus; 341-270 BCE)[1].

The PHM's implications for our species go somewhat further than they do for other living beings. As well as proscribing cruelty and carelessness, the principle requires that we strive to ensure that human beings are *never* harmed, except to prevent them from suffering or doing unwanted harm. It also requires that any preventive harm that is administered is never more than the minimum necessary to forestall whatever unwanted harm could reasonably have been expected in the circumstances. These requirements bring human judgement into the picture, both in respect of assessing the likelihood of unwanted harm, plus its nature and extent, and in respect of determining the minimum harm required to forestall it. Quality of moral judgement is largely a function of personal character, which will be discussed in the next chapter. Here we will probe the concepts of 'unwanted harm' and 'preventive harm', partly by employing the principles of reciprocity and justice. Having done that, the PHM will have been fully defined. Some case studies showing how the PHM may apply in practice conclude the chapter.

Unwanted and Preventive Harm

'Unwanted harm' means simply what it says. Most people have an aversion to being harmed, most of the time. To want to be harmed would be contrary to the self-preservation and happiness that we generally desire. Masochism aside, it would be contrary to human nature. But it so happens that harm is sometimes necessary to prevent harm being done or suffered; in cases of self-defence, for instance. The unwanted harm in such circumstances would be the harm that the person under attack

---

1 Epicurean Principal Doctrine XXXI, as listed by Diogenes Laertius. See Brad Inwood and L. P. Gerson (translators and editors), *The Epicurus Reader* (Indianapolis: Hackett Publishing Company, Inc., 1994), p. 35.

believes he or she is likely to suffer. Because of its insistence on our 'striving to ensure', the PHM requires that beliefs about what might happen be reasonably formed and held. Preventive harm would itself probably be 'unwanted' by the would-be assailant, but 'wanted' by the intended victim. Wherever preventive harm is administered, the PHM also requires that it be no more than the minimum necessary for the desired effect to be realised. More fully, it requires that we strive to ensure that the least possible (but still efficacious) harm is inflicted. Judgement must be exercised there as well: judgement that employs presence of mind, accompanied by self-restraint.

Some kinds of harm are clearly worse than other kinds. An arson attack on someone's unoccupied home may prove to be more harmful than slandering its owner, but never as bad as murdering him. The basic human needs categorised by Maslow point to a way in which degrees of harm might be assessed. Actions that exacerbate needs towards the bottom of his hierarchy (e.g., survival, safety) would usually be regarded as worse in kind than those that violate relatively higher-order needs (e.g., aesthetic experience, cognitive achievement). But that is not to deny the importance of the higher-order needs: when it comes to human nature, they are just as fundamental as all of the other needs. Nevertheless, it is clear that most people most of the time would choose to be slandered in preference to being murdered. As well as measuring harm by kind, it may also have a quantitative aspect. For instance, the harm done by murdering two or more people would be greater than that arising from murdering one person. Given that degrees of harm exist and are discernible, the infliction of harm by someone in anticipation of harm being done or suffered by someone else brings reciprocity into play, and with reciprocity comes justice.

Reciprocity and Justice

Aristotle had a lot to say about reciprocity, but dismissed it from moral significance. According to him, the Pythagoreans who preceded him had mistakenly 'defined justice without qualification as reciprocity.'[2] While

---

2 Aristotle, *Nicomachean Ethics*, V, 5, 1132b.

reciprocity in the sense of give and take might be thought to imply equity, for Aristotle it meant returning same for same, an eye for an eye—to the detriment, he believed, of the stability of the body politic. In his view, what should be sought is proportionality between offence and punishment. Aristotle's 'proportionality' is what we would now understand as 'even-handedness': the two notions entail the return of one thing for another thing, where the thing returned is fitting in the context though not necessarily the same as the other thing.

Reciprocity is central to various systems of ethics. Confucians, for example, maintain that 'when a man carries out the principles of conscientiousness and reciprocity he is not far from the moral law.'[3] Conscientiousness is akin to the kind of attentiveness and care that I have been talking about, while reciprocity is encapsulated in the so-called Golden Mean. According to the Mean, whatever you would not have done to you by other people you should refrain from doing to them. The Golden Rule of Christianity is of course very similar, pointing to the value accorded to reciprocity by widely divergent cultures. Indeed, the same principle can be found in an influential branch of atheistic ethics, that of naturalism, where again we find it being associated with 'gold'. As described by Thomas W. Clark (founder and director of the Centre for Naturalism in the U. S.), the 'Golden Rule of Reciprocity' answers to our need for community involvement coupled with individual flourishing.[4] Flourishing through reciprocity fits comfortably with the ideas I am promoting. Individual flourishing is a Maslovian need. Reciprocity within a community is a means of satisfying our need for social order. In the same way that we need to give respect as well as receiving it, we need both to be humane and to be treated humanely (more on this follows in the next chapter).

Reciprocity involves giving or receiving something by one person in return for something received from or given to another person. The exchange will be adjudged fair (i.e. just) if the respective parties benefit equally (or nearly so) from the things they receive in return for what they give. The substitution of one harm for another harm in cases

---

3 Lin Yutang, *The Wisdom of Confucius*, p. 110.
4 Thomas W. Clark, *Encountering Naturalism: A worldview and its uses* (Cambridge, MA: Centre for Naturalism, 2007), p. 85.

of preventive harm constitutes a form of exchange, and may therefore be viewed under the aspect of reciprocity. However, instead of being determined by equality or thereabouts between preventive harm and forestalled harm, the appropriateness of the former will depend on whether it exceeds a reasonably determined minimum. Infliction of preventive harm will always be attended by the threat of inappropriateness, i.e. of overstepping the mark and causing more suffering than the circumstances warrant. Hence the PHM's 'no worse than the minimum' stipulation. We will be acting rightly if the harm we inflict in order to prevent ourselves from being harmed is no worse than the minimum harm we (reasonably) believe to be necessary. We will also be acting rightly if the harm we inflict in order to prevent someone from suffering unwanted harm is likewise no worse than a reasonably determined minimum. Right is the aim whenever harm is administered in order to prevent the person harmed from either suffering or doing unwanted harm.

Punishment for harm that has been done can also be viewed under the aspect of prevention. For it to accord with the PHM, harm inflicted in the form of punishment must be no more than the minimum adjudged necessary to prevent the culprit from re-offending. Such would be the basis of humane punishment. If vengeance is to be given a place (and human nature may demand that it be so) then let it consist in the fact of the harm that is meted out to the offender, in line with the stated principle. Any harm inflicted under the principle may also serve the interests of societal lawfulness, by deterring others of similar propensity from offending.

Having led to some ideas about punishment, the discussion of reciprocity has brought us to a point where justice has become the issue. From the standpoint of an individual, justice has an external dimension and an internal one. Externally, interactions between the individual and other people may be described in terms of just or unjust. Internally, the individual may be similarly described: 'she is a just person'; 'he is unjust'. The Greek concept of justice (dikaiothyne in a Romanised version of the original lettering) encompasses both dimensions. It entails a sense of order, both external and internal—externally, orderly relations between the individual and his or her natural and social environments; internally, harmony between an individual's reason, feeling and will. Plato considered justice to be inseparable from the virtues of wisdom, courage and temperance; either a person is just, wise, courageous and temperate, or is none of these.[5]

As will be shown in a moment, the Platonic virtues are implicit in an externally focused conception of justice advanced by the philosopher and legal scholar John Finnis (b. 1940). In Finnis's view, justice consists essentially of three elements—other-directedness, duty, and equality. Other-directedness is concerned with one s interactions and relationships with other people; duty stems from one s indebtedness to others, and their rights vis-à-vis that indebtedness; and equality is aligned with the notions of proportionality, equilibrium and balance.[6] Justice, Finnis maintains, will have been served where the things that are fitting for and needed by a person to survive and to live well are forthcoming.[7] Where, then, are the Platonic virtues to be found in Finnis's formulation? Well, a certain amount of wisdom would be required in determining what is fitting; a certain amount of courage in obtaining what is fitting; and a certain amount of temperance in providing those in need with that which is fitting. Outward-looking other-directedness can therefore be seen to be deeply conditioned by internal qualities; which is to say, by personal character.

Like Finnis, the philosopher John Rawls (1921-2002) also focused on the external dimension of justice. For him, a just society is a 'rightly ordered' society,[8] and the concept of justice is concerned with fairness in the resolution of competing claims.[9] Very briefly, justice as fairness in a society requires that equal basic liberties (for example freedom of conscience and speech) are enjoyed by everyone, that social and economic opportunities are the same for everyone, and that no-one benefits

---

5 Plato, *Republic*, translated by Paul Shorey, in *Plato: The Collected Dialogues*, edited by Edith Hamilton and Huntington Cairns, IV, 427e.
6 John Finnis, *Natural Law and Natural Rights* (Oxford, Great Britain: Oxford University Press, 1980), pp. 161-163.
7 Finnis, p. 163.
8 John Rawls, *A Theory of Justice* (Cambridge, Massachusetts: Harvard University Press, revised edition 1999 [first published 1971]), p. 20.
9 Rawls, *A Theory of Justice*, p. 9.

from altered socioeconomic arrangements unless the least advantaged members of society also benefit.[10]

In contrast to Finnis and Rawls, Maslow turned his psychologist's gaze inwards and attended predominantly to the internal dimension of justice. He associated several so-called 'metapathologies' with injustice, including insecurity, anger, cynicism, mistrust, lawlessness and total selfishness.[11] These are all personal characteristics, for it is perfectly conceivable that a person might be described as cynical, or mistrustful, or insecure, or 'metapathological' in any other way, without any particular action on his part having been in mind. For Maslow, the effects of injustice are very similar to those of disorder, which include lawlessness, breakdown of authority, insecurity, wariness, loss of safety, necessity for vigilance, alertness and tension. Then there is 'total selfishness', which would certainly be contrary to both Finnis's and Rawls's conceptions of justice. Selfishness works against other-directedness, duty, equality and fairness, all of which contribute to the principle of reciprocity. Total selfishness could be regarded as a cause of injustice as well as being an effect of it; both cause and effect, or reciprocally reinforcing, where one's own selfishness precipitates selfishness in someone else.

Summing Up

Let us put all of the bits of the PHM back together and remind ourselves of what it says:

> *In your dealings with the world, firstly strive to ensure that no living being is harmed either cruelly or carelessly. Secondly, strive to ensure that no human being is ever harmed, except to prevent unwanted harm being done or suffered by the person who is harmed. Thirdly, strive to ensure that any preventive harm administered in accordance with the second stipulation never exceeds the minimum necessary to forestall whatever unwanted harm could reasonably have been expected in the circumstances.*

---

10 See Rawls, *A Theory of Justice.*
11 *The Farther Reaches of Human Nature*, p. 308.

Some fairly straight-forward questions that can be asked of actions by human beings can be extracted from the principle, to facilitate adjudications of wrong and right. First, in respect of all living beings, (1) Is harm inflicted either cruelly or carelessly? And in respect of human beings, (2) Is the action harmful without being intended to prevent the person being harmed from doing or suffering harm? (Call this the 'non-vindicated harm test'.) (3) Where the intention was to prevent harm being done or suffered, is the preventive harm more than the minimum necessary to forestall whatever harm could reasonably have been expected in the circumstances? (Call this the 'no-worse-than-minimum' test.) Wrong would be the decision if the answer to any of the questions is yes. For an action to be adjudged right the answer to all three questions would have to be no.

You might think that a principle of behavioural-governance would be better framed positively instead of negatively ('do this!' rather than 'do not do that!'). For example, the following would seem to be saying much the same kind of thing. *In your dealings with the world, strive to ensure that the basic needs of all living things (including oneself) are maximally satisfied*—the 'principle of the greatest good', as it might be termed. But no. Expressed in that manner, the principle would quickly be shown up as being impracticable, for it would surely be the case that maximum satisfaction for some of us could only be attained at the expense of other living beings: our natural selfishness would see to that. The negative formulation is therefore better. In any case, the two formulations are not equivalent. Maximum need-satisfaction is not the same as harm-minimisation: harm-minimisation may go some of the way towards satisfying one's needs, without maximising their satisfaction.

As we have seen, the Principle of Harm-Minimisation readily lends itself to a three-question test for moral guidance. In some circumstances a simpler two-step rule could suffice: first, do no harm (*primum non nocere*); then, secondly, if harm is unavoidable, act on the least harmful of the possible courses of action. As has been mentioned, a rough measure of relative harmfulness may be established by identifying the kinds of needs at stake. Working against a person's need to survive by murderously attacking him would usually be regarded as being more harmful than violating his need for shelter by burning down his house. The more basic the need (i.e. the closer to the bottom of Maslow's hierarchy) the greater the potential harm.

Some examples of how the rules might be applied follow.

Case Studies

Coal and Global Warming

It is widely believed that global warming induced by coal-burning will cause harm in the form of ill-health, shortened life-spans, and all of the social and economic costs associated with the various pathologies. The question that one must ask oneself of any action is whether greater harm will befall living beings if it is not undertaken. For as long as it lasts all of us bear some responsibility for coal-burning. So the question that we coal-burners need to ask ourselves is whether the harm to future generations exceeds the harm we would suffer if the coal industry were shut down. Although this might seem to be merely a kind of negative utilitarianism (least harm instead of maximum happiness), the degree to which future harm is quantifiable for comparison with the present benefits of coal-burning should be given serious consideration. Harm may be more amenable to measurement than happiness.

Drug Crops and their Destruction

In the discussion of harm in Chapter 4 the question arose as to whether it is right to destroy poppy and coca fields that form the livelihood of growers in Third World countries, in order to impede the flow of drugs to other nations. We can now answer that it is. In the first instance, cultivation of the drugs would be deemed wrong under the PHM, because the harm they do is not of a preventative nature; or, more precisely, the harm is not inflicted with the intention of preventing the person harmed from either doing or suffering harm. Conversely, the harm that destruction inflicts on the growers is designed to prevent them from doing unwanted harm to others, and would therefore be deemed *prima facie* acceptable under the PHM (only *prima facie*, because an assumption that I will mention shortly would also have to be tested). Alternatively, if the proxies of the user-sufferers decline to destroy the crops when they have a chance to do so, unwanted harm would be inflicted on the user-sufferers in order to prevent harm being suffered by other parties, namely the growers; so non-destruction (as an instance of morally relevant non-action) would be wrong. That of course rests on the assumption that destruction is the only effectual course of action, and the least harmful one (to the growers).

Harming the Dead
Sophocles' (d. 406 BCE) tragedy *Antigone* illustrates how the violation of non-living entities can harm living beings. In the play, the tyrant Creon is opposed in battle by Polyneices. Polyneices is slain, but retrieval of his body is forbidden by Creon. Polyneices cannot be buried and is therefore dishonoured according to the custom of the day. His sister Antigone loses her life in an attempt to obtain justice for her brother's memory. The three-question test is required here. Creon's action would fail the non-vindicated harm question, and could also be adjudged cruel.

Hate-Speech
Is a bigot wrong when he vilifies people because of their ethnicity? The victim of racial abuse is harmed by being deprived of the respect that he believes he deserves from other people. The harm inflicted is not of a preventive nature and therefore constitutes a violation of the PHM. The bigot is wrong to vilify. A side-issue is whether those who advocate unrestricted freedom of speech might themselves be wronged by restraints on hate-speech. If they feel the need to be able to say anything they like, they might regard any such restraints as an obstacle to self-fulfilment. Here some kind of weighing the respective kinds of harm is required. To my mind, restraints on free-speech would be the lesser of the two: self-fulfilment is higher Maslow's scale of needs than respect, in which case any harm suffered from its non-satisfaction would be less severe in kind than that arising from lack of respect.

Holy Book-Burning
Living beings are harmed when something they value is harmed or violated. A devotee of Islam would be deeply offended by a public (and

publicised) Koran-burning, say by an official of another religion. Let us imagine that an official is driven by his belief that his is the only true religion and that anything precious to people of other faiths constitutes fair game. The need motivating his action may have been self-actualisation, either in the form of a desire to harm through an exercise of power, or by means of expressing the religious zealotry that is fundamental to his character—it is hard to think of anything else that could inspire such a deed. The need of the Muslim would be lower and therefore more basic on Maslow's scale, a mixture most likely of respect and belongingness, both of which are violated by the desecration of the beloved object. Clearly, instead of book-burning, far less harmful ways of expressing disagreement could have been found. For anyone with the merest smattering of humaneness, the official's action would not be seen as having harm-prevention as its aim. The action would therefore be morally condemnable. Matters would be worse if the desecration provoked revenge attacks, resulting in collateral death and injury. If such attacks were predictable, then the Koran-burner would be culpable, as would the assailants. The basic right to life would have been violated.

Meat-Eating

Provided the killing is neither cruel nor careless, the use of other organisms as food would be permissible under the PHM. Vegetarians and vegans would probably be among the first to disagree, but anyone who seriously and sincerely believed their health to be dependent on a diet that included meat could argue that harm in the form of killing was necessary to prevent a similar kind of harm befalling them.

Runaway Rollercoaster

Might do's and don'ts along the lines suggested help an agent faced with having to choose from a set of alternative courses of action where all of the probable outcomes are open to moral objection? Some conundrums posed by the evolutionary biologist Marc Hauser (b. 1959) illustrate the problem. In one of them, a rail-car carrying five people is hurtling towards a collision that would certainly kill everyone on board. An onlooker named Denise could, if she so chooses, throw a switch that would divert the rail-car onto a siding; but there is a person on the siding who would be killed when the car hits him. Should Denise throw the switch, thereby saving five people at the cost of one person's life? In a variation of the dilemma, instead of having a diversionary switch at her disposal, Denise could, again if she so chooses, push a very fat man onto the track before the car reaches the point of collision. The man's body mass would be sufficient to stop the car without injuring the passengers, but he would be killed. Should she push? Surveys conducted by Hauser revealed that the majority of respondents would throw the switch, but not push. In other words, throwing the switch was regarded as right and pushing as wrong.

By simple accounting, the consequences of the switching and the pushing are identical—five lives saved, one lost. Bare numbers therefore fail to explain the different responses. What is more, application of the PHM cannot resolve the matter: switching and pushing would yield the same answers to the various test-questions. Perhaps switching was deemed acceptable because it was less 'hands-on' than pushing. Also, the pushing option could be regarded as unrealistic, thereby solving the problem—by dissolving it. For one thing, even to think that someone's body mass would be able to stop a speeding rollercoaster seems improbable. The respondents could have intuited the unlikelihood of the thought ever entering Denise's mind. Furthermore, if the man were really so gross, would Denise be able to move him onto the track in the split second available to her? That too seems unlikely.

But the PHM provides a clear-cut solution of a deeper problem, namely whether Denise should switch or push at all. Should she prevent the crash, or would she be doing better to let it occur? Whichever way, in either set of circumstances, she could be held responsible for at least one death. (Remember that refraining from possible action is equivalent to actually acting when it comes to morally relevant behaviour.) Denise is at risk of being damned if she does and damned if she doesn't. But resolution is straightforward. Switching and pushing would both result in harm being done to a human being, not in order to prevent the person concerned from doing or suffering unwanted harm, but rather to prevent other people from being harmed. Either action would fail the non-vindicated harm test, and accordingly be adjudged wrong. Perhaps one should say the lesser of two wrongs, since allowing the rail-car to crash also has its drawbacks. Nevertheless, Denise could not reasonably be held responsible for the circumstances leading up to the crash, where-as she most certainly would be responsible for the switching or pushing, and their consequences. Denise should neither switch nor push.

  Note that the case could be viewed under the aspect of human sac-rifice, such as that involving the mythological Greek princess Iphigenia. Iphigenia's father Agamemnon had offended against one of the gods, who by way of retribution demanded that he kill her. Like the potential victims of Denise's switching or pushing, the harm inflicted on Iphigenia had nothing to do with preventing any harm that she herself might have done or suffered. Human sacrifice is morally wrong.

Self-Defence (1)

What about an armed householder who confronts an unarmed burglar? The burglar flees into the bathroom and locks the door. The household-er fires his gun through the door, killing the intruder. (The similarities to the South African case involving the athlete Oscar Pistorius are inten-tional.) The bare facts suggest that the moral scales would weigh heavily against the householder: death entails much greater harm than what might reasonably have been thought necessary to prevent harm being done to himself. The householder could (and should) have bailed up the burglar and called the police.

Self-Defence (2)

An armed robbery is under way when a security guard enters the build-ing and sees the cashier being threatened; murder seems imminent. The guard shoots the thief. It is later found that the thief's gun was a toy, albeit a very realistic one. The three-question test is needed here. 'No' would be an appropriate answer to the first two questions, since the shooting was neither cruel nor careless, and it was intended to prevent harm being done. But the no-worse-than-minimum test is more prob-lematic. Clearly the shooting injury sustained by the thief is worse than anything he could have inflicted with the toy, but how could the guard have known that? Whether the thief could reasonably have been expect-ed by the guard to shoot the teller would decide the issue. On the bare facts of the case it appears that he could, so no wrong on the guard's part would be involved.

Telling Porkies

I want now briefly to consider the morality of falsehood. Falsehoods are lies, and are the opposite of truth. Following Bernard Williams, I understand truth to involve both sincerity and accuracy, and falsehoods their opposites. If we are sincere, then our assertions accord with our beliefs. If we are accurate, our beliefs are in reasonable accord with the facts.[12] Imagine truth and falsehood to be the poles of an axis, and that the axis is intersected at right angles by another axis, the poles of which are moral right and moral wrong.

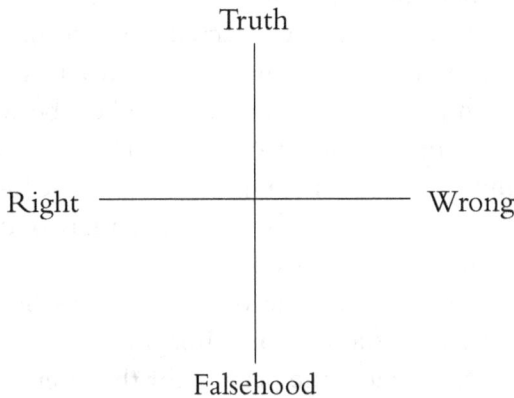

Truth

Right ———————————— Wrong

Falsehood

Figure 2: Morality of Truth and Falsehood

Perhaps counterintuitively, the picture thus presented indicates that as well as falsehoods being wrong and truth good, there are some falsehoods that are right and some truths that are wrong. But instances of the latter two are not hard to find. Morally right falsehoods constitute the region of the white lie, for example where a person misleads a would-be assassin with regard to the whereabouts of his intended victim. Conversely, by

12 See Bernard Williams, *Truth and Truthfulness* (Princeton: Princeton University Press, 2002), p. 94.

normal standards of decency and humanity, a person would be wrong
to respond truthfully to the assassin's inquiries. The other two sectors
of the chiasmus are uncontroversial: truth/right and falsehood/wrong.
Harmless truth-telling is precisely that, harmless, and therefore right;
injurious falsehood is by definition harmful and therefore wrong. I will
give two examples of the latter.

First let us consider some poorly made clothes using inferior material that are placed on the market by their maker. A customer is tricked
into believing the clothes will meet all of her needs, including comfort.
Business has been slow, and the sale will help the tailor to keep afloat.
Being gullible the customer takes him at his word. By seeking to augment his means of livelihood the tailor is primarily motivated by the
need for sustenance; there is nothing more basic than that. The customer's physiological needs are also affected, because of the financial loss
she suffers. Besides that, and more seriously, when she realises that she
has been duped her self-respect would also likely be wounded, perhaps
aggravated by a general mistrust of others. The waste of money might
have been minimal, but that in conjunction with the loss of respect both
for herself and for other people would conceivably outweigh the tailor's
gain; his lie would be adjudged wrong.

Perjury is my second example of injurious falsehood, although less
straight-forwardly than the first one. Imagine that a drug-runner is on
trial in a jurisdiction where the penalty for the offence is death. He lies
under oath in an attempt to save his life. Leaving aside for a moment
the question of whether the death penalty itself can ever be justified,
should the lies be adjudged right or wrong? The perjuring agent's need
is survival, but that of the respondent—is what? And who exactly is
the respondent? With respect to the perjury (as distinct from the drug
trafficking), perhaps the community as a whole, in the form of the state,
should be seen as respondent, either in its own right or on behalf of
potential victims of drugs should the perjury have the desired result,
i.e. acquittal. In its own right, the state could conceivably suffer some
kind of harm at the hand of an agent (for example breach of its perjury laws), and therefore nominally qualify as respondent—but harm of
that nature may not be morally significant. Rather, for the harm to be

morally significant, it would also need to impact on individual human beings, or other kinds of living beings. The state is an abstraction, and it is hard to imagine how abstractions could be harmed in a moral sense— none of the Maslovian needs are applicable to them. Taking, then, the potential future victims of the agent's drug-running to be respondent to the perjury, it would seem that the needs under threat centre on survival, i.e. the same need that is at stake for the agent. The case involves significant harm on both sides.

To settle the question of the rightness or wrongness of the perjury, a position would first have to be taken on the death penalty, especially if one accepts the principle propounded by Rawls to the effect that obligations cannot issue from unjust institutions. If the death penalty were sufficient to render a social system as a whole unjust, then perjury in the circumstances of the case would seem permissible, notwithstanding the possibility of future harm.

Terrorism and Torture

Should a terrorist be tortured in an endeavour to find out where he planted his bomb? In other words, should the terrorist be harmed in an attempt to prevent harm being suffered by the victims of the bomb? Which is the lesser of the two harms? Application of the two-step rule under utilitarian principles clearly points towards torture—if torture is eschewed, a great many people might be killed or otherwise injured, harm that could have been avoided if the vital information had been extracted. The case sits under the rubric of self-defence. The PHM would mandate the use of force to obtain the required information, on the proviso that cruelty remains off limits. (Sanctioning torture would seem to conflict with the Universal Declaration of Human Rights; for discussion, see p. 123.)

The Death Penalty

Application of the PHM is clear-cut on this issue. Inflicting death in order to prevent someone who is in custody from committing further crimes would rarely if ever constitute the minimum harm necessary to achieve the desired result. On the stated principles, imposition of the death penalty would always be wrong.

Voluntary Euthanasia

Medically-assisted suicide for the terminally ill could be considered under the two-step rule. Because of the existence of harm, morally relevant behaviour is clearly involved. Two parallel instances thereof, in fact. On the one hand, where the person providing the assistance to die performs the role of agent and the patient that of respondent. On the other hand, where the patient is both agent and respondent. In both instances, for the action of the agent to be morally right under the principles that have been set down, it would have to be based on the alternative that is least harmful for the patient. Two kinds of harm are at stake. One consists in the pain and possible loss of dignity that accompanies protracted dying; the other is death itself. Which is the lesser of the harms? That is something that only the patient can (and should) decide, in his or her particular circumstances. Any legal sanction of assistance-to-die would have to include safeguards ensuring that suicide was the authentic choice of the patient, at the time assistance was provided. Such safeguards could prove very difficult both to formulate and to implement, given the possibility of a person's views on the subject changing over time. Comatose patients would present a particular problem in that regard, perhaps resolvable to some extent by the use of medical powers of attorney.

Conclusion

From the case studies we can see that many kinds of moral issues are susceptible to treatment by the PHM and the various tests emanating from it. But now the question arises, what kind of people, if any, might be committed to the principle? And should any such commitment be found to exist, where would it come from? Some answers are suggested in the chapter that follows.

Chapter 7: Motivation and the PHM

One is a slave to things in which one places one's highest values (St Augustine).[1]

To be committed to the PHM is to be committed to performing certain kinds of morally relevant behaviour, and refraining from other kinds. Behaviour, we recall from Maslow, is motivated by the interaction between personal character and needs; in which case, the commitment in question might reasonably be expected to be associated with a particular kind of personal character and a particular kind of need. In this chapter we will see that adherence to the PHM is coincident with goodness of character and a need for humaneness. Conversely for non-adherence, where badness of character and inhumaneness are the rule.

Good Character, Bad Character

Personal character is a determinant of the rightness or wrongness of a person's morally relevant actions, i.e. whether or not the actions conform to the PHM. Reciprocally, the moral tenor of a person's actions forms the basis of our assessment of his or her character. As the philosopher Jean-Paul Sartre (1905-80) once proclaimed, we are the sum of our acts. Substitute 'character' for 'we' in the formula, and we would have character consisting in what our actions say about us, plus, if one wanted to dig a little deeper, the beliefs that lie behind our actions. It is only through our dealings with the world that our character can become known to others, and possibly also to ourselves.

Someone whose actions are predominantly or habitually good will be adjudged a person of good character, while a habit or predominance of evil dealings with the world will be regarded as the work of a person of bad character. In speaking thus, there is an obvious need to

---

1 See Paul Vincent Spade, 'Medieval Philosophy', in Anthony Kenny (editor), *The Oxford History of Western Philosophy* (Oxford: Oxford University Press, 1994), p. 65.

come to an understanding of what 'good' and 'evil' mean when used to describe a person's behaviour. Otherwise we risk going round in circles: good behaviour issues from good character; good character is the result of good behaviour, and so on. We have made a start on breaking the circle, by aligning goodness with observance of the PHM and evil with non-observance thereof. Some ideas from Aristotle on the notions of virtue and vice will help unravel it a little further. Virtue, of course, is tantamount to goodness, and vice to evil.

According to Aristotle, virtue 'is a state of character concerned with choice, lying in a mean, i.e. the mean relative to us, this being determined by a rational principle, and by that principle by which the man of practical wisdom would determine it.'[2] Since a 'man of practical wisdom' is nothing more or less than a good man, we seem to have found ourselves in the same kind of circle, where the good consists in that which is recognised as being such by a good person. But let us press on: an escape route will be suggested in a moment.

The mean spoken of by Aristotle is one that charts a course between two extremes, both of which are vices; one being a vice of 'excess', the other a vice of 'defect'. Example: If one course of possible action would be prodigal (excess) and another course niggardly (defect), then a middle course would be described as liberal. Of the two Aristotelian extremes, one is generally more erroneous than the other. The mean that constitutes virtue is not simply the mid-point (the median) between them, but a context-sensitive judgement that steers action towards the lesser of the two vices. This is consonant with the PHM's 'no worse than' stipulation in respect of preventive harm. Interestingly, two centuries before Aristotle, Buddha in the East was also exhorting his followers to adhere to 'the middle way,' according to which 'excessive mortification [is] as unreal and unworthy as mere desire and pleasure.'[3]

The virtue of courage provides a more concrete example. Courage, Aristotle maintained, lies between cowardice and foolhardiness: cowardly acts would rarely if ever be seen as courageous while foolhardiness is inconsistent with rational decision-making. A foolhardy person might

---

2 Aristotle, *Nicomachean Ethics*, II.6, 1106b-1107a.
3 William James, *The Varieties of Religious Experience: A Study in Human Nature* (London: Folio Society, 2008 [first published 1902]), p. 308.

appear to be courageous, but it would not be courageousness as Aristotle understood it. In a similar vein, the literary critic Walter Benjamin (1892-1940) once noted how courage (*Mut* in German) is polarised in fairy tales, so that it occupies the middle ground between low cunning (*Untermut*) and high spirits (*Übermut*).[4] It is not hard to see how coward-ice might be associated with cunning, and foolhardiness with high spirits. Benjamin and the fairy tales on which he was commenting appear to have been on the same wavelength as Aristotle.

Why, though, should foolhardiness and cowardice be considered wrong? Or, for that matter, any of the extremes condemned by Aristotle. Looking beyond the labels, I think the answer is that such extremes are contrary to different aspects of our fundamental nature. Foolhardiness, for example, flies in the face of rationality, and cowardice undermines sociableness. That foolhardiness is akin to irrationality is easy to see, while cowardice is brought into conjunction with unsociableness through its inherent selfishness. A coward is someone intent on looking after his own interests whilst beggaring those of others; he or she is also likely to be equipped with a severely attenuated sense of shame. Ultimately, both foolhardiness and cowardice are forms of disorder—of the personality on the one hand, and of society on the other hand. I will have more to say on the goodness of order later, especially in Chapter 11, but here it can be noted that the relationship between goodness and order points to a way of escaping the circles that have been alluded to. If the relationship holds, goodness both of character and of behaviour would be assessable in terms of orderliness, rather than merely each other. To conclude with Aristotle, a person will be virtuous if his or her character is such that reason is exercised and a middle path between two extremes is chosen, and action is then undertaken in accordance with the choice.

Character was also prominent in Hume's discussions of morality. He gave this as a maxim: 'no action can be virtuous, or morally good, unless there be in human nature some motive to produce it, distinct from its sense of morality.'[5] What might that motive be? Hume again: 'An action, or sentiment, or character is virtuous or vicious; why? because its view

---

4 Walter Benjamin, *Illuminations: Essays and Reflections,* edited by Hannah Arendt; translated by Harry Zohn (New York: Schocken Books, 1968), p. 102.
5 Hume, *Treatise,* 3.1.1.

causes a pleasure or uneasiness of a particular kind.'[6] So we see virtuous behaviour, i.e. morally right action, being associated with pleasure,
and wrong with its opposite. Virtuous action and virtuous character are
inextricably linked, and together are responsible for a 'particular kind' of
pleasure. As Philippa Foot observed, the foundation of moral philosophy
for Hume consists in the action-guiding nature of moral judgement,[7]
and personal character would clearly have a large bearing on the quality
of moral judgement. This is a very important aspect of morality. From a
moral perspective, a person's character consists in the degrees to which
it is marked by natural goodness and natural evil. As such, character
influences moral judgement and guides action consequent upon moral
judgement.

The notion of character entails a sense of personal identity. If everyone
existing at a particular moment of time were not *in some way* identical
to the person they think they were a moment before, or a day before,
or whatever other sensible unit of time before, then there would be no
point in talking about character. I have italicised 'in some way' because
of the large number of theories on offer with respect to continuity of
identity. As mentioned earlier, there are theories that focus on physical
continuity, others that look to psychological continuity (especially with
regard to memory), and some that consider both of these kinds.

Some ideas on the notion of psychological continuity from the philosopher Derek Parfit (b. 1942) are worth noting. According to Parfit,
changes of character can come about either deliberately or non-delib-
erately, and either normally or abnormally.[8] Deliberate normal changes
would include those arising, say, from voluntary character-building exer-
cises. Non-deliberate normal changes would be those that are induced,
for example, by the aging process, and by one's dealings with the world.
Deliberate abnormal changes of character would include those brought
about by brain surgery such as lobotomies, and by forced indoctrination.
Changes resulting from illness (for example, dementia) and injury could
be regarded as non-deliberate and abnormal.

---

6 Hume, *Treatise*, 3.1.2.
7 See Foot, p. 9.
8 Derek Parfit, *Reasons and Persons* (Oxford: Clarendon Press, 1987 [first published 1984]), p. 207.

Regardless of the cause, a person's character can change radically. Think, for example, of the lascivious Augustine (354-430) before his conversion to Christianity and eventual accession to sainthood. Some of Augustine's pre-conversion behaviour was certainly contrary to the tenets of Christian virtue, but post-conversion he was quite a different person. Would the later Augustine have deserved to be punished for his earlier behaviour? Parfit maintains that desert should vary directly with the degree of psychological connectedness between past and present selves.[9] With regard to Augustine, since very little connectedness is apparent, there would on Parfit's principle be no justification for punishing him.

Whether Parfit's principle itself is applicable in all circumstances could be another matter. If the past actions were particularly heinous, then any apparent disconnection of character may be incapable of excusing them. The case of John Demjanjuk (1920-2012) can be cited in this regard. After a series of trials beginning in 1986, Demjanjuk was convicted in 2011 of complicity in the deaths of many thousands of Jewish prisoners of the Nazi regime in occupied Poland. Demjanjuk steadfastly maintained his innocence, and died whilst the conviction was being appealed. After the war, Demjanjuk had lived for many years in the USA, where he was widely regarded as a model citizen. Nevertheless, if he was in fact guilty of the crimes attributed to him, then his apparent change of character would seem irrelevant.

Augustine's and Demjanjuk's histories, indeed all of our histories, can be considered in light of the question of whether human beings are fundamentally good or fundamentally evil. Variability of character is a fact of life—within individuals themselves as we have just seen, but also across the human species. In which case, one would seem to be skating on very thin ice if a generalisation were ventured with regard to the goodness or badness of human character. Nevertheless, I will soon offer an argument for the predominance of species-wide goodness, in the form of a need for humaneness. Before getting to that, we will see that some very great thinkers, the likes of Hume and Kant, have believed goodness to be the norm; or perhaps better to say, believed in the *possibility* of goodness

---

9 Parfit, p. 326.

being the norm. I will explain the qualification after outlining the ideas of the two men.

Hume first. According to the philosopher Marcia Lind (1951–2000), Hume can be seen as having wanted to secure the 'normative power' of the natural, in the absence of any kind of support from God.[10] (Which, of course, is precisely what my project is about, in its search for naturalistic grounds on which morality might be based.) Lind goes on to list some of the things Hume asserted about the natural, including its universality and inseparability from the species; its foundational role in human nature; the impossibility of its not 'holding' (i.e. it inexorably asserts itself); and its correctness, in contrast to the nonnatural, which is 'perverted.' In relation to the last, Lind notes that Timon the man-hater was given by Hume as an example of someone with a *perverted* sense of morality,[11] and that such perversions were understood by him as a form of malady, or malfunctioning—indeed, as being nonnatural. On that basis, normal and natural functioning would include the moral sense of benevolence that Hume promoted. Benevolence would count as a law of (human) nature.

Turning now to Kant, we find that he spoke of three predispositions in the 'fixed character' of humankind: animality, humanity and personality. Animality was described in terms of 'physical and purely *mechanical* self-love, wherein no reason is demanded,'[12] and characterised by self-preservation, propagation of the species and community with other people. Humanity as a predisposition was said to consist in self-love derived from comparing oneself with other people; practical reason is involved in making the comparison, and equality the main desideratum. Finally, personality was distinguished from the other predispositions by 'the capacity for respect for the moral law as in itself a sufficient incentive of the will.'[13] Moral feeling was considered by Kant to be an aspect of personality, a feeling that is assimilable by the free will 'into its maxims;' i.e., inculcated as a principle of conduct. The assimilation

---

10 Marcia Lind, 'Hume and Moral Emotions', in Flanagan and Rorty (editors), *Identity, Character, and Morality: Essays in Moral Psychology*, pp. 136-137.

11 Lind, p. 140.

12 Immanuel Kant, *Religion within the Limits of Reason Alone*, translated and introduced by Theodore M. Greene and Hoyt H. Hudson (New York: Harper & Row, 1960 [translation first published 1934]), p. 42 (text henceforth referred to as 'Religion'), p. 22.

13 Kant, *Religion*, pp. 22-23.

culminates in good character, which is something that is acquired rather than occurring spontaneously or fortuitously. Since the capacity for respect of the moral law could only be described as good, the predisposition that is personality is itself also good; moreover, good in a morally relevant way. But neither animality nor humanity were regarded by Kant as being inconsistent with the moral law. Therefore, the complete package of Kantian predispositions was associable with moral goodness. If human nature is fundamentally predisposed towards the good, how could Kant possibly account for moral evil? His answer was that we have a *propensity* for evil, as distinct from a *predisposition* for it. Predispositions were seen by him as being essentially innate, while propensities were held to be either innate or acquired. Self-love, when 'taken as the principle of all our maxims,' was considered by Kant to be the main source of evil.[14] Respect was prescribed as its remedy. Respect for others, that is. Should that become the 'principle of all our maxims,' then there would be much goodness in the world, goodness of will, goodness of deeds, and goodness of character.

Now the qualification that I said I would return to. It is simply this. Instead of goodness actually being normal to human nature, it might be better thought of as a human potential. There has been enough misery, wrongdoing and downright evil in the world to entitle one to think that the moral sense propounded by Hume has been swamped or at least dulled by insensitivity to the suffering of others. And enough of those things to believe that the Kantian propensity for evil has overwhelmed any innate predisposition to goodness that we might possess—that, as a species, respect for others has yet to become the principle of all our maxims, and that good character therefore remains a possibility rather than a fact.

A somewhat darker assessment of human character than whatever might be inferred from Hume and Kant was offered by Spinoza, for example when he wrote 'Anyone with any experience of the capricious mind of the multitude almost despairs of it, as it is governed not by reason but by passion alone, it is precipitate in everything, and very

---

14 Kant, *Religion*, p. 41.

easily corrupted by greed or good living.'[15] The 'multitude Spinoza refers to encompasses nearly everyone, specifically all of us who are incapable of reaching the heights of rationality and philosophising attained by the likes of Spinoza himself. And yet Spinoza can still be found enjoining the multitude (and true philosophers as well) to abide by the moral directive 'love your neighbour as you love yourself'. To love one's neighbour would be to refrain from wronging him, i.e. to avoid harming him; in other words, to practise goodness towards him. For Spinoza, the multitude were to conform to the directive through obedience (whether religiously or civically inspired), while philosophers were to discover and endorse it through rational inquiry. But the main point I want to make here is this: by virtue of the injunction Spinoza obviously assumed that such love and goodness are humanly possible. Had he not made that assumption, his words would only have been so much hot air, and he was not one to waste his breath in that manner. Again, therefore, we have before us the potential for (if not actual) goodness of character; in this case in the form of the capacity for love, or charity, which in the final analysis may not be so very different from Humean moral sense and the Kantian predisposition to goodness. For each of us, the extent to which any of these takes hold and predominates will depend, very generally, on both nurture (familial, cultural and geopolitical circumstances) and nature (biology, including genetics), plus interaction between the two.

What might be called the Tennyson principle pretty well summarises matters from the perspective of nurture. In Alfred Lord Tennyson's poem *Ulysses* (1842) we find the line 'I am part of all that I have met;' which is to say, 'I am part of you', and presumably 'you are part of me'. The Tennyson principle could be seen as a special case of Sartre's formula mentioned a short while ago, since our meetings with the 'others' of whom we are a part should assuredly be counted among the 'acts' that constitute our character. The 'that' in Tennyson's text encompasses the effects that others have on our need–satisfaction, and those effects include attitudes of mind towards the people concerned, and perhaps the world in general. Attitudes of mind are inscribed on our character. From

---

15 Spinoza, *Theological-Political Treatise*, Chapter 17 Paragraph 4.

the perspective of nature, the Tennyson principle could be expanded to include 'and I am part of those who met to make me'.

A good person, Philippa Foot maintained, is someone whose actions are guided by what she called 'practical rationality,'[16] a quality that aims at the propagation of good, having derived from goodness of character. Goodness of character entails goodness of will: goodness of will is definitive of character and is a factor in moral judgement. All of that sounds very much like Kant, for whom the will was the only thing that can be unqualifiedly good. But goodness of will is not the only kind of good:[17] goodness of will pertains specifically to human beings, while good in general may apply to anything that is consistent with an organism's natural purposes. My influenza would be good for the virus concerned, but bad for me.

Might personal character be the predominant, even sole, determinant of the way we behave? A criticism of the philosopher Friedrich Nietzsche (1844-1900) made by Foot is worth noting in this regard, for it raises the possibility of character being paid excessive attention. In Foot's view, Nietzsche claimed that the worthiness of an action depended more on the nature of the individual who did it than the act itself.[18] For Nietzsche, on Foot's reading, behaviour that would generally be regarded as reprehensible may be excusable, even considered meritorious, on the condition that the agent is someone above the 'herd'; i.e., an intrinsically virtuous 'master' rather than an intrinsically non-virtuous 'slave' (Nietzsche couched his theory of morality in terms like these). Against that, Foot insisted that actions may be bad in their own right, either because of their nature or because of their objective, or because they diverge from the agent's beliefs with regard to right and wrong.[19] Murder, for instance, is bad by nature; inducing someone through hypnosis to kill one's enemy would be bad because it has murder as its ultimate objective; and, on the assumption that the hypnotist did what he did because of his reluctance to commit murder by his own hands, his action would be bad also on the grounds of moral inconsistency, which

---

16 Foot, p. 62.
17 Foot, p. 51.
18 Foot, p. 110.
19 Foot, p. 76.

is a form of character-failure. The nature of human actions, the ends of such actions, and personal character are all relevant to issues of moral right and wrong.

Consonant with Nietzsche, one's character contributes to the nature of one's acts; contrary to him, Foot held that the nature of one's acts helps to define character. Character and action are reciprocally influential; it is a matter of both/and, not either/or. Foot also maintained that children cannot be taught norms merely by fostering in them such qualities as courageousness and authenticity, important though these be. More than that, children need to be made to understand that some things simply must not be done, such as murder and theft.[20] If Foot's theory of natural good is predominantly of the nature of virtue ethics, then it is a form of virtue ethics that embraces a large measure of deontological prescriptiveness.

I will soon argue that humaneness of character takes the form of a Maslovian Being-need. My principal claims are that a person of good character is a humane person, and that a person of bad character is someone who is inhumane. However, before proceeding with those matters there is a problem that requires attention. If character is such a strong a determinant of one's morally relevant behaviour, where might one find room for freedom to choose and to act? Since freedom to choose from alternative courses of action is necessary to moral relevance, an inconsistency seems to have arisen.

Character and Freedom

Maslow can be seen as having pointed to the problem of freedom in the distinction he drew between coping (need-motivated, goal-directed) behaviour and expressive (of personality) behaviour. Usually, Maslow says, a person's behaviour is a mixture of both kinds of behaviour, but its expressive aspect would seem to militate against freedom—we do what we do simply because we are what we are, and we are what we are because of such determinants as biology, environment, and cultural circumstances. We may have little choice with regard to any of these, and

---

20 Foot, p. 114.

all of them affect our values (as well as our needs, wants, preferences and interests).Values are embedded in one's personal character and are therefore reflected in the character of one's deeds. As seen in the epigraph, it was Augustine's view that we are slaves to the things that we value highly. If our values and therefore character do in fact makes slaves of us, how could we possibly be free? In particular, where could a place be found for the freedom of choice (between alternative courses of action) that is necessary to moral decision-making? The PHM would appear to be closed to freedom. How, then, might the kind of morality I am promoting be served, or even get started?

The answer, I suggest, can be found in the matter under discussion in this chapter, the personal character of agents. Good character, bad character; good will or ill will, rather than free will. Freedom in the form of self-determination is a Maslovian Being-need—everyone needs freedom, good and bad people alike (see Chapter 9 for further discussion). In light of Augustine's dictum, we might even say that the needs that determine our behaviour include our need to be free. If that seems paradoxical, the problem can be circumvented by recognising that a good person has a need to be good, or as it might be called, a need to be humane. A good person's decisions in respect of how preferences and wants should be met will be guided by that need. The freedom involved is of the kind Spinoza had in mind when he wrote, 'That thing is called free which exists from the necessity of its nature alone, and is determined to act by itself alone [whereas] a thing is called necessary, or rather compelled, which is determined by another to exist and to produce an effect in a certain and determinate manner.'[21] The actions of a good person are constrained (or, more strongly, determined) by his or her character, but that is no impediment to morality. Goodness of character inclines a person towards choosing courses of action that do not deny the needs of others, especially when those needs are more pressing than the person's own needs. Goodness of character also encompasses the power of self-restraint, the exercise of which contributes to the satisfaction of the need for freedom.

---

21 *The Ethics*, 1def7.

In view of the deterministic nature of a person's actions, would a good person's good deeds be deserving of praise? Perhaps not, but the actions would nevertheless be commended by similarly disposed people. Philippa Foot eschewed tying goodness to commendation,[22] but I believe the two may nevertheless be related. Commendation, or praise (and their opposites) are ineradicable components of our moral vocabulary, as are good and evil. Reason would be brought to bear in the moral decision-making of a good person, but it would not be the be-all and end-all of morality. A certain level of mature rationality would be necessary to the formation of moral character, either good or bad. Young children and people with severe cognitive disabilities are not part of the goodness–badness scenario. They may be regarded as mischievous, or loving, or withdrawn (as in cases of autism), or naïve, and so on; but few of us would regard traits or conditions such as these as being relevant to morality.

It would seem to follow from what I have been saying that a bad person, i.e. someone of an immoral character, has a need to be bad. If the person could not have done otherwise, on what grounds could he reasonably be blamed for his vicious action? This is really just the obverse of the commendation of good actions. An agent's evil behaviour will be held to be reprehensible by the same people who praise the actions of a good person.

Some actions that we perform will be of no moral relevance, including those that have little or no effect on anyone else. But many actions will be morally relevant—they will be instances of morally relevant behaviour, because of the non-trivial effects they have on others. On the basis of the foregoing ideas, morally relevant behaviour could be re-defined as behaviour that is either condemned or commended from the perspective of a person of good character. Behaviour will justifiably be condemned if it has an adverse impact on the satisfaction of someone else's basic needs—an adverse impact is a harmful impact. If there is no such impact, then the action will not be condemnable, and may in fact be commendable (although it may also be neither).

Before moving on, a possible problem with the nexus between condemnation and harm needs to be addressed. Is it always the case that

---

22 See Foot, p. 39.

harm must precede condemnation? Breaches of trust, for instance, will generally be thought to be wrong, but their connection with harm could be obscure. In Philippa Foot's book there is a story about an anthropologist who, whilst on expedition, promised his indigenous assistant that he would not take a photograph of him. He refrained from doing so, thereby respecting his assistant's wishes. The photograph could have been taken unbeknown to the assistant, but the anthropologist felt that the promise had to be kept. The trust to which upheld promises contributes is an aspect of human good, and the anthropologist's self-restraint was that of a good person. Untrustworthiness, by contrast, is a bad human disposition (as is disrespectfulness, when respect is due).[23]

To see why the putative nexus might be questionable, let us suppose that the photograph was in fact surreptitiously taken, contrary to the anthropologist's undertaking. A breach of trust would have occurred, but, by being unaware of what had happened, the assistant would seem to have escaped harm—an application, perhaps, of the adage about people not being hurt by what they don't know. People of good character would presumably want to condemn the anthropologist's action, but condemnation appears to have been detached from harm. If that were indeed the case, there would be trouble for any harm-oriented theory of morality, such as the one I am promoting.

The problem is resolvable in either of two ways. First, although the assistant seems not to have suffered any immediate harm, he would have been exposed to the risk of finding out about the photograph sometime in the future. If he does eventually learn of it, the harm that he had feared at the time of the anthropologist's promise could then eventuate. Exposure to significant risk of non-trivial harm would often amount to harm. More than that, however, breach of trust arguably always entails some kind of present or future harm, on the proviso that someone finds out about it (if it remains forever undiscovered there would be no-one to pass judgement, either for or against). Secondly, then, assume that someone does learn of the breach, someone other than the assistant. Assume also that the person making the discovery is someone of good character, in which case condemnation would presumably follow; but

---

23 Foot, pp. 47–48.

on what grounds? The answer, I suggest, involves widening the net of respondency. Anyone who learns of the breach is drawn into the net, and having been drawn in, feels their own safety and well-being to be under threat. They understand that social cohesion is impaired by untrustworthiness, and that breaches of trust therefore either directly or indirectly constitute an assault on their own need for safety and belongingness. It is they who suffer harm, along with other like-minded people, even if the person initially deceived remains unaffected—thereby preserving the nexus between condemnation and harm.

I now wish to expand on the notion that a good person has a need to be good. As foreshadowed, the contention is that a person of good character is a humane person, and that humaneness is experienced in the form of a need to be humane, a need that is expressed in behaviour that conforms to the PHM. According to the philosopher J. L. Mackie (1917-1981), the core of morality consists in humaneness.[24] I believe that to be correct, and will back up that belief by explaining what humaneness consists in and how it comes about.

Humaneness

If we were asked to define 'humaneness' we would probably start by talking about such qualities as 'kindness', and 'empathy'. And we would be correct to do so, but if we were to think a little more deeply about it, we might also find something along the lines of 'principled consideration of the needs of others' coming into view. I think it can be shown that that notion pretty well sums what humaneness is about.

Setting aside 'principled' for a moment, humaneness is 'consideration' in two of the term's customary senses, thoughtfulness and tolerance. Thoughtfulness consists in thinking before acting. It entails the strenuous attention to conduct that Confucius compared to compassion. By means of attentiveness, humane people take in as much relevant information as they can. Attentiveness is contrary to the carelessness that is proscribed by the PHM. Thoughtfulness also entails reflectiveness. By means of

---

24 J. L. Mackie, *Ethics: Inventing Right and Wrong* (London: Penguin Books, 1990 [first published 1977]), p. 194.

reflectiveness we become aware of alternative courses of action from which to choose, and by the same means determine what kind of action would best serve our interests. Reflectiveness would also raise awareness of the possibility of our own interests being best served by attending to the interests of relevant others, for example those to whom we are bound by ties of affection and duty. In so far as it is humane, thoughtfulness occurs against a morally acceptable background.[25] The same applies to consideration in general, with tolerance providing material for the background, i.e. tolerance as revealed by one's actions (and through them one's character), including the words one uses when referring to others. A tolerant person will understand that other people have needs that are similar to his or her own needs, but also that the needs of others may be subject to different hierarchical arrangements; in some cases so different that ultimate ends also differ. The same person will also understand that people may feel compelled to satisfy their needs in different ways, exemplified by a Muslim's refusal to eat pork and the vegetarianism practised by Buddhists. Being thoughtful and tolerant, a humane person recognises that the needs of others may sometimes outweigh one's own needs.

Now the term 'principled'. Humane consideration is principled because, when adopted as a guide to the conduct of one's life, it is fully informed by reason and it is maintained and acted upon with consistency. Consistency is a mark of order, of conformity between a person's beliefs and actions. When one's beliefs include beliefs about the legitimacy of the basic needs of other living beings, actions that stem from them will tend to enhance orderliness in the world, rather than undermining it. Part of that orderliness will be attributable to the mitigation of harmful unintended consequences arising from our actions. Unintentional infringements of the basic needs of others may be seen as instances of unintended consequence. I will take a moment to explain how humaneness can contribute to their mitigation.

First I should note that the notion of unintended consequence was conceived in the twentieth century by the sociologist Robert K. Merton (1910-2003). The idea is not complicated, but the consequences

---

25 Cf. Owen Flanagan, 'Identity and Strong and Weak Evaluation', in Flanagan and Rorty (editors): *Identity, Character, and Morality: Essays in Moral Psychology*, p. 59.

themselves can be very great indeed. Unintended consequences can arise either because they were unforeseeable, or because they were unforeseen, or because they were foreseen and ignored on the grounds of triviality. Derek Parfit uses 'the fisherman's dilemma' to illustrate the last.[26] There is one lake and many fishermen obtain their livelihood from it. A few of them decide to increase their daily catch by a handful or two, in the belief that the effect will be imperceptible. When the other fishermen become aware of what has happened, an increasing number of them do the same. What was once imperceptible soon develops into a glaring catastrophe: the lake is emptied of fish. How might humaneness help?

Principled consideration by a humane agent would serve to prevent consequences from being unforeseen and would guard against trivialisation of them. Overfishing is a widely known phenomenon. If Parfit's fishermen had taken notice of the issues, and perhaps discussed them among themselves, they might have changed their practices—they might even have helped to expand the wider community's awareness of ecological interconnectedness. The case involves what Philippa Foot labelled 'culpable ignorance,' i.e. not knowing something that one should have known, and acting reprehensibly because of it.[27] Carelessness would be another name for it. Compared with the unforeseen and the foreseen-but-trivialised alternatives, unforeseeable adverse consequences would seem simply to be unfortunate. But again, what was once unforeseeable might become foreseeable if one were to think carefully about the relevant issues.

To this point a humane person has been presented as being thoughtful and tolerant, in a principled manner. Kindness and empathy have also been mentioned, but there is another characteristic that I would also like to discuss, namely 'cooperativeness'. Cooperativeness could reasonably be regarded as a natural outgrowth of the tolerance that comes with reflectiveness, but it is important enough in its own right to warrant discussion.

I will begin with Spinoza, whose work can be viewed as an attempt to reconcile self-interest with ethical life. In Spinoza's view, human

---

26 Parfit, pp. 84–85.
27 Foot, p. 71.

behaviour is fundamentally motivated by striving for self-determined action, which may be presumed to arise from self-interest. While that might seem to be an unpromising foundation for an ethics in general and cooperativeness in particular, Spinoza nevertheless managed to find a place for both. His was a kind of rationally-based moral egoism, in so far as acts that superficially appear to be contrary to one's interests come to be justified by demonstrating that the acts concerned are or were—all things considered—in fact consistent with them.[28] According to Spinoza, a being capable of rational thought realises that its power of acting may be enhanced by other beings, so that 'The good which every-one who seeks virtue wants for himself, he also desires for other men . . .'[29] Rational beings understand that their power of acting is enhanced or facilitated by enhancing or facilitating the power of acting enjoyed by other beings. Consequently, rational beings strive to bring into effect conditions that are conducive to the satisfaction of the needs of others as well as their own needs. In other words, consistent with their own interests and with the interests of others—a community of interests, one might say, where cooperativeness is the rule.

The same underlying principle is evident in a proposition from Hume to the effect that obligations should be fulfilled in order to secure the trust of one's fellow beings,[30] because it is in one's interests to be trusted. It is in one's interests because of one's reliance on cooperative effort for the satisfaction of needs; and, as the philosopher Bernard Williams (1929-2003) pointed out, cooperative effort depends on trust, where one party is willing to rely on another party to do certain things.[31] Cooperation also depends on acknowledgement of the interests of others, and perhaps suppression of one's own interests, at least temporarily. Cooperativeness and trust would feature strongly in a humane community.

People can be more or less humane, depending on the extent to which they interact with the world in a principled and considerate manner, which in turn depends on the degree to which the needs of other living beings are respected and perhaps even assimilated by them. 'Assimilate' is

28 See Kurt Baier, 'Egoism', in Singer (editor): *A Companion to Ethics*, p. 201.
29 *The Ethics*, 3p37.
30 See Finnis, p. 301.
31 Williams, p. 88.

used here in the sense ascribed to the term by the scientist David Bohm (1917–92), namely 'to digest.'[32] By digesting them, the needs of others are, so to speak, metabolised, and made into an inseparable part of oneself. Having assimilated them, a person would resist acting in ways that are detrimental to the satisfaction of the needs of others. Detrimental action would amount to self-harm. Accordingly, a person would be unlikely to treat anyone whose needs are also now his own needs merely as means to the attainment of his ends. Indeed, others' ends form part of his own ends—a small 'kingdom of ends' would have come into being, in keeping with an ideal promulgated by Kant. A capacity for assimilating the needs of others (i.e. other living beings, and the inorganic environment for reasons explained in Chapter 5) would be there from the start, in the form of a (perhaps latent) need for humaneness.

A question that might be asked here is whether one's degree of humaneness is fixed, i.e. invariable over the course of a person's mature life-span. That would be the same as asking whether one's character is variable; between good and better, or better and worse, and so on. Clearly, variations occur. Augustine's conversion from licentiousness to saintliness is one example. How might variations be brought about? A short answer would be, by means of changes to any of the determinants of character: i.e., very broadly, changes at the level of biology or psychology, changes to one's social circumstances, and changes of cultural setting. Biologically and psychologically, a once-gentle person afflicted by dementia could become violent. Socially, a person known for her gregariousness may become morose, perhaps even vindictive, after falling victim to a crime. Culturally, brighter educational opportunities might enable someone to develop a greater awareness of the interconnectedness of things and the needs of living beings.

A heightened awareness of interconnectedness in the world would conceivably foster imaginative insight into the problems that confront other living beings. Imaginative insight is akin to empathy—it involves the emotions. Were it to eventuate, the emotions would also be elevated; emotions ranging across the entire spectrum spoken of by Spinoza,

---

32 See David Bohm, *Wholeness and the Implicate Order* (London: Routledge Classics, 2002 [first published 1980]), p. 178.

from joy to sadness. Joy, such as the esteem that is elicited by evidence of supererogatory goodness; sadness, such as the disgust that is evoked by acts of cruelty; the first might be followed by emulation, the second by amelioration. Also joy commingled with sadness, witness the widespread generosity with which people often respond in the aftermath of natural disasters, including those in distant lands.

In sum, norms that reflect humaneness include thoughtfulness, tolerance, empathy, reciprocity, and cooperativeness, all of which are implicit in the PHM. Such norms provide ample guidance for the conduct of a decent and good life. More so because, as I have suggested, humane people would not be the people they are unless they felt the need to be humane. To pursue that matter we return to Maslow.

The Need for Humaneness

Humaneness as it has been defined here is reflected in several of Maslow's B-values, goodness first and foremost. Other relevant B-values are wholeness, and what Maslow refers to as 'dichotomy-transcendence.' The dichotomy he had in mind is the one that divides *us* from *them*, where everything is seen in terms of rivalry and warfare.[33] Transcendence overcomes dichotomy by inducing a sense of wholeness. All-encompassing fellow-feeling is the result, bringing empathy into play—as someone who overcomes the dichotomy might express it, 'we are all in this together'. Justice is another of Maslow's B-values—reciprocity as even-handedness is a feature of justice. All of that being the case, inhumaneness would presumably correspond to the converse of the B-values; which is indeed what we find. Evil, the converse of B-valued goodness, is said by Maslow to emerge in the form of nihilism, selfishness, hatred and cynicism.[34] The stated characteristics are all contrary to humaneness. Nihilism, as the French intellectual Albert Camus (1913-60) observed, is indifferent to life, one's own as well as that of others.[35] Selfishness is contrary to

---

33 *The Farther Reaches of Human Nature*, p. 308.
34 See *The Farther Reaches of Human Nature*, p. 308.
35 Albert Camus, *The Rebel*, translated by Anthony Bower (Harmondsworth, Middlesex: Penguin Books, 1962 [first published 1951]), p. 14.

justice—it works against empathy, duty, equality and fairness. Hatred and cynicism also serve as barriers to empathy.

From a formula provided by Mary Midgley, values can be said to be expressions of needs. They 'register' needs, to use Midgley's word.[36] If we need X then X will be valued by us. Accepting that to be the case, our values, or some of them, will reflect our needs (we may also value things that are not needed, such as fine wine and luxury cars). On that basis the constellation of B-values proposed by Maslow can be aligned with a particular set of needs, a set that I am saying consists in the need for humaneness. For Maslow, the putative need would fit under the umbrella of self-actualisation, but it can also be thought of as a need in its own right. And it might be helpful to think precisely along those lines, for the need for humaneness would then be found comfortably to accommodate Humean moral sense and Kant's predisposition to goodness. With this bonus. To view the 'sense' and the 'predisposition' as a need would bring Maslow's principle of prepotency into play. And having done that, it would become clear that all of the lower-order needs, the need for food and shelter, the need for belongingness, the need for respect, and so on—all such needs would have to be met, to a reasonable degree, before the need for humaneness could assume full motivational force. Which, to my mind, makes sense, especially if we recall Orwell's tramps and Levi's Auschwitz prisoners. It is also reminiscent of an aphorism of Nietzsche's, one that bears thinking about, to the effect that virtue comes from happiness (rather than the other way round, as proclaimed by the Stoics amongst others). In the form of an actualisable need, humaneness could be regarded as a human possibility, not an automatic given—the need may be there, but only latently. For the species as a whole, in order for the actualisable to become actualised, something akin to Rawlsian justice-as-fairness might have to be realised, far more widely than happens to be the case today. Justice-as-fairness would be predicated on satisfaction of all of the lower-order needs, 'to a reasonable degree'.

But we must nevertheless ask, even if a need for humaneness were disturbed from its latency, what would induce us to act upon it? Simply this: the satisfaction that we believe or feel would be attained from meeting

---

36 Midgley, *Beast and Man*, (Introduction to the first edition, p. xlii).

an erstwhile unsatisfied need. Furthermore, because of our fundamentally rational nature, for the most part we act in ways that are consistent with our needs. We act rationally when we attempt to satisfy our needs. Philippa Foot in her book imagined a sceptic doubting whether sufficient reason could be found for confining one's actions to those for which 'good human beings must aim,' for instance doing good rather than harm to others.[37] As I see matters, the word 'must' points to how to the sceptic might be answered. 'Must' implies need; for example, if we *must* have food in order to survive, which we assuredly do, then food is *needed* by us. So we get back to needs. Perhaps the sceptic's question should be envisaged as having emanated from a person of bad character, for it is hard to imagine why a humane person would ever ask it; except perhaps in a rhetorical sense, or in the role of devil's advocate. As well as being rationally justifiable, attempts to satisfy a need are also emotionally justifiable, because of the pleasure that follows upon satisfaction of the need. As Kant defined it, pleasure 'is the idea of the agreement of the object, or the action with the subjective conditions of life . . . .'[38] Satisfaction of the need is our object (in the sense of 'objective').

As well as pleasure, self-respect would also serve as a motivational objective. To deviate from ways that are consistent with our mode of self-actualisation could (almost certainly would) imperil our self-respect, and possibly also the esteem that others may feel for us. Self-respect and the esteem of others are needed by us, and we value having them. Note that the 'us' and 'we' being spoken of here are assumed to be people of good character. Those of bad character could by the same logic be said to be acting rationally when pursuing their nefarious goals.

By virtue of their registration in values, our needs influence our decisions with regard to choices between alternative courses of action. In other words, and in the terminology of this book, needs and values are inescapably implicated in morally relevant behaviour. Individual needs and values become embedded in social standards and rules of behaviour; i.e. in norms. Some norms are moral norms, i.e. standards whose breach

---

37 Foot, p. 53.
38 Kant, preface to *The Critique of Practical Reason*, translated by Thomas Kingsmill Abbott ((Chicago: The University of Chicago, Great Books of the Western World, 1952), Vol. 42, p. 293.

attracts moral censure. Norms affect behaviour for reasons that range from avoidance of censure to decency and basic goodness.

The need for humaneness can be viewed as something that is characteristic of normal human functioning (cf. Hume), or as 'instinctoid' (cf. Maslow), or as constitutive of our empathetic core (cf. Mackie); or as an aspect of the life form of our species (cf. Foot). Taking that as our cue, the need could be regarded as something that has evolved, more or less in step with the evolution of all of our other basic needs, and alongside the emergence of rationality and freedom. In sum, the need for humaneness could be considered as something integral to normal human nature, something that exists in nearly all of us, though sometimes ineffectually because of the straitened circumstances that can beset us. Should the need become activated, i.e. were it to attain motivational force, magnanimity would come into view, magnanimity in the sense of 'greatness of spirit' (this is the etymological basis of the term). Magnanimity in turn conjures up notions of human excellence and sheer goodness of character. In a world devoid of a beneficent deity, which is the world I am assuming we inhabit, humane human beings are the only source of moral goodness.

Conclusion

I have to admit that none of what I have been saying about humaneness confirms its existence, but the mere fact that it is conceivable in the terms that I have been using provides the concept with a measure of plausibility. Plausibility does not constitute proof, and perhaps the best evidence in favour of its existence would be to point to people demonstrably of a humane disposition, people like Mahatma Gandhi, Martin Luther King Jnr, and Nelson Mandela. Their actions were largely concerned with the welfare of others, often to their own personal disadvantage. No doubt numerous exemplars could be cited, including many from the ranks of ordinary people. As well as that, the putative need fits comfortably into Maslow's scheme.

Moral right and wrong has been seen in Part I to have a very great deal to do with needs. In Part II, which now follows, needs will be further examined, with a view to establishing a link between them and the phenomenon of order. Order, I will argue, provides a naturalistic foundation upon which morality may be erected, thereby providing a means of satisfying our metaphysical need.

PART II:
Metaphysical Support for the Principle of Harm-Minimisation

Chapter 8: Let's Get Metaphysical

The question as to the origin of moral values is a question of primary importance (Friedrich Nietzsche).

The idea that morality possesses origins that are susceptible to explanation has a long history. Explanation is the business of philosophers, scientists and theologians, and it is of interest to many other people as well. Explanation can help locate philosophical grounds on which beliefs may be based; it helps us make sense of what is going on around us. The Stoics, Plato, Spinoza and Kant are some of the many schools and thinkers who have felt the need to establish a philosophical basis on which morality might rest. Resort was commonly made to the gods. For example, in the *Laws*, Plato maintains that living well depends on 'thinking rightly about the gods;'[1] while not everyone would agree with him on what 'thinking rightly' consists in, the root idea can be applied more generally. Spinoza, for instance, placed great store in the acquisition of 'adequate ideas', and he also thought very deeply about 'God'. Spinoza is justly famous for his contribution to moral philosophy, most extensively articulated in *The Ethics* (published posthumously in 1677). The appendix of Part IV of his book deals with social order and moral order. The moral standards promoted there are held to emanate from nature, and since nature is all there is, supernaturalism can be discounted. Spinoza's attempt to find a basis for ethics in nature was one of the inspirations for the present book.

I obviously have a lot of explaining to do, but there is a question that can be broached here: might the idea of a philosophical ground be indicative of a need for one? I believe that could well be the case. In the absence of an anchor in fundamental reality, ethics could be regarded as an intellectual abstraction; hence a warning from Albert Camus, to the effect that virtue requires justification in order not to be abstract (from his 1951 book, *The Rebel*). Virtue is justified when we can explain why

---

1 Plato, *Laws*, translated by A. E. Taylor, in *The Collected Dialogues of Plato*, X, 888b.

one should abide by what one believes virtue to consist in. The search for answers to the *why* and *what* questions are the business of ethics, as distinct from metaethics. The latter, metaethics, is more concerned with *how* and *whence* questions: how did we come to be the moral beings that we undoubtedly are, or, as it might be put, where did morality come from; from what ground did it spring? Even to ask the last question, let alone trying to answer it, is symptomatic of the conjectured philosophical need.

This second part of my book is largely metaethical in tenor. One of its aims is to explain further the origins and nature of our moral beingness. A moral being is someone who understands what it means to be moral. What it means to be moral consists in having beliefs about what is morally right and morally wrong. Ethics, as distinct from metaethics, is concerned with describing what moral right and wrong consist in; Part I addressed that matter, by linking wrong to harm and harm to needs, and establishing right as the absence of wrong. With regard to metaethics, Derek Parfit expressed the hope that conclusions for ethics would be forthcoming from work in that field.[2] Since any metaethical inquiry conducted by a human being is likely to entail some kind of understanding of what it means to be moral, it seems to me that the conclusions aspired to by Parfit are nigh on being inevitable. My principal metaethical claim is that we are moral beings because of our need for a uniquely human kind of order. I will also argue that the need is real, and that it is therefore something that is objectively true about us. The need gives rise to morally relevant behaviour when attempts to satisfy our need impacts on the needs of others, and we have seen how morally relevant harm arises from such impacts.

Philosophical need could be regarded as a kind of 'metaphysical need', a notion that some people would baulk at. Nietzsche, for instance, wrote about taking an axe to the 'root of the "metaphysical need" of man,'[3] but very soon after wielding his axe he can be found in the same book advancing the proposition that was foreshadowed in the epigraph. More fully, the point that he was making was this: the 'question as to the

2 Parfit, p. 447.
3 Friedrich Nietzsche, *Ecce Homo*, 'Human All-Too-Human', in *The Philosophy of Nietzsche* (New York: The Modern Library, 1927), s. 6.

origin of moral values is . . . a question of primary importance to me because it determines the future of mankind.'[4] In view of his rejection of metaphysical need, the proposition could be seen as something of an admission; or a back-tracking. In my opinion, the search for origins is symptomatic of philosophical needfulness. What were the origins for Nietzsche? Eschewing the traditional 'selflessness', he gave pride of place to 'self-preservation and the increase of bodily energy.'[5] Satisfaction of the philosophical need by a Nietzschean would be attained without reference to the supernatural. My approach also avoids supernaturalism, by finding a route to morality via the concepts of needs and order. The chapter that follows continues the story of needs.

---

4 *Ecce Homo*, 'The Dawn of Day', s. 2.
5 *Ecce Homo*, 'The Dawn of Day', s. 2.

Chapter 9: More about Needs

Freedom, Sancho, is one of the most precious gifts that Heaven has bestowed upon men. With it all the treasures locked in the earth, or hidden in the depths of the sea, are not to be compared (Miguel de Cervantes, Don Quixote Part II Chapter 58).

Different things are valued differently by different people at different times—whence the possibility of moral relativism, which could be seen to pose a threat to any project seeking to endow a particular moral code with universal validity and applicability; i.e., any project such as the one I am engaged in. In this chapter we will examine whether the threat can be countered. We will also consider whether there are any basic needs that are missing from Maslow's schema, and then take a look at the relationship between needs and other aspects of human psychology, such as preferences, wishes and desires. Rights will also be discussed, with particular reference to the Universal Declaration of Human Rights. But first relativism.

Moral Relativism and Needs

Moral theory distinguishes between two kinds of moral relativism, 'metaethical' on the one hand, 'normative' on the other.[1] Metaethical moral relativism acknowledges that moral beliefs and values are contingent upon cultural and historical factors, because of which no moral code can be said to have universal validity. Normative moral relativism holds that divergent beliefs and values should be respected, and that moral judgements issuing from them deserve to pass without condemnation. Now while the two kinds of relativism might be 'distinguished' from one another in theory, in practice it is not a matter of either/or between them. Rather, as their titles suggest, they are instantiations of the metaethical/ethical divide mentioned a short while ago. Where a metaethical position is taken, it is likely to be consistent with whatever beliefs are

---

1 See David Wong, 'Relativism', in Singer (editor), p. 442.

held about right and wrong, i.e. one's normative beliefs, and why one should act in accordance with those beliefs.

Abstention from all judgements that involve divergent values could be described as an extreme form of normative relativism. A more reasonable position, in the view of the philosopher David Wong, would permit the passing of judgement on those who have substantially different values, and even leave open the possibility of moral judgements with respect to certain facts being objectively correct or incorrect.[2] Judgements of objective correctness would presumably have to be based on some kind of pre-existing standards of conduct, which would previously have passed the test of objective correctness. To speak of objective correctness involves a move away from relativism and towards absolutism, which opposes relativism by insisting on the universal validity of particular moral principles. The PHM is of that nature.

Absolutism might be described in terms of 'ethical exclusiveness', where a single code of ethics amongst a number of alternative codes is believed to be the sole possessor of validity. Nihilism, according to which all ethical codes are equally invalid and therefore rejected holus bolus, could also be described as absolutist. Against absolutism of either kind there would be ethical inclusiveness, or pluralism. Because of their inclusiveness, pluralists would likely embrace the sort of moderate normative moral relativism mentioned by Wong. The philosopher Philip Kitcher (b. 1947) is pluralist in this sense—he defends a position in ethics that is close to that advocated by the historian of ideas Isaiah Berlin (1909-97), a position in which the fundamental values of various rival traditions are duly recognised by each of them.[3] Recognition of another's fundamental values need not, in Kitcher's view, prevent one from believing that some codes of ethics are better or worse than others. Codes of ethics will be 'better', he maintains, if they advance the interests of justice and cooperation and 'worse' if they retard them.[4] 'Better' and 'worse' involve the kinds of judgements of objective correctness and objective incorrectness that are characteristic of moderate normative relativism.

---

2 Wong, p. 448.
3 Philip Kitcher, *The Ethical Project* (Cambridge, Massachusetts: Harvard University Press, 2011), p. 249 (footnote).
4 Kitcher, p. 210 ff.

I have suggested that a person's ethics is likely to be consistent with his or her metaethical position (should one be adopted). Kitcher is a case in point; his pluralism is interlaced with metaethical relativism. The good, he maintains, evolves from the circumstances in which people find themselves, and their endeavours to solve the problems that confront them.[5] In other words, that which is held to be good is variable depending on circumstances; in which case, codes of ethics emanating from the various conceptions of good would likewise be variable. What might not be variable in the scenario depicted by Kitcher, or indeed any other scenario (apart from nihilism), is the sheer existence of some kind of code of ethics, ever since the beginning of ethical consciousness fifty thousand years ago (the time-scale is Kitcher's).

Mention has already been made of Mary Midgley's proposition to the effect that values stem from needs. Assuming for now that the relationship holds, Kitcher's pluralistic assertion with regard to the reciprocal recognition of fundamental values may be paraphrased along the lines of 'recognition by members of rival traditions of the needs taken as fundamental by the others'. And with the recognition of needs come the order-based theory of morality, and its derivative PHM. As is the case with Kitcher, the order-based theory also contains fixed and variable elements. Fixed is the existence of our basic human needs, and our vulnerability to harm because of them. All of the basic needs will be shown in Chapter 12 to emanate from the need for homosapient order (basic needs may evolve, but basic they remain). Variable are our ways of satisfying our needs, and our hierarchies of needs. The hierarchical arrangement of needs may vary from one age or culture to another; and if variation occurs, ultimate values would likely differ.

As a counter-measure against absolutism and extreme normative relativism, differences in hierarchies of needs could be transcended by focusing on needs of the most basic kind—basic in terms of the hierarchies of respondent persons. Ultimate values may vary, but violation of them would always be morally suspect; though not necessarily intolerable, because of the possibility of 'perverted' (to use Hume's expression) scales of value. For instance, in the present context, a scale of values that

---

5 Kitcher, p. 288.

encouraged inhumane behaviour, i.e. behaviour contrary to the PHM, would be adjudged perverted, and it would be tolerable to act against it. To what extent, then, should different moral standards be accepted? For a proponent of the PHM the answer would be, with a wide degree of tolerance; subject always to the injunction against inhumane behaviour. Relativism is at the centre of important moral issues, but thinking about them in terms of needs and values would seem capable of shedding light on them.

Maslow's rankings are themselves indicative of the pervasiveness of relativism. In middle and upper class mid-twentieth century Western civilisation, i.e. Maslow's milieu, self-actualisation may well have become the supreme goal, but that has not always been the case, and still is not for many people. Honour and esteem, for instance, would probably be ranked ahead of everything else in warrior cultures, including modern criminal societies such as the Mafia. However, to repeat, while hierarchical rankings of needs may vary from one age or culture to another, the basic instinctoid needs themselves remain unaltered. The fact that they are basic attests to the point—they help define what it means to be human. The possibility of changes in basic needs arising from genetic mutations and subsequent adaptations must be acknowledged, but whether we would then still be 'human' in the present sense of the term could become questionable. Would we be 'human' if the need for belongingness were to disappear? I don't think we would; likewise for all of the other Maslovian needs. Awareness of the commonality of our basic needs may contribute to an understanding of others, including people from different ages and cultures. Appreciation of the variability of hierarchical rankings could help us understand how and why ultimate values differ.

Another possible criticism of Maslow is that his catalogue of basic needs is incomplete. The list shown on p. 39 makes no mention of some things that would commonly be regarded as fundamental to the human condition, including the need for freedom, the need for play, and the need for power. I will now argue that each of these can in fact be accommodated within the Maslovian schema.

More Needs: Freedom, Play and Power

Freedom is a need that is felt by most of us, and it would certainly be a serious matter if Maslow had omitted it. It is indeed a 'precious gift', as Don Quixote proclaimed to his squire Sancho Panza (see the epigraph). Direct reference to the need for freedom is hard to find in Maslow's writings, although 'aliveness' is listed among his B-values, and is contrasted with 'feeling oneself to be totally determined.'[6] On the basis of the contrast, self-determination can be understood as a B-value, and therefore also as a B-need. Self-determination consists in autonomy (literally, 'self-legislation'), and while not the same as freedom, the two concepts are closely related. As John Rawls might have said, autonomous action is made possible by our nature as free and rational beings, the same nature that enables us to make principled choices between alternative courses of action.[7] If we were not free, we would be unable to choose; if we were not rational, we would be unable to comprehend whatever alternatives might be available to us. Like slaves, we would be fully determined by external forces, and that would be wrong. As the scientist Alexander von Humboldt (1769-1859) once remarked, in an excoriation of slavery, 'what is against nature, is unjust, bad and without validity.'[8] Humboldt's objection to slavery on the grounds that it constitutes an offence against our essential (i.e. natural) freedom can be applied more widely: simply broaden the concept of nature and we would soon find environmentalists like Aldo Leopold nodding in assent. Me along with them, because of the relationship between the connectedness of nature (another of Humboldt's principal tenets) and order.

Play would also seem to be a universal need. The philosopher Martha Nussbaum (b. 1947) lists it among her so-called 'constitutive circumstances of the human being,' a list that otherwise bears a strong resemblance to Maslow's catalogue.[9] John Finnis also considered play

6 *The Farther Reaches of Human Nature*, p. 308.
7 See *A Theory of Justice*, p. 222.
8 Quoted by Andrea Wulf, in *The Invention of Nature: The Adventures of Alexander von Humboldt the Lost hero of Science* (London: John Murray, 2015), p. 108.
9 See Martha Nussbaum, 'Aristotelian Social Democracy', in Gillian Brock (editor), *Necessary Goods: Our Responsibilities to Meet Others' Needs* (Lanham, Maryland: Rowman & Littlefield Publishers, Inc., 1998), pp. 146-151.

to be a basic human good, i.e. something upon which human fulfilment depends and therefore something we need. (In addition to play, the
goods identified by Finnis are life, sociability or friendship, practical reasonableness, knowledge, aesthetic experience and religion.[10]) Maslow's
schema would indeed be gravely deficient if it failed to accommodate
play. But Maslow does in fact allow a place for it, not specifically as a
need but again as a B-value. The absence of play is said by Maslow to
lead to the loss of zest in life and an inability to enjoy[11]—outcomes that
would almost certainly prevent one from achieving self-actualisation.
Maslow would have agreed with Kant's assessment of the benefits of play,
such as recovery of energy spent in work, sociability via party games, and
physical health through athletic games.[12] (Notwithstanding the benefits,
Kant was generally critical of play.) That leaves the need for power.

The need for power will here be understood to refer to the need
that one has for control over oneself, as well as over other things and
other people. It finds expression in either of two ways, malign or benign,
which are portrayed by the psychologist David C. McClelland (1917-
98) in terms of 'two faces'. Malignity comes into view as an unsocialised
'concern for personal dominance;' exploitative sex and aggression are
both symptomatic of malignant power. Benign power is more socialised,
typified by running for public office and the empowerment of followers.[13] Education is a key to empowerment. (Leadership and education
are linked etymologically through the Latin *educare*, which means 'to
lead out.'[14]) Socialised leadership, McClelland asserts, takes its educational
function seriously. Effective leaders tend to steer their followers towards
becoming leaders themselves.

In its concern with learning and teaching socialised power ties in with
the Maslovian need for intellectual achievement, and therefore also with

---

10 Finnis, p. 86 ff. Practical reasonableness is concerned with bringing 'an intelligent and reasonable order'
into one's life, by infusing one's actions, habits and attitudes with freedom, reason, integrity and authenticity.

11 *The Farther Reaches of Human Nature*, p. 309.

12 See Mihai I. Spariosu, *Dionysus Reborn: Play and the Aesthetic Dimension in Modern Philosophical and Scientific Discourse* (Ithaca: Cornell University Press, 1989), pp. 49-50.

13 David C. McClelland, 'The Two Faces of Power', in David A. Kolb, Irwin M. Rubin, James M. McIntyre
(editors), *Organizational Psychology: A Book of Readings* (Edgewood Cliffs, New Jersey: Prentice-Hall, 1974),
pp. 167-168.

14 McClelland, p. 175.

self-actualisation. It also shares common ground with Spinoza's principle of *conatus*, according to which everything strives for self-preservation and joy. While self-preservation and joy are aims of the striving, they can also be regarded as needs. Seen as such, they permeate Maslow's entire hierarchy—the first is especially concerned with physical needs, the second with social and being needs.

The need for power issues in commands either to oneself or to others, to fall into line with one's conception of what constitutes proper order. But power can go beyond the means employed in attaining it; it can also become an end in itself. Should that happen, the dominance–submission aspect of power described by McClelland becomes active, whereupon followers tend to be treated as 'pawns rather than origins.'[15] Instead of 'origins' McClelland might have said 'ends'; either way, a breach of morality would probably have occurred. Empathy would also have probably gone missing, thereby diminishing the prospect of humane interaction and increasing the likelihood of violation of the PHM.

To look upon someone as a pawn is to belittle the individual's humanity. It is to deny his or her essential freedom, perhaps to the point of enslavement. In saying that, it must be acknowledged that the vast majority of us are 'pawns' for much of the time, serving the ends of those with whom we are connected in the complex webs of relations that enmesh us. The critical question is whether we are 'mere' means, contrary to the Kantian imperative; and the answer will depend on the attitude of those who 'use' us. If there is recognition on their part that they too are means to the ends of others, perhaps even the ends of those they employ through some kind of reciprocal or synergistic relationship, then there would be a good chance of their regarding us as something other than 'mere' means. Recognition along those lines would likely be reflected in humility, a quality that Lao Tzu (601-531 BCE), the founder of Taoism, regarded as the source of true leadership. Humility in turn would be reflected in cooperation rather than conflict; in inclusiveness rather than exclusiveness; in helping in the satisfaction of the needs of others rather than acting as a hindrance—in short, in benign power rather than malign

---

15 McClelland, p. 172.

power. Likewise for us, of course, in respect of those who serve our ends—reciprocity of means, reciprocity of ends.

Power can be perverted in various ways, at each of the levels of the Maslovian hierarchy. At the physiological level, it may find expression as lechery or greed; at the social level, it would be marked by covetousness, envy and sloth; and at the level of being, by spiritual pride. What have been known since biblical times as the seven deadly sins can all be understood as perversions of the will to power, and therefore of the need for power. If one is lecherous or greedy, then one aims at the satisfaction of inordinate appetites for sex or material goods. If one is covetous or envious, then one lusts after things that properly belong to others. If slothful, then one may fail to fulfil one's social functions. In these ways, covetousness, envy and sloth are all disruptive of social order. Finally, if one is spiritually proud, then one's sense of self-importance tends to reach gargantuan proportions. Theologically, spiritual pride consists in the denial of God; secularly, it consists in the denial of the worth of other people and the world in general. Both theologically and secularly, spiritual pride is characterised by extreme self-centredness and selfishness.

The need for power need not result in evil. Think, for example, of compassionate leaders like Mahatma Gandhi, Martin Luther King Jnr and Nelson Mandela, all of whom attained power and arguably therefore needed it. In a letter written from prison in 1975 to his wife Winnie, Mandela maintained that a person's development as a human being depends on several qualities, humility among them; others included honesty, sincerity, simplicity, generosity, and a preparedness to serve. Such qualities, according to Mandela, 'are the foundation of one's spiritual life.'[16] These are hardly the ideas of a power-hungry fiend. But the need for power does indeed reach pathological degrees in some individuals. Milton's Satan, in *Paradise Lost* (1667), is archetypical, summed up in the proposition 'Better to reign in Hell, than serve in Heaven.'[17] Regardless of whether good or evil, the attainment of power would assuredly contribute to the satisfaction of the need for self-actualisation in those motivated by some form of power, which is probably to say nearly everyone.

---

16 Mandela, p. 211.
17 John Milton, *Paradise Lost*, Book 1, 263.

All of the needs that seemed to be missing from Maslow's hierarchy are in reality firmly entrenched in it. His list appears to be comprehensive, with the exception of what I will refer to as the 'need for malignant self-actualisation', which will be found to be a close relative of malign power. Malignant self-actualisation consists in the kind of self-fulfilment that a patently evil person attains by inflicting harm on others, something that all too many of us appear to be capable of, at least some of the time. As well as being destructive towards individual beings, evil impinges on the entire system of good; in Mary Midgley words, it damages 'the proper arrangement of the whole.'[18] One could substitute 'order' for 'arrangement' without distorting Midgley's meaning. Evil in the form of malignant self-actualisation is an affront to order.

Although Maslow's theory focuses more on motivation than morality, his ideas feed directly into significant issues that are germane to moral theory. The sequence is simple and direct: from needs to harm to morality. According to the philosopher Michael Ruse (b. 1940), so-called hard-line Darwinians regard biological needs as being directly connected to ethics.[19] The sequence I have just set out would seem to be enough to make me a hard-line Darwinian, especially if needs arising from our social and spiritual make-up were classed as 'biological', alongside our physiological needs. But that could be stretching the concept 'biological' too far.

Besides needs, there are other aspects of human psychology that are commonly spoken of in terms of moral relevance, including preferences, wishes, wants, values and interests. Validly so, because any of them may lead to behaviour by agents that impacts on others in ways that invite moral judgement. In the next section I argue that the basic needs delineated by Maslow are either prior to or equivalent to each of the others. By 'prior to', I mean 'a determinant of'.

18 Mary Midgley, *Beast and Man: The Roots of Human Nature*, p. 77.
19 Michael Ruse, Darwin and Design: Does evolution have a purpose? (Cambridge Massachusetts: Harvard University Press, 2003), p. 238.

Preferences, Wishes, Desires, Wants, Values, Interests

Preferences are attitudes of mind that derive from some sort of internal ranking of wants, interests, values and needs. We generally prefer to have some wishes, wants and needs met before others are met. Some values and interests inevitably take precedence over other values and interests. Unless we are like Buridan's ass, a choice will be made based on what we prefer when faced with having to decide which of our wants to act on. But preferences are posterior to needs, as well to wants, interests and values. For example, statements about needs and preferences may take the form, 'I need P more than I need Q therefore, if both cannot be obtained together, I would prefer to have P rather than Q'. Any of the terms 'want', 'interest', 'values' and 'desire' could be substituted for 'need' in the formula and it would still make sense.

'Wish' is close in connotation to 'desire'. Something that is desired will be something that is wished for, and that which is wished for will be something that is desired. Fundamentally, we will desire that our basic needs be met, since it is by having them met that we will survive and perhaps even prosper.[20] The things required to satisfy our basic needs—food, water, shelter, friendship, love, and so on—could be described as being naturally good for us: to desire something is to adorn it with the mantle of goodness. Hobbes was again prescient: 'whatsoever is the object of any man's appetite or desire, that is it which he for his part calleth *good* . . .'[21] Apart from that, however, the object of our immediate desire may not be desirable in the long run.[22] If we are experiencing a cold snap, we might warm ourselves by lighting a coal-fire; and we do that in full knowledge of the fact that prolonged and widespread use of coal will be detrimental to the health and well-being of ourselves and our progeny. The desirable is that which ought to be desired, where 'ought' is determined by one's beliefs with regard to goodness and right. Although satisfaction of our basic needs will be always be desired, it may not be desirable. That which

20 Cf. Steven Pinker, *How the Mind Works* (New York: W. W. Norton & Company, 1997), p. 143.
21 Hobbes, chapter 6.
22 See William D. Casebeer, *Natural Ethical Facts: Evolution, Connectionism, and Moral Cognition* (Cambridge, Massachusetts: The MIT Press, 2005), p. 28.

is good for us now may prove harmful in the longer term; and perhaps harmful to others at either time.

The term 'want' is ambiguous. On the one hand, when I say 'I want Y', Y may be of no consequence to my well-being; it could even be harmful. 'I want a cigarette', for example. My wanting a smoke would seem to have little or nothing to do with my basic needs. However, if I am a nicotine addict, I may indeed feel in need of a cigarette; my wanting one is a demand emanating from my physiology. In such instances, wants would be a close approximation of basic needs. On the other hand, 'to be in want of X' would generally be understood to be in need of X, and that our well-being depends on obtaining it. To put it another way, the want is equivalent to a basic need.

The philosopher James Griffin (b. 1933) distinguishes between 'mere wanting' and 'the sort of wanting that connects with values,'[23] which is fair enough, for the sort of wanting that connects with values would be that which also links up with basic needs, in the same way as the desirable (as distinct from desire) does. By way of further linkage, Mary Midgley maintains that our deepest concerns are reflected in wants, which she regards as 'the deepest structural constituents of our characters.'[24] The depth that Midgley attributes to wants makes them sound very much like Maslovian instinctoid needs.

Values and interests are closely related. If we have an interest in something it will be because we value it. It is hard to imagine how we could be interested in anything that was of no value to us. If something is valued, then its interests are likely to be promoted. If we disvalue something, then we may act against its interests, or wish that others would so act. The relationship between interests and values is very strong. Where, then, do they stand in relation to needs? Simply put, they derive from them. To repeat Midgley's formulation 'values register needs.' If something is needed then it will be valued, and we will have an interest in seeing that the need is satisfied. Maslow was seen earlier to have been of a similar mind when he equated metaneeds with B-values. I will have more to

---

23 James, Griffin, *On Human Rights* (New York: Oxford University Press, 2001 [first published 2008]), p. 115.
24 Midgley quoted by Stephen J. Pope, *The Evolution of Altruism & The Ordering of Love* (Washington DC: Georgetown University Press, 1994), p. 36.

say about values in Chapter 11, under the heading 'N-order' ('N' stands for 'normative'). Although interests stem naturally from basic needs, they can also have shallower roots. For instance, a new book from a favourite author would be of interest, but would we really need it? Often we would not. In the event of a clash, interests stemming from needs would likely take precedence over those that do not. Again, therefore, it can be concluded that needs are prior to interests; and prior to values as well, based on Midgley's proposition.

Preferences, wishes, desires, wants, values, and interests all rest on a foundation of needs. The fact that we have a need for something—for example a drink—causes us to do something to satisfy the need. Need precipitates purposeful action, mediated by feelings and beliefs about the kind of action that might (or should) be taken. Given the opportunity, we might quench our thirst with wine rather than orange juice, a choice that expresses our preference. Viewed from the perspective of the preference, our choice of wine expresses a want, which in turn can be traced to our need for physiological equilibrium, or homeostasis. If asked why we want the wine we will say, 'because I am thirsty'—that is the reason for having a drink. Homeostatic disorder (felt as thirst) causes us to find a means of quenching the thirst. Preference kicks in when we are given a choice as to how to quench it, but need precedes preference. Our preference for wine could be due to contextual (for example cultural) factors, although biology may also play a part (for example, an allergy to citric acid). Another example: We see someone collapse in the street and rush to help them. Why? Because, I would say, of our basic need for humaneness. If asked for a reason for our helping behaviour, we might refer to our belief that matters should be so. Given a choice, we prefer to lend a hand rather than turning a blind eye. At bottom, however, or from the other direction, the need provides a causal explanation for our action.

Needs, then, are either prior to or close approximations of preferences, wishes, wants, interests and values. And all of the latter would seem to be morally relevant; to the extent that they are, needs would also be morally relevant. They become morally relevant when we engage in morally relevant behaviour in order to satisfy our needs and their proxies. And, to repeat, it is our needs that make us vulnerable to harm.

A connection between needs and morality might also be forged by medium of politics. Aristotle famously regarded ethics and politics as being continuous because of a shared principal objective—attainment of the good. We saw this earlier in the opening words of his *Nicomachean Ethics*.' In another of his major works, the *Politics*, he proclaims: 'Every state is a community of some kind, and every community is established with a view to some good; for mankind always act in order to obtain that which they think good.'[25] For Aristotle, then, individuals and political bodies are similarly concerned with attainment of the good; such is their purpose, or end. Justice is a particular form of the good that is relevant to both—just individuals are virtuous individuals, and just societies are societies whose laws encourage people to live well together.

Now if needs are assumed to be relevant to politics, then needs would also be relevant to morality. The assumption seems reasonable: citizens install a government they believe capable of providing or enhancing the means required to satisfy their need for food, shelter and security, and whatever else is of fundamental importance to them, e.g. education and freedom. A government that ignored the basic needs of its subjects might not last very long. Nelson Mandela was alert to the matter, as demonstrated by the self-addressed memorandum that was mentioned earlier. Politicians are similarly interested in having their basic needs satisfied, including, in their case, the need for power. I will not pursue this line of thought any further, except to note that it would be congenial to David Braybrooke's position on the relevance of needs to social policy.

As well as being prior to preferences, wishes, wants, interests and values, needs may also serve as a basis on which to ground rights. The Universal Declaration of Human Rights (UDHR) will be used as a springboard for discussion of the matter.

<hr>

25 Aristotle, *Politics*, translated by Benjamin Jowett (Chicago: The University of Chicago, Great Books of the Western World, 1952), Vol. 9, I.1.

Needs and Rights: The Universal Declaration of Human Rights

First some background. The UDHR was ratified by the United Nations in 1948; it consists of thirty articles, and addresses such matters as life and liberty, freedom from slavery, equality in person and before the law, and education. The UDHR has served as the basis of the International Bill of Human Rights (IBHR). The Bill was proclaimed in 1966 in the form of two covenants supplemented by two voluntary protocols, the first also in 1966 and the second in 1989. Bearing in mind the profound cultural, religious and political differences among the nations that voted for it, the UDHR is a remarkable achievement. Philosophical differences also. Christians and Jews, liberal democrats and Marxists, and others of various religious and political persuasions, all had recourse to a multitude of sources for their views. How the UDHR ever came to pass is cause for wonder; but pass it did. The UDHR has been used as a model for bills of rights in the constitutions of many now-independent countries, especially within the British Commonwealth. Although the UDHR and the IBHR could reasonably be held to be concerned more with political right than with moral right, the two kinds of right are arguably continuous with one another, especially in light of Aristotle's views on the relationship between ethics and politics. More than that, however, I will endeavour to show that the rights specified in the documents tie in with the concept of needs.

Given its background and influence, the UDHR has understandably not escaped criticism. James Griffin, for example, disapproves of Article no. 24, which promulgates the right to paid holidays; but he believes most of the other rights to be acceptable.[26] One might also observe that consensual stipulations like those of the UDHR must be seen as products of their times and places, and therefore prone to being relativistic—later generations could well stipulate differently. But that is only to say that morality evolves, and will continue to evolve, more or less in step with the evolution of the species from which it emanates (us).

---

26 Griffin, p. 202.

If, as I suggest, the UDHR is to serve as a platform for needs-based moral precepts, then I must show how rights and moral good (and evil) are related; and how needs and rights are related. I think the first relationship will be clear to everyone. If people have a right, say, to be treated fairly, then it will be morally right to treat them fairly, and wrong to treat them unfairly. I should acknowledge that the argument assumes coincidence between the concepts of *rights* and *right*; a coincidence that may not always be precise. For example, the philosopher Onora O'Neill (b. 1941) argues that the two concepts converge only at an abstract level: i.e., where whatever an agent is obliged to do because it is right is the same as that which a respondent has a right to expect—such is the vocabulary of right. A gap opens up in the vocabulary of rights where obligations to respondents remain unallocated to an agent.[27] Nevertheless, there is at least justification on an abstract level for treating rights as a surrogate of right, because of the very close relationship between the two concepts.

Some meat will now be put on the bones of the relationship between needs and rights, based on a sample of the UDHR articles.[28] Before beginning, I should note that a similar exercise was conducted in 2005 by the philosopher Gillian Brock. Brock's aim was to demonstrate that a needs-based account is more fundamental to global justice than a human rights account. Her point being, before rights can be sensibly defined and codified, we must have knowledge of what our needs are.[29] I believe that to be correct, but I also wish to establish that there is something even more fundamental than the various needs that Brock, like Maslow, identifies; namely the need for homosapient order. Philosophers have a penchant for fundamentals: the more fundamental the better.

Needs and Rights: the Question of Priority

The first UDHR Article for discussion is no. 2, which states, 'Nobody should be discriminated against on the basis of race, religion, gender,

---

27 See O'Neill, 'Rights, Obligations, and Needs', in Brock (editor), *Necessary Goods: Our Responsibilities to Meet Others' Needs*, Chapter 5.
28 The UDHR in its entirety can be accessed at *www.un.org/en/documents/udhr/*
29 Gillian Brock, 'Needs and Global Justice', in Soran Reader (editor): *The Philosophy of Need* (Cambridge: Cambridge University Press, 2005), p. 65 ff.

politics, or on any other grounds.' Discrimination stems from prejudice
and intolerance. In condemning discrimination on the basis of qualities
like race and gender, which lie beyond the control of the individual, the
second article aims at the advancement of fairness and justice; accordingly, it addresses the need for esteem and possibly self-actualisation.
Religion and politics may also be beyond the control of the individual in some circumstances, for example in theocracies and dictatorships,
where contrary views can attract severe punishment; otherwise, choice
would generally be exercisable, at least to some extent. However, regardless of whether religion and politics are matters of individual choice,
the article insists that one should keep an open mind towards them. A
difficulty arising from this is whether one would be entitled to be intol-
erant of credos that are themselves discriminatory, for example Nazism
and various kinds of fundamentalist religion. The article's position is that
one would not be so entitled; it does not follow, however, that rational
disapproval would also be out of line.

Next, UDHR Article no. 3 stipulates that 'Everyone has the right to
life, liberty and security of person.' Again, there could hardly be rights
more fundamental than these. The article addresses very basic needs, such
as survival and safety. The inclusion of liberty with the right to life and
security suggests that it too is basic. And so it is, for without it opportunities for self-respect would be severely curtailed. Liberty, or freedom,
is a Maslovian B-need, and therefore answers to the need for self-actualisation in the form of human flourishing. Observance of these rights
would help satisfy needs from one end of Maslow's hierarchy to the
other.

Another set of fundamental needs is the subject of Article no. 5, which
states that 'No one shall be subjected to torture or to cruel, inhuman or
degrading punishment.' This article speaks against an especially grievous
form of harm. The pertinent needs are homeostasis and safety, belongingness and esteem; in other words, all of the designated Maslovian
deficiency needs. Maslow was of the view that the lack of gratification
of such needs can diminish one's humanness, by destroying some of the
characteristics that define what it means to be human.[30] The diminution

---

30 *The Farther Reaches of Human Nature*, p. 365.

could also be an effect of cruelty, through vitiation of self-respect. Note that we are talking here about diminution, not total loss. A person who is subjected to torture or inhumane punishment would still be a person, i.e. a human being, regardless of the severity of his or her suffering. Back in Chapter 7 the question was raised as to whether it is permissible for a terrorist to be tortured in an endeavour to locate the bomb he is believed to have planted. An argument was given there in favour of permitting it, albeit with minimum force. This particular conflict between the UDHR and the PHM may be unresolvable, although PHM would debar the use of torture as punishment. Cruelty would also be proscribed, but whether there can be torture without cruelty would be debatable. Judith Shklar's definition of cruelty as the infliction of pain on a weaker being in order to humiliate would seem to leave the door open to torture in some circumstances, including the case in question. The terrorist would not necessarily be humiliated by the pain he is made to suffer, and he may in fact be stronger rather than weaker than his assailants, for example in the strength of his resolve.

Finally, Article no. 14 is pertinent to the vexed issue of asylum-seeking. The article specifies that 'Everyone has the right to seek and enjoy in other countries asylum from unjust persecution.' Safety and belongingness are clearly at issue here, and a straightforward case of right and wrong would appear to be involved. But the politics surrounding asylum-seeking complicates matters. While it would seem to be unequivocally wrong to refuse to accommodate someone attempting to escape persecution, the conventions of the UN Refugee Agency (UNHCR) oblige refugees to fit in with the laws and customs of the host nation. In particular, the prospective host has the right to refuse entry to criminals and the like. In other words, the social stability of the host nation is assumed to be paramount, and that could conflict with the aims of Article no.14, from which the UNHCR takes its lead. Whence *real politick*.

In 2012 there were 45 million displaced persons in the world, more than nine hundred thousand of whom were classified as asylum-seekers—by the end of 2014, those numbers had grown to almost 60 million and 1.8 million respectively. An unqualified reading of Article 14 would seem to require a nation to permit entry to anyone who made it their destination. But what would happen if all of the refugees were to select just one country? Any attempt to accommodate such a large number would obviously give rise to the kind of social disorder legislated against in the refugee convention. The scenario is of course unrealistic, but a principle is involved—it is a matter of where to draw the line. What would be the right number? To maintain order the number would have to be such as not to encroach on satisfaction of the needs of the host's citizens, especially their needs for homeostasis and safety. How many refugees, then, would be too many? That would be a question for social scientists to answer, but some sort of reasonable estimate would seem possible.

The foregoing discussion demonstrates how the rights prescribed in the UDHR connect up with Maslovian needs. Indeed, all of the UDHR articles can be read in a similar fashion. Physical needs are at issue in the rights to life, security, work, and an adequate standard of living. Social needs are relevant to the rights to a family life, participation in public affairs, freedom of movement, a fair hearing in legal affairs, privacy, and freedom from discrimination on the grounds of religion, race, gender and politics. The various freedoms are vitally concerned with self-esteem. Being needs are concerned with the rights to work, self-determination, gender equality, education and participation in the aesthetic and intellectual achievements of the community. Even the right to paid holidays rejected by James Griffin could be seen to contribute to satisfaction of a worker's need for belongingness within his or her family and other social needs, plus the need for play.

The connection between needs and human rights is very strong, and that, in conjunction with the aforesaid connection between rights and morality, suffices to show how moral prescriptions can be derived from basic needs. From the articles that have been discussed, prescriptions such as the following could be deduced:

- Avoid discriminating against others because of their race, religion or gender.
- Pay respect where respect is due.
- Be kind. Offer help to those in need.

The stated prescriptions augment and are consistent with the rules-of-thumb given earlier; namely, in the first instance, avoid doing harm, and, in the second instance, where harm is unavoidable endeavour to minimise it. Prescriptiveness requires that a necessary connection be made between moral judgement and action.[31]

Another conclusion can be drawn from the close relationship between needs and rights; namely, that everyone has the same basic needs. Universality of basic needs follows from the principle that rights are equal across the human race, a principle that was put into practice with the promulgation of the UDHR, especially its injunctions against discriminatory and unfair practices. Equality in this regard has an absolute aspect and a relative one. That rights are held to be equal in an absolute sense is evident from the UDHR's stipulations that the various entitlements should be enjoyed by 'everyone' and 'anyone.' We see that they are relative in the constraints that are placed on the exercise by an individual of his or her rights.

John Finnis observes that the UDHR and derivative documents generally employ two principal canonical forms: first, that everyone 'has the right to...' and, second, 'no one shall be....'[32] Finnis goes on to point out that the two forms arise from the notion that the rights and freedoms are subject to limitation.[33] The limitations stem from UDHR Article no. 29, which stipulates that the various rights must be exercised within the ambit of laws that protect the rights of others. One might add that the idea that freedom involves limitation or constraint corresponds to the notion that personal autonomy entails self-restraint; but the point at issue here is that the limits placed on fulfilment of rights and needs help bring equality into effect. For example, if my rights are successfully constrained by your rights, and yours by mine, then parity (as well as peace) between us should prevail. Equality of rights as surrogates of needs means that everyone is entitled to have their need for food satisfied as much as any other person is entitled to have the same need satisfied; likewise the need for love, the need for esteem, and all of the other needs in the Maslovian schema. I am speaking here in general terms, and the qualifier 'other

31 See Foot, p. 18.
32 Finnis, p. 211.
33 Finnis, p. 211.

things being equal' would apply in particular cases. For example, a person who has been without food for several days would probably be in greater need than someone who has been fasting for just one day; their levels of satiety, prior to receiving sustenance, would not be equal. Nevertheless, based on the general point at issue, it follows that an ethics based on needs is essentially egalitarian.

So strong is the relationship between human needs and human rights that one might ask whether moral theory and moral practice should begin with rights rather than needs. Assuming the mantra 'values register needs' to be valid, the question becomes one of rights versus values. And on that score, I believe that Gillian Brock's subordination of rights to values was correct. 'We have a right to X because we value X' makes more sense than 'we value X because we have a right to X'. That would hold, I believe, on the proviso that values are truly grounded in basic needs. Without the proviso, we could find rights being based on spurious or superficial values. But, then, how should one decide what is spurious or superficial? The question of priority is obviously complex: fortunately, it and any answer we might come up with are irrelevant to the kind of morality I am proposing. Even if rights were accorded priority, the foregoing analysis of the UDHR suggests that they too could be shown to revolve around the principle of harm-minimisation. The main point to be taken from the discussion in this section is that the rights specified in the UDHR are very closely related to basic human needs, from which it follows that the prescriptions and proscriptions of the UDHR can be understood as proxies of the do's and don'ts of needs-based morality. Or, more fully, a need-for-order-based morality. It is time that we looked at what the term 'order' entails.

Chapter 10: Order

I know noble accents
And lucid, inescapable rhythms;
But I know, too,
That the blackbird is involved
In what I know (Wallace Stevens).[1]

Why Order?

Why indeed. The answer for present purposes is that consideration of the notion of order can help explain the origin and nature of morality. Stories about order and its relation to morality began a long time ago, perhaps with Plato, for whom the so-called 'forms' constituted eternal realities. A person whose mind is fixed on those realities was said to have the eternal, unchanging order in his sights. From that, the possibility of abiding harmony was thought to arise,[2] in effect by approximating the eternal order. The existence of universal order was explained as an act of God,[3] in which case, in so far as God is a moral being, the resultant order would also likely be of a moral character. Soon after Plato, Aristotle was also looking upon order as a kind of goodness, but full consideration of the moral relevance of order seems to have been delayed until Nicolas Malebranche (1638-1715) broached the issue.

A philosopher-priest, Malebranche administered a thorough dose of Platonist reality to the concept of order, thereby turning it into an eternal and immutable truth—that is to say, into something that exists independently of humankind and everything else besides. He even subordinated God's will to it: in the words of the philosopher Stephen Nadler (b. 1958), it was Malebranche's view that 'God's wisdom, the dwelling place of Order, stands above his will and guides it.'[4] That would

---

1 From the poem *Thirteen Ways of Looking at a Blackbird* (way no. VIII).
2 Plato, *Republic*, VI. 500.
3 Plato, *Statesman*, 273.
4 Malebranche quoted, in Stephen Nadler, *The Best of All Possible Worlds: A Story of Philosophers, God, and Evil in the Age of Reason* (Princeton: Princeton University Press, 2010), pp. 137-138.

seem to be an almost heretical position for a Catholic priest in France to take (thereby exposing its author to danger from the Inquisition), but it follows from it that morality, as commanded by God, would have its origin in order.

Not long after Malebranche, the poet Alexander Pope was declaring, 'Order is Heaven's first law,'[5] and going on to proclaim that wealth and wisdom are fostered by it. Morality is not among the things Pope explicitly makes contingent upon order, but the 'first law' of a deity generally regarded as beneficent would at least have to have been consistent with it. Around the same time as Pope was singing the praises of order, Jean-Jacques Rousseau (1712-78) and his contemporary David Hume were also speaking of it in glowing terms. Not that they would have endorsed the elevation of the idea to the height that their philosophical predecessor Malebranche had raised it, but they certainly believed it to be of great significance. In Rousseau's words, 'the love of order which produces order is called goodness, and the love of order which preserves order is called justice.'[6] And from Hume, 'the same love of order and uniformity, which arranges the books in a library, and the chairs in a parlour, contribute to the formation of society, and to the well-being of mankind. . . .'[7] The sentiments behind these statements are so similar that one might wonder whether they grew out of the time of Rousseau's and Hume's brief friendship. But that occurred in 1766, many years after the words first appeared in print. A century and a half later the philosopher and psychologist William James (1842-1910) seems to have been thinking along similar lines when he wrote, 'The course of history is nothing but the story of men's struggles from generation to generation to find the more and more inclusive order.'[8] An 'inclusive order' would encompass morality, since morality is assuredly involved in 'men's struggles.'

Morality was clearly part of the story of order for Malebranche, Rousseau and Hume, and arguably James as well. However, in spite

---

5 Alexander Pope, *An Essay on Man* (1734).

6 Rousseau quoted by Ryan Patrick Hanley, 'Rousseau's Virtue Epistemology', in *Journal of the History of Philosophy*, Vol. 50, no. 2 (Baltimore: The Johns Hopkins University Press, 2012), p. 256. The quotation is from *Emile*, which was first published in 1762.

7 Hume, *Treatise*, 3.1.3.

8 William James, 'The Moral Philosopher and the Moral Life', in Susan Haack (editor) with Associate Editor Robert Lane, *Pragmatism Old & New: Selected Writings* (New York: Prometheus Books, 2006), p. 264.

of the importance that order held for eminent thinkers such as these, its connection with morality appears never to have been subjected to extensive treatment. A gap in our knowledge has been left by the inattention, one that is worth trying to fill. But we must first look more closely at the nature of order, and to that end I will start with what it is not. An inkling of what things are can often be obtained by contrasting them with their opposites.

Order, Chaos, Harmony

Order and chaos are opposed to one another. Both have appeared in philosophy, literature and science in various guises—in poetry also, as can be seen in the excerpt from Wallace Stevens's poem (first published in 1917) in the epigraph to this chapter. Nobility and lucidity as invoked by Stevens are certainly fine things, and are more associable with orderliness than with chaos. But chaos always lurks, in the form of the blackbird. It is probably inappropriate to speak of 'form' in connection with chaos; 'formlessness' would be better, and more consistent with the origin of the term itself, since *Chaos* is the name that was given to an ancient god, whose substance consisted of the unformed matter of the world. Staying with the ancients, the pre-Socratic philosopher Empedocles (490-430 BCE) believed that the world oscillates between periods of strife and periods of peace and love, a notion that is reflected in the Manichean creed, and in Hinduism's perpetual battle between the gods Kali and Vishnu. Disorder can be thought of as the natural partner of strife, and order as an accompaniment of lawfulness, or peace.

Despite the opposition between their characters, or perhaps because of it, order and chaos were brought together by the ancient Greeks in the form of harmony. In Plato's *Phaedo*, Socrates gives an account of the dual nature of Harmonia,[9] daughter of Aphrodite and Ares, respectively the gods of love and war. She was given in marriage to the mortal Cadmus, king of Thebes; among her wedding gifts was a necklace that brought calamity to all who wore it. Mortality was one of the misfortunes visited upon her: when she and Cadmus died, both of them were

---

9 Plato, *Phaedo*, 95.

turned into serpents. What is interesting about the legend is the two-fold combination in the person of Harmonia of, on the one hand, love and war; and, on the other hand, of eternal idea ('eternal' because of its godly origin) and perishable being. With regard to the first, harmony can be seen to encompass the extremes of human nature, as revealed in love and war; with regard to the second, harmony is an expression of both permanence and transience. Like Wallace Stevens's poem, the Harmonia legend reminds us that order and chaos are never far apart. The moral is that order requires work of an organising kind to be performed if it is to prevail over disorder. I will return to this theme later this chapter, in the section 'Origins of Order'.

In speaking of harmony I should point out that many thinkers have looked upon the notion as having nothing whatsoever to do with chaos and everything to do with order. That was especially so for the ancient Chinese, for whom order and harmony—primarily cosmic in scale, but also with social and aesthetic ramifications—were largely coextensive. For example, Lao Tzu was predominantly concerned with harmonious primal union as part of the natural order, while Confucius looked to social order for moral harmony to be brought into being. Order in the physical world was believed by the Confucians to be restorable by the principles of harmony.

At roughly the same time Lao Tzu and Confucius were promoting the notion of cosmic order in China, Pythagoras and Plato were doing much the same in ancient Greece. With differences, of course. Perhaps where the Greek thinkers diverged most sharply from their Chinese counterparts was in the mathematics that permeated their accounts of the cosmos's structure and our relation to it. For the Greeks, mathematical concepts were either integral to the structure (Pythagoras) or regarded as a means of describing and explaining it (Plato). Many strands of Pythagorean thought are evident in Plato's philosophy: their views on the after-life were similar, and Plato's ideal state, as described in his *Republic*, emulated Pythagoras by encouraging a collective form of social life, in which men and women were considered equal and property was held in common. But the employment of mathematics in the *Timaeus*, which was published several years after the *Republic*, is probably the most striking manifestation of Plato's Pythagoreanism.

Cosmic order was believed by Pythagoras and Plato to have been the work of a divine creative force. Were it not for the deity's work, they maintained, the world would have remained in a state of primal chaos. Plato was forthright on the matter, especially in the *Timaeus*, where it is said 'when all things were in disorder God created each thing in relation to itself, and in all things in relation to each other, all measures and harmonies which they could possibly receive;' before that happened, the only proportion that existed was by accident.[10] The *Timaeus* is an account of the creation of the cosmos, and it came to form the basis of Western cosmology until mediaeval times, when Aristotelianism began to take over. Interestingly, as well as referring to the universe at large, in ancient Greek the word *kosmos* stood for beauty and order.[11] Just to think about the cosmos was also to think about beauty and order.

Closer to our own time, Friedrich Nietzsche in the nineteenth century drove a dichotomising wedge between chaos and order, calling the first existent and relegating the second to the category of illusion. In his words:

The total character of the world . . . is in all eternity chaos—in the sense not of a lack of necessity but a lack of order, arrangement, form, beauty, wisdom, and whatever other names there are for our aesthetic anthropomorphisms. . . . Let us beware of attributing to [the universe] heartlessness and unreason or their opposites: it is neither perfect nor beautiful, nor noble, nor does it wish to become any of these things; it does not by any means strive to imitate man. None of our aesthetic and moral judgements apply to it.[12]

By contrasting the world's chaos with the direction in which our human hearts and minds take us—i.e., towards order—Nietzsche may be seen to have perceived orderliness in the world, but only as something construed by human beings. Aesthetic judgements and moral judgements are notably given as examples of such constructions. In saying that, I am

---

10 Plato, *Timaeus*, 69.
11 See Wulf, p. 235.
12 Friedrich Nietzsche, *The Gay Science*, translated by Walter Kaufman (New York: Vintage Books, 1974), s. 109.

assuming that the line between the world and human beings is no more than an imaginary one, and was drawn by Nietzsche partly to make the point that humans are the only beings in our godless world (as he believed the world to be) capable of conceiving of order, and of chaos, as Nietzsche himself does. From a naturalistic perspective the division is not sustainable, and to the extent that the ideas of human beings are part of the world, at least some order would have to be attributed to it.

Two centuries before Nietzsche, Spinoza was also expressing scepticism with regard to the reality of order. He maintained that 'because those who do not understand the nature of things, but only imagine them, affirm nothing concerning things, and take the imagination for the intellect, they firmly believe, in their ignorance of things and of their own nature, that there is order in things.'[13] Now to view order as nothing more than a figment seems to me to sit rather uneasily alongside the pantheistic (or pan-naturalistic) principles that Spinoza espoused. God (or nature) was the totality of things for him, and therefore as real as anything could be. Would Spinoza want to say that nature (or God) was not in itself orderly? Perhaps he would, but it would be a strange position to take. The reason it would be strange is that, from a pan-naturalistic viewpoint, grounds would become readily evident for investing order with reality and relegating disorder to the category of human fabrication. One would only have to view matters from the perspective of nature. If that were done, everything would be found to exhibit certain law-like regularities, especially in the form of cause and effect—regularities that merit the ascription 'order'.

From our own perspective, that of humankind (a perspective necessarily taken from within nature), both order and disorder can be seen to exist. Our perspective is necessarily limited—we are not all-seeing and all-knowing; if we were, our vantage point would be identical to that of nature as a whole and we would find order everywhere. Nevertheless, in spite of our limitations, part of what an anthropomorphised nature would see as orderly we also see, i.e. that which conforms to natural law as we understand it. Together with the order that exists in the form of regularity within nature, our powers of analogy enable us also to see that

---

13 *The Ethics*, 1app.

the concept has application to other phenomena, including some aspects of human behaviour and endeavour. We analyse the concept thereby establishing criteria for orderliness (to be discussed shortly). We then say that that which conforms to the criteria is that which is orderly; that which does not conform is disorderly, or chaotic.

The notion of universal orderliness within nature contrasts sharply with the positions taken by Nietzsche and Spinoza—although it must be acknowledged that theirs was strictly a human perspective, not that of nature. Nevertheless, I believe the case for the reality of order (and disorder) to be strong, from either perspective. Order is something that is perceivable by us as representatives of nature in the form of natural law, and conceivable also as the counterpoint of disorder. Disorder reveals itself to us all too frequently, in such forms as ugliness, bodily malfunction, and unruly behaviour—Nietzsche was right in that respect. Order is the converse of such tribulations, and can emerge from the things we do to counteract them. Beauty, proper functioning, and humaneness are the results.

These reflections on chaos and harmony have had us skirting around some important aspects of the nature of order, especially social order and aesthetic experience. I will sharpen up the thinking on these matters shortly. But before moving on, I should make clear that order and harmony are not synonymous. Harmony necessarily entails order, but the reverse does not apply: only some order entails harmony. In an example that I will use again later, a prison environment may be orderly, but not harmonious. Nevertheless it can be safely said that wherever order does entail harmony, it will be either aesthetic or ethical in character: beautiful order, good order.

It is time to bring this preliminary exposition of the nature of order to an end. Although some insight into the matter might be obtained from consideration of what order isn't (chaos) and what it is like (harmony), we are still a long way from having a full description of it. Whether a full description is even possible might be doubted. Definitions of the term abound—thirty-six of them in its noun form can be found in the

Web-based *Dictionary.com*; similarly in other dictionaries.[14] Nevertheless, in spite of the difficulties, some general characteristics are apparent.

General Characteristics of Order

I will begin with Aristotle, according to whom order consists in (or arises from) inter-contact between things.[15] As we saw in the epigraph to Chapter 2, all of the things of which the world is composed were thought by Aristotle to be connected to one another. Here is more of what he had to say on the matter:

We must consider in which of two ways the nature of the universe contains the good and the highest good, whether as something separate and by itself, or as the order of the parts. Probably in both ways, as an army does; for its good is found both in its order and in its leader, and more in the latter; for he does not depend on the order but it depends on him. And all things are ordered together somehow, but not all alike,— both fishes and fowls and plants; and the world is not such that one thing has nothing to do with another, but they are connected. For all are ordered together to one end. . . .[16]

The passage raises many issues of interest, including the inherent goodness of order, and the interconnectedness of things. The goodness of order will be discussed later, in the section 'Humaneness and Homosapient Order' (Chapter 11); for the present, I want to focus on the notion 'order of parts'.

From what Aristotle says, it seems that parts that are interconnected may be ordered either in terms of time or place, or in terms of both time and place. With regard to time, using an illustration provided by Aristotle, we would know something was wrong if dinner were served when we would normally expect breakfast. With regard to place, the positions of participants in a ceremonial procession would often be determined by their rank, or status. With regard to the conjunction of time and

---

14 See http://dictionary.reference.com (accessed 3 March 2010). The *Macquarrie Dictionary* has an almost identical list.

15 See Aristotle, *Metaphysics*, translated by W. D. Ross (Chicago: The University of Chicago, Great Books of the Western World, 1952), Vol. 8, VIII.2, 1042b.

16 *Metaphysics*, XII.10, 1075a.

place, we would believe, other things being equal, that queues should be ordered in accordance with the times people join them. We can infer from Aristotle's account that order denotes a kind of connective relationship between entities, whereby wholes are assembled from two or more parts. Therefore, we may say that order consists fundamentally as a relation between at least two interacting things; on those grounds, it can be described as a complex phenomenon.

Six of the dictionary entries for order relate to the notion of 'command', and are of no immediate concern here; in that sense, the reference is to a *cause* of order (a command is given with a view to creating some kind of order). Homosapient order, as I will be defining it, excludes order in the sense of command, although some kind of internal command (an act of will, say) might be required to bring it into effect. And it may be the case that the said internal commands stem ultimately from one's need for homosapient order. Moral commands are like prescriptions (such as the PHM and its derivatives) that guide one's moral affairs, ideally towards a morally tolerable end.

Several of the definitions of order have general application. They refer to the notion of order in terms of arrangements or dispositions of things, and classes of things (including persons) that 'are distinguished from others by nature or character.' Aristotle's concept of prioritisation is explicit in one of the definitions: 'the disposition of things following one after the other, as in space or time; succession or sequence.' Broadest of all we have 'state or condition generally.' Any of these could be applied to physical matter, to social arrangements, and to personal dispositions; in other words, to the various domains of need identified by Maslow. The notions of composition, coherence, wholeness and integration are implicit in the definitions, as I will now attempt to demonstrate.

Beginning with composition, a thing that is a composite is a 'state or condition' that consists in an arrangement or disposition of other things; in other words, it is a whole of some kind. Some composites may also be groups. A group is an assemblage of things, i.e. a composite, but it is a composite that is invested with a characteristic that distinguishes it from other assemblages. Grouping requires an act of abstraction, whereby things that constitute a group are considered to be related in some way. The very act of abstraction means that some things are set apart from other things—of positioning them in a particular way within space and time. In other words, spatial and temporal prioritisation occurs, and with it comes some kind of order. To illustrate, otherwise disparate human beings might form a group because of a common characteristic, or a perception of such, for example shared aims.[17] A measure of orderly integration might be expected of such entities, and their aims are what distinguish them from those who do not share them.

The concept of orderly integration is a close relative of two of the other general characteristics of order, coherence and wholeness. My discussion of them begins with a text from Spinoza.

By the coherence of parts I understand nothing but that the laws or nature of the one part so adapt themselves to the laws or nature of the other part that they are opposed to each other as little as possible. Concerning whole and parts, I consider things as parts of some whole insofar as the nature of the one so adapts itself to the nature of the other so far as possible they are all in harmony with one another. But insofar as they are out of harmony with one another, to that extent each forms an idea distinct from the others in our mind, and therefore it is considered as a whole and not as a part.[18]

If parts fail to cohere, Spinoza tells us, each of them would be viewed as a whole in its own right, while the entity in which they are combined would not be seen as such. Coherence connotes good order, for example through an appropriate prioritisation of parts, which in turn is cognate with harmony. Coherence is very important to us. We need to be able to make sense of things, and it is in our nature to attempt to understand what is going on around us. Coherence can be welcome, even when it is founded on a misconception. Long-standing trust was placed in the Ptolemaic geocentric understanding of the planetary system, until it was displaced by the Copernican heliocentric interpretation. Although Copernicus's system was in many ways simpler and more elegant, the old

---

17 See Finnis, p. 152.
18 Curley (editor and translator), *A Spinoza Reader: The Ethics and Other Works*, pp. 82–83. The extract is from a letter written by Spinoza to his friend Henry Oldenburg, an official of the British Royal Society.

ideas were in their time widely respected and served their purposes, for example in navigation.[19]

Coherence signifies that parts have been brought together in such a way as to form a whole. In other words, it is a mark of integration and consequently of integrity, in the sense of good *working* order. Coherence, wholeness, and integrity therefore have a functional aspect. They may also have an aesthetic one. We find, for instance, Thomas Aquinas associating wholeness with perfection, and calling the latter one of three conditions of beauty; the others being due proportion and clarity. Due proportion is equated by Aquinas with harmony (in that sense, it is cognate with coherence and order). Clarity is likened to brightness, whence, Aquinas maintains, 'things are called beautiful which have an elegant colour.'[20] The mention of elegance of colour suggests that Aquinas had aesthetic beauty in mind when he was writing this. On his reading, a beautiful thing is necessarily an integrated coherent whole. But the reverse does not apply: a whole need not be beautiful (just as order need not be harmonious).

The concept of *unity* can also help explain that of *whole*. In his treatise *Metaphysics*, Aristotle defines unity—or oneness—in terms of individuality, or distinctiveness, of 'being essentially a "this" and capable of being isolated either in place, or in form or thought.'[21] Various kinds of unities are catalogued, including those that exist by virtue of being continuous (such as dots that are joined to form a line), those whose substrata are identical (water and ice would be an example), and those with parts that together constitute a particular form (Aristotle's example is that of a shoe and the materials used to make it). With regard to formal unity, the composite entity is such that the totality of the parts is not 'a mere heap:' the parts come together under the guidance of a cause consisting in form.[22] A thing's form, Aristotle says, is its shape,[23] which can be understood to

19 See Umberto Eco, *Signs of the Times*, in Catherine David, Frédéric Lenoir, Jean-Philippe de Tonnac (editors); Ian Maclean, Roger Pearson (translators), *Conversations About the End of Time* (London: Allen lane The Penguin Press, 1999), p. 214.
20 Thomas Aquinas, *The Summa Theologica*, translated by Fathers of the English Dominican Province, revised by Daniel J. Sullivan (Chicago: The University of Chicago, Great Books of the Western World, 1952), Vols. 19-20, I.Q39, Art.8.
21 *Metaphysics* X.1, 1052b.
22 *Metaphysics* VIII.6, 1045a.
23 *Metaphysics* X.1, 1017b.

refer to its structure; and a whole is said to be a thing that has unity of form.[24] A unified whole is a particular kind of composite entity, from which it would follow that a unified entity, in at least one sense of unified, is an entity that evinces order.

All of this might look like ancient history, and of course that is what it is. But the fact remains that we still talk about order in very similar terms to those used so many years ago, by the likes of Aristotle and Spinoza. For example, in the last decade of the twentieth century we find the biologist Stuart Kauffman (b. 1939) observing how interactions and connections between organisms and goods and services in ecosystems and economic systems open the way to incorporation of new organisms, goods and services, so giving rise to newly integrated wholes.[25] Interaction between parts, joining of parts to make integrated wholes; such are the properties that define order. But there is one more property that must be considered, namely 'goodness'.

The etymology of the term *good* is indicative of its connection with *order*. As Robert Nozick observed, *good* stems from the root *Ghedh*, which means 'to unite, join, fit, to bring together.'[26] The relationship between unity and order again comes into view, now with the addition of goodness, in some sense of the term 'goodness'. What sense might that be? It is apparent from the quotations on p. 128 that Rousseau and Hume were clear about the goodness of order, and that, for them, its goodness extended to the moral sphere. I will address the question of whether order is morally good in the next chapter; here I wish simply to note that order is good in a very general way. General goodness may or may not be moral goodness.

Two of the dictionary entries for order are concerned with general goodness. First, we find that order is 'a condition in which each thing is properly disposed with reference to other things and to its purpose; methodical or harmonious arrangement.' Second, we have 'proper, satisfactory, or working condition.' Orderliness is good because it contributes to the fulfilment of a thing's purpose; disorderliness is bad because

---

24 *Metaphysics* V.6, 1016a.
25 Stuart A. Kauffman, *The Origins of Order: Self-Organization and Selection in Evolution* (New York: Oxford University Press, 1993), p. 370.
26 Nozick, p. 418.

disorder works against attainment of a thing's purpose. I am being mindful here of something Spinoza wrote: it was his understanding that that which is good is that which 'we certainly know to be useful to us.'[27] If the shoes mentioned by Aristotle fail to fit their intended wearer, they fail in their purpose—they are bad, although *prima facie* without moral significance (if the shoe-maker intentionally puts a shoddy product onto the market, morality would then be involved).

Order consists in organised complexity, arising from interconnectivity of the parts of a whole. Perhaps the most complexly ordered thing that we can think of is the very thing that enables us to think, the human brain, with its immense number of neurons and synapses. Synaptic connections play a major role in the brain's functionality—break a significant number of them, perhaps even just a few, and functionality would surely be impaired. In sum, order is an organising principle whose end is fitness for purpose of orderly objects. For an organising principle to take effect, something or someone is needed to exercise it: an organiser, one might say, along the lines of Aristotle's army leader, i.e. a commander capable of whipping the parts of the whole (the troops in this case) into shape. As we will now see, it is this aspect of orderly organisation that is critical to the distinction between life and non-life.

Order and Life

Life on Earth is widely believed to have begun approximately 3.5 billion years ago, and our planet and the universe of which it is a part is thought to be several times older than that. Everything that now exists can be understood to be composed of material that has existed since the beginning of time—material in the form of either matter or energy. This might come as something of a surprise, in view of the fact that much of life as it is now understood is based on the processes of cell division and cell differentiation (in mitosis and meiosis). Where does the material for new cells come from? Science tells us that its primary source is the sun's thermonuclear conversion of atomic particles into the light energy that plants use to convert carbon dioxide and water into life-giving

---

27 *The Ethics*, 4def1.

carbohydrates, by means of photosynthesis. Plants serve as food for our mothers and us, and for the animals eaten by us and our forebears. On this view, our universe and everything in it consists of ever-changing assemblages of a constant supply of material. Material that was energy and which becomes matter takes the form of particles (quarks, electrons, and so forth) that in turn become aggregated into the composites we perceive as physical entities, such as stones, trees, birds, and people. All of this is fully consistent with what the scientist Antoine Laurent de Lavoisier (1743-1794) posited as the supreme principle of chemistry: 'matter is neither created nor destroyed, all it knows is transformation.'[28]

Compared with non-life, life is characterised by the ability to replicate and by the ability to create order through the use of energy;[29] non-life possesses neither characteristic. The journalist and science writer Matt Ridley (b. 1958) regards these as 'two very different skills,'[30] but I think order can be shown to be involved in both of them. I will begin with the ability to replicate.

Deoxyribonucleic acid (DNA) is the *sine qua non* of replication. Things that have forever been devoid of life are devoid of DNA. DNA in its own right could be viewed as a form of life, demonstrated most remarkably by the still-potent DNA often retrieved from dead organisms, including fossilised ones. DNA can be used to replicate a dead organism, or some part of it. But for that to happen the DNA would first need to be implanted in a living host, perhaps a cell of some description—which is what genetic engineering is about.

In the early 1950s Francis Crick (1916-2004) and James Watson (b. 1928) found order to be central to fundamental life processes. DNA was the key, but instead of being explained merely by the chemical constituents of the molecule, life and genetic inheritance were shown by them (assisted by others, sometimes without due recognition) to depend on the way base elements are symmetrically arranged along its two helical strands. The term 'symmetry' is used here in its general sense of harmony of proportions, which derives from its etymological basis

28 Quoted in Ken Alder, *The Measure of All Things: The Seven-Year Odyssey that Transformed the World* (London: Abacus, 2004 [first published 2002]), p. 143.
29 See Ernst Mayr, *What Makes Biology Unique?* (New York: Cambridge University Press, 2004), p. 210.
30 Matt Ridley, *Genome: The Autobiography of a Species in 23 Chapters* (London: Fourth Estate, 2000), p. 12.

'similarity of measure', i.e. commensurability. (Mathematically, symmetry obtains when an object remains perceptibly the same after having undergone some kind of motion, for example rotation.[31]) As well as symmetry, equivalent amounts of the four base elements of the molecule and identically shaped pairings of them were found to be features of its organisation.

Symmetry, equivalence, identical shapes; all are suggestive of order. Perhaps more than merely suggestive, for some scholars have considered the relationship to be very close indeed. The astrophysicist Mario Livio (b. 1945) states that the orderliness of an object is often determined by its symmetries.[32] He notes also that orderliness contributes to an object's so-called 'aesthetic value', on the basis of a formula proposed by the mathematician George Birkhoff (1884-1944). According to the formula, aesthetic value is proportional to the result obtained from dividing order by complexity—implying that aesthetic value increases when order increases relative to complexity.[33] Now if that were treated as a standard algebraic equation, and both sides were multiplied by 'complexity', we would find order consisting in the product of aesthetic value and complexity. Or, as it might be expressed, order would equate with beautifully rendered complexity. On that account, an increase in order would emerge from an increase in either beauty or complexity (assuming that the other remains constant), or both beauty and complexity. I must say that I find the idea attractive, but I will leave it there and move on.

The relationship between symmetry and order has long been the subject of comment. In his book *The Garden of Cyrus* (1658), Sir Thomas Browne marvels at the symmetry that is evident in animals and plants. This, he writes, 'doth neatly declare how nature Geometrizeth, and

31 For the sake of completeness I should point out that physicists regard order and symmetry as *opposing* tendencies. Roughly speaking, symmetry is akin to absolute uniformity, such as exists where a closed system is in thermodynamic equilibrium. Order, by contrast, is something that emerges from symmetry, in the form of a structure or pattern. For a useful account see Martin H. Krieger, *Doing Physics: How Physicists Take Hold of the World* (Indiana: Indiana University Press, Second Edition 2012), especially Chapter 4. Krieger acknowledges that symmetry is commonly identified with order, and that is the way I am using the term.
32 Mario Livio, *The Equation that Couldn't be Solved: How Mathematical Genius Discovered the Language of Symmetry* (New York: Simon & Schuster, 2006), p. 13.
33 Nozick also refers to Birkhoff's theory, noting that it bears some resemblance to his description of organic unity as 'unity in diversity.' Organic unity is central to Nozick's ethical theory, and is equated with 'value'. See Nozick p. 415.

observeth order in all things.'[34] *All* things, it should be noted, non-living as well as living. Science in our own time has shown that the tendency towards order within non-living nature occurs at a very elementary level, typified by the stability of molecules that are formed after atoms either gain or lose electrons; stability so attained is described as a state of minimum energy. The sinuosity of rivers provides another example of non-living natural order. Sinuosity is the ratio between, on the one hand, the distance travelled by a river along its entire winding course, and, on the other hand, the distance as the crow flies between mouth and source. For an average river, sinuosity works out to be about the same as the ratio between a circle's circumference and its diameter, i.e. *pi*.

From the realm of living nature, there is the so-called principle of dynamic equilibrium that pertains to biological cells, according to which the parts that come together to form highly complex systems such as biological cells must fit together 'both precisely and loosely.'[35] As well as that, mathematical regularity has been found to obtain between the number of different kinds of cells (eye cells, hair cells, liver cells, etc.) in a multitude of organisms and the number of genes characteristic of the respective organisms—the number of different kinds of cells is approximately the square root of the number of genes.[36] Snail shells reveal yet another kind of mathematical regularity, so much so that the philosopher Gaston Bachelard (1884-1962) was in awe of them, and regarded them as 'the clearest proof of life's ability to constitute forms.'[37] Snail shells, indeed mollusc shells in general, take the form of spirals which conform to the Golden Ratio, whose emblem is the Greek letter *phi*.[38] As defined by Euclid more than two thousand years ago, the Golden Ratio is the ratio between the greater segment and the lesser segment of a straight line that has been divided in two in such a way that the ratio thus obtained is the same as the ratio borne by the whole line to the greater segment: its approximate value is 1.6. The form taken by a shell is largely

34 Browne quoted by D'Arcy Thompson, in *On Growth and Form* (Cambridge: Cambridge University Press, 1997 [first published 1961]), p. 103.
35 See Natalie Angier, *The Canon* (New York: Houghton Mifflin Company, 2007), p. 204.
36 See Kauffman, p. 35.
37 Bachelard quoted by Jonathan Bate, *The Song of the Earth* (London: Picador, 2000), p. 155.
38 Refer Mario Livio, *The Golden Ratio: The Story of Phi, the Extraordinary Number of Nature, Art and Beauty* (London: Review, 2003), p. 9.

governed by the organism's genetic components, which are themselves structured symmetrically—symmetry and order, therefore, from beginning to end. The formation of molecules and the sinuosity of rivers show that order is evident in at least some non-living entities, but the genetic conveyance of information that finds expression in successive generations remains the exclusive property of life.

The mention of successive generations brings the notion of *fitness* into view. From the perspective of genetics, order just *is* fitness, where fitness is a value ascribed to chromosomes to indicate the ability of the corresponding organism to produce surviving offspring.[39] Genetic orderliness translates into reproductive capacity, and must be regarded as part of the overall story of order. However, outside of genetics, matters are different. The context only has to be broadened slightly, to that of biology, to see that order means much more than reproductive capacity. Think for example of organisms that are for some reason unable to reproduce, such as mules and eunuchs; neither is capable of producing offspring, but does that alone make them disorderly? No, it does not. For as long as they survive, everything apart from their reproductive parts would be working in reasonable harmony. They might be considered to be defective in some way, but they are not chaotic; if they were, they would not be alive. Consider also sexually immature organisms. Infants cannot reproduce, but we would not on that account regard them as disorderly. While fitness in the sense employed by geneticists constitutes only part of the story, the term nevertheless lends itself to a useful extension. 'Fitness' derives from 'fit', and its associated sense of 'fitting together', and from that, 'best fit'. Fitness has very broad application to the notion of order.

Order in nature runs deep, so deep that it reaches into human nature and from there to morality. But these are matters for later parts of the book; the other factor that differentiates life from non-life still has to be considered. Besides genetics, life is also distinguished by the capacity to make use of energy from either the sun or certain kinds of molecules. Organisms take in energy and they also discharge it. The processes involve what I will refer to as 'entropy-avoidance'. The concept of

---

39 See John H. Holland, *Hidden Order: How Adaptation Builds Complexity* (New York: Basic Books, 1995), p. 65.

entropy comes from physics and cosmology, where the Second Law of thermodynamics stipulates that closed systems such as the universe tend towards disorderliness. Closed systems are those that are unable to interact with their external environment (the universe as a whole has no external environment). Disorderliness culminates in what is called thermodynamic equilibrium, i.e., within a system, an even spread of matter that is utterly devoid of structure, just an undifferentiated blob. Thermodynamic equilibrium is the ultimate entropic condition; it is the state of maximum thermodynamic disorder, and is generally held to be irreversible.

In the 1940s Erwin Schrödinger (1887-1961), whose work is known to have influenced Watson and Crick, equated 'fairly high levels of orderliness' with 'fairly low levels of entropy,' and argued that organisms maintain their orderliness by continually 'sucking' order from their environments.[40] By sucking in orderliness, life-forms are able to avoid (or forestall) thermodynamic disequilibrium. Organisms are living entities; non-living entities are not organisms. Entropy is an inevitable concomitant of life; to compensate for it, thereby avoiding death, organisms on Schrödinger's theory extract what is called 'negative entropy', or orderliness, from the external environment. To illustrate, life depends on nutrition, which involves the absorption of energy from foodstuffs, in exchange for an increase in energy in the form of heat in the surrounding environment. The initial absorption represents the extraction of orderliness, and the consequential heat contributes to the disorderliness of the encompassing system. The process of exchange is what we call *metabolism*.

In recent years the exchange of orderliness has been couched more in terms of 'Gibbs free energy' than Schrödinger's 'negative entropy'. Schrödinger himself referred to free energy (see Note to Chapter 6 of his book), but felt that the technicalities involved were beyond the grasp of the average reader. The technicalities are not important here; what is important is the fact that life necessarily involves the transfer of entropy (i.e. disorder) to the external environment, whereas non-life does not. Orderliness in this general sense is fundamental to life, including the

---

40 Erwin Schrödinger, *What is Life?* (London: Folio Society, 2000 [first published 1944]), p. 91.

life of our species. Order contributes to the achievement of a very basic purpose of living entities—namely, to stay alive. This effectively completes the answer to the question that was posed at the beginning of the chapter, Why Order? Order is pertinent to morality because, firstly, it is necessary to life in general, and secondly, it is critical to various aspects of human life. How critical will become clearer in the next chapter.

To sum up, life as distinct from non-life is generally characterised by disorder-avoidance. As a consequence, life is always structured in an orderly fashion, at least to some extent, whereas non-life need not be. The biologist Steven Rose (b. 1938) encapsulated the point in an assertion to the effect that order must be maintained if life is to persist: order within both the cell and the organism, and in the relationship between the organism and the external world.[41] It is this dependence on order— the *need* for it—that distinguishes life from non-life. And, as we will soon see, it is humankind's need for a particular kind of order—homosapient order—that distinguishes us from other life-forms. The need in question will be found in Chapter 12 to be implicated in the various human needs identified by Maslow, which were earlier found to be at the bottom of morally relevant harm.

Hopefully by now I have succeeded in convincing you of the importance of order, perhaps by augmenting your knowledge of what it consists in. But we might not be able to claim that we truly or even adequately know a thing unless we can pinpoint where it came from. Spinoza certainly thought that to be the case. Some comments on the aetiology of order would therefore be timely.

The Origins of Order

What, if anything, first brought orderliness into being? What was its first cause? Plato had an answer—in the *Phaedo*, he notes that the philosopher Anaxagoras (500-428 BCE) had asserted that 'it is mind that produces order and is the cause of everything,' and then goes on to say, through his spokesman Phaedo, 'mind in producing order sets everything in order

41 Steven Rose, *Lifelines: Life Beyond the Gene* (London: Vintage, 2005 [first published 1997]), p. 137.

and arranges each individual thing in the way that is best for it.'[42] In other words, order is the result of conscious effort rather than unconscious forces, or blind chance. Whose effort is responsible for it? Initially, to Plato's way of thinking, things were ordered by the creative Demiurge in accordance with an eternal Form in the shape of the Good, thereby ensuring the best possible arrangement. And thereafter? Presumably everyone acting individually, again in accordance with the Form, or the best possible approximation thereof. Order on that basis would consist in the parts of a whole being arranged in the best possible manner; in short, order is harmony *(harmonia* in Greek means 'fitting together').[43]

Anyone who believes in an infinite deity would probably be satisfied with thinking along lines similar to those set down by Plato—it was God who created order. Some people might even identify order with God, in which case order would be eternal. The last might be regarded as a Spinozistic solution, one that is amenable to a naturalistic interpretation. But the notion of eternity is itself problematic, especially if time is considered to have begun with the Big Bang, as proposed by the physicist Stephen Hawking in his book *A Brief History of Time* (1988). If Hawking is right, timelessness may be presumed to have preceded the Big Bang, and in a timeless state there would be no arrow of time and therefore no entropy. If order is understood to be equivalent to the absence of entropy, then, in these circumstances, order would have prevailed before the Big Bang—timelessly and therefore eternally. This is all very speculative, and I will not pursue the line of thought any further.

Something that is not so speculative is the Big Bang's part in bringing the laws of nature into existence. And we can thank our lucky stars (literally, since it is the stars that provide much of the elementary matter from which we and everything else are made) that the laws that were instigated culminated in the laws as we now find them. If the universe and Earth within it were subject to ever-so-slightly different laws of nature, then there would be a strong possibility that life would never have got

---

42 Plato, *Phaedo,* translated by Hugh Tredennick, in Edith Hamilton and Huntington Cairns (editors), *The Collected Dialogues of Plato* (Princeton: Princeton University Press, Bollingen Series LXXI, 1999 [first published 1961]), 97c.
43 Milton C. Nahm, (editor), *Selections from Early Greek Philosophy* (USA: Appleton-Century-Crofts, 1947), p. 73.

off the ground, let alone evolved. This is known as the 'weak anthropic principle', according to which our small segment of the universe happens to have been endowed with just the right conditions to enable life first to begin and then to develop. If, say, our planet's orbit had brought it significantly closer to the Sun than it has until now (or farther from it), then the extreme heat (or cold) may well have made life impossible. But we exist, and we have reached a high level of organisation. We are very complex beings.

So our initial question can be rephrased: How did our just-right universe ('just right' like Goldilocks's porridge) and the organisation that we both instantiate and perceive come about? Was it all by chance, or was it intentional? If the latter, then it may be said to have been designed, i.e. purposeful; and if designed, then there must have been a designer (such as Plato's Demiurge). But that would be contrary to what we have learned from Darwin, at least from the atheistic position I have chosen to adopt. In any case, regardless of how order arises, whether by accident or by design, it would seem to be fundamental to nature.

Atheistic thinkers would of course have to look to something other than a divine designer for the origin of order. Schrödinger might be able to help here. We know that one of the steps crucial to the emergence of life is the development of mechanisms that provide energy.[44] Photosynthesis is one such mechanism: photons from sunlight are used by plants and some bacteria to produce food. Sunlight, Schrödinger noted, is the most powerful supply of 'negative entropy' accessible to plants.[45] More generally, energy is needed to convert disorder into order, so it would seem that energy was implicated in some way in the first appearance of order. But no more than as an efficient cause thereof: 'supply' as used by Schrödinger connotes 'source', which connotes 'cause'. Energy alone is not sufficient to produce order; other factors or materials are also required.

Life itself might be sufficient for order to come into being. According to Stephen Jay Gould, any harmony and order that the world might display is only the by-product of the struggle amongst individuals to

44 Richard Southwood, *The Story of Life* (Oxford: Oxford University Press, 2007 [first published 2003]), p. 12.
45 See Schrödinger, p. 92.

increase 'the representation of their genes in future generations.' [46] Such is the nature of Darwinian natural selection. Gould's position is that of a representative of one side (called *adaptionist*) of a contemporary debate about the origin of living order. Opposed to the strict adaptionist reading are complexity theorists like Stuart Kauffman. For Kauffman and like-minded individuals, the order that is perceptible in an organism results directly from a tendency for order to emerge spontaneously in 'massively complex systems.' Having emerged, order becomes available for natural selection to work on,[47] but the main point is that complexity (i.e. wholes comprised of many interacting parts, as defined by Aristotle) is sufficient for order to come into being. Parts combine to form wholes, which themselves become nested like Babushka dolls in formations of other wholes; and so on, with all of the wholes fitting together in 'proper array' thereby functioning more or less smoothly.

Living physical order is the point at issue in the adaptionist-complexity debate, but there were of course massively complex systems in existence before life first surfaced: the universe just after the Big Bang would be one such instance. As we have seen, order is evident in many of nature's lifeless purlieus; and, in the absence of a supernatural artificer, it too can be looked upon as having emerged spontaneously. Similar comments would apply to social order, since socioeconomic systems also tend to be 'massively complex', with people forming families, families forming institutions, institutions in proper array, and so on. It would also extend to individual human beings, who, besides the complexity of their physical and psychological make-up, also contribute to the formation of complex social and economic systems. On the complexity principle, order would evolve spontaneously within all of these separate (but interconnected) domains. Precisely how this happens is a very involved process that is still the subject of investigation; interested readers may wish to consult Kauffman's and other relevant works.

Can any conclusions with regard to primal order be drawn from the foregoing? If entropy-avoidance were the only means of producing order,

---

46 Stephen Jay Gould, *Hen's Teeth and Horse's Toes* (New York: W. W. Norton & Company, 1983), p. 122. See also Gould's *Ever Since Darwin: Reflections in Natural History* (New York: W. W. Norton & Company, 1979), p. 12.
47 Kauffman, pp. 173, 409.

then the origin of order would consist in 'life processes' themselves, for example metabolism; or, more succinctly, in life *per se*. On that basis, while disorder (i.e. entropy) certainly existed before life, order (negative entropy) would only have come into being with the emergence of life. After its inception, life's reproductive processes would have brought further instances of entropy-avoidance into being. As one of the section headings in Schrödinger's book proclaims, order is based on order.[48] As Schrödinger saw it, whilst life is obedient to overarching thermodynamic laws, and in that sense can be regarded as orderly, it also brings order into being through the maintenance of existing order. Furthermore, the life-processes by which order is maintained also answer to laws of nature, and are therefore orderly in the same sense as the entropic processes are orderly.[49] For its beginning, life depended on the capacity of carbon to form chains, rings and polymers,[50] all of which are composite structures; their various shapes suggest that they were (and still are) non-random, i.e. orderly. The order that was characteristic of the first life-forms was therefore based on the orderliness of their constituent non-life forms. Vestiges of order predate even such rudimentary forms of life as single-celled organisms with their organelles. In other words, while life is sufficient for order it is not necessary for it; and, conversely, although order is necessary for life it is not sufficient for it.

We are probably no closer to finding the source of primal order, and the inconclusiveness could lead one to suspect that there is no such thing as primal order, in vindication of the positions taken by Spinoza and Nietzsche. However, assuming that order does exist, the inconclusiveness also leaves the door ajar for a supernaturalistic explanation, perhaps from an advocate of Intelligent Design. The possibility cannot be dismissed, but neither can the prospect of a naturalistic explanation. Complexity theory may offer the best hope for the latter. If order can indeed emerge spontaneously from complex systems, then the origin of order would be tied in with the origin of complexity; in other words, it would be

48 Schrödinger, p. 84.
49 Schrödinger, p. 85.
50 See Richard Fortey, *Life: An Unauthorised Biography* (London: Folio Society, 2008 [first published 1997]), p. 67.

coincidental with the Big Bang. If the physicists are right, the Big Bang transformed something that was infinitely non-complex ('singularity' is the technical term) into a profoundly complex and multi-layered phenomenon. From that came entropy and the possibility of order, and Schrödinger's distinction between non-life and life on the basis of disorder-avoidance. Life's ability to avoid disorder is what enables it to satisfy its need for order. Life can be seen as having first come into being when a particular arrangement of matter enabled a composite, complex thing to resist the effects of the Second Law of thermodynamics, i.e. to resist physical disorder.

Of course, physical disorder is not the only kind of disorder that confronts human beings. Social disorder and psychological disorder are also very common. Successful resistance against disorder on all fronts will be rewarded with homosapient order. It is time that we found out more about this uniquely human kind of order.

Chapter 11: Homosapient Order

Men by nature strive for a civil order (Spinoza).

Because the concept of homosapient order is new, any attempt to find support for it (or refutation of it) in the existing literature would presumably be futile. We can nevertheless affirm from the previous chapter that order of some kind is fundamental to life. We might also infer from Rousseau, Hume and others that the relevance of order (again, 'order' of some kind) extends beyond the physical. My aim in this chapter is to show how its relevance reaches into the social, spiritual and normative domains of human life. For reasons that will soon be made clear I will refer to spiritual order as *eudaimonic* order. Homosapient order, therefore, can be understood to consist of four parts: physical order, social order, eudaimonic order, and normative order. Each of the parts will now be described and explained.

P-Order

'P' = Physical. P-order refers to arrangements of the elementary parts of which composites exist. The parts range from sub-atomic particles (or whatever else the smallest or most fundamental components of nature might happen to be) to composites thereof. The orderliness involved in genetically controlled propagation and entropy-avoidance is physical in nature. P-order would be impossible in the absence of coherence and integration of the parts of which the composite is composed. All of the general characteristics of order outlined in the previous chapter must be present.

Various kinds of composites can be P-orderly, non-living as well as living. Within each realm, there are things that are in a state of nature (i.e. things whose basic structure is uninfluenced by human beings), and other things that are not in a state of nature (i.e. things whose basic structure has been influenced by human beings). P-orderly composites in a state of nature include mountains (non-life) and trees (life). P-orderly composites not in a state of nature include machines (non-life) and genetically-modified crops (life). Non-living composites that are not in a state of nature are wholes whose parts are sufficiently integrated for them to be able to fulfil their functions; for example, houses and all of the mod-cons inside them. Similarly for living composites, for example well-structured anthers and carpels that contribute to the reproduction of flowering plants.

P-order is necessary to life, including human life, but non-living entities have no need of it: non-living entities have no needs whatsoever. P-order is good in the general sense of the term good—its existence is a mark of orderliness with respect to purpose. For living entities, harm in the form of death would follow upon non-attainment, or destruction, of P-order. Enough was said about physical order in the discussion of the orderliness of life and the origins of order to enable us to move on to the next component of homosapient order.

S-Order

'S' = Social. S-order is confined to the realm of life. It refers to the grouping of organisms in ways that help them satisfy some kind of need or serve a particular purpose. S-orderly groups can be found in many branches of life, including insects, birds, chimpanzees and human beings. They can even be found in inanimate life-forms, such as slime mould. A multicellular body of slime mould can emerge from a collection of individual single cells, the transformation occurring when food becomes scarce.[1]

Many kinds of insects are what we call social insects, including honeybees and ants. The colonies they form are complex systems. They are complex by virtue of being wholes that consist of large numbers of non-randomly structured parts.[2] Non-random agglomeration brings order into existence, or enhances whatever order might previously have existed. Complex patterns of division of labour contribute to the orderliness of colonies. Members take on specific and specialised tasks such as

---

1 See Sandra D. Mitchell, *Biological Complexity and Integrative Pluralism* (New York: Cambridge University Press, 2003), p. 155.
2 Mitchell, p. 210.

cell-cleaning, brood and queen care, food storage and foraging.[3] Insects such as these are described by biologists like Edward O. Wilson (b. 1929) as being *eusocial*, meaning that their colonies contain multiple generations, and that altruistic acts are performed in the course of their various labours. Eusociality has evolved only infrequently in the animal kingdom, and is rarer among vertebrates than it is among the invertebrate insects.

Eusociality is of course a feature of *Homo sapiens*.[4] People of all ages inhabit our societies, division of labour is universal, and altruism is sufficiently common to entitle one to believe that many of us are more inclined towards tolerable moral behaviour than towards its opposite. Human communities that are S-orderly are composed of people who have been more or less socialised. Socialisation is accompanied by what Philip Kitcher calls 'psychological altruism,' which occurs when the desires that a person might have harboured in a solitary context are modified by the presence of other people; and modified in such a way that fulfilment of the perceived desires of others is made an objective of the person's actions. Well-socialised people, Kitcher observes, tend to take others' wishes seriously and feel 'sympathetic emotions' towards them; they are also respectful of authority and identity with groups; and, finally, they are anxious to avoid the effects of breaking the rules. All of which serve to motivate helpful behaviour on their part.[5] Empathy is mixed up in this, especially in the sympathetic emotions mentioned by Kitcher. Well-socialised people would generally be regarded as people of good character, and empathy is a constituent of such a character.

Most of the definitions of order found in dictionaries are applicable to human S-order, in either of two senses—on the one hand, orderliness of social organisations themselves; on the other hand, orderliness of relations between members of social organisations. Under the aspect of organisation we find, 'a rank, grade, or class of persons in a community;' and 'a group or body of persons of the same profession, occupation, or pursuits.' What we see here might be termed social differentiation. With

---

3 Mitchell, pp. 210-211.
4 Edward O. Wilson, *The Social Conquest of Earth* (New York: Liveright Publishing Corporation, 2013), p. 137.
5 Kitcher, p. 131.

regard to social relations, the main item refers to 'conformity or obedience to law or established authority; absence of disturbance, riot, revolt,
unruliness.' Peace and S-order are close in connotation but they are not
synonymous; as mentioned earlier, a prison environment may be orderly
but not peaceful.

Institutional order contributes to civil order, i.e. orderliness of society
at large. Civil order, in turn, is critically important to individual survival.
As seen from Spinoza in the epigraph, our nature is such we strive for
it, and that is because 'fear of isolation is innate in all men inasmuch
as in isolation no one has the strength to defend himself and acquire
the necessities of life.'[6] Two thousand years earlier, in his treatise *Politics*,
Aristotle had already famously described human beings as 'social animals'. When isolated, a person is said by Aristotle to be 'not self-sufficing,'
and is therefore 'like a part in relation to the whole.'[7] He continues, 'he
who is unable to live in society, or who has no need because he is sufficient for himself, must be either a beast or a god . . . .' In view of what
we now know about insects, birds and other social animals, one might be
inclined to think, not even a beast.

To condemn self-sufficiency might seem a little strange, especially
when we find Maslow placing it with the qualities that are of most
value to us.[8] For Maslow, self-sufficiency is a positive trait that human
beings should aspire to—apparently in stark contrast to Aristotle. As
I read Maslow, the opposite of self-sufficiency amounts to over-reli-
ance on others, on which grounds self-sufficiency would certainly be
commendable. But Aristotle's position also appears to be correct—the
overwhelming majority of us are clearly not self-sufficient. Therefore,
Maslow and Aristotle are both right, each in his own way. While self-sufficiency for Maslow entails a sense of 'doing the best one can for oneself',
recognition of one's self-*in*sufficiency from Aristotle's perspective would
involve appreciation of the fact that doing the best for oneself almost

---

6 Spinoza quoted by Hasana Sharp, 'Eve's Perfection: Spinoza on Sexual (In) Equality', *Journal of the History
of Philosophy* Vol. 50, no. 4 (Baltimore: The Johns Hopkins University Press, 2012), p. 571, footnote no. 82.
The quotation is from Spinoza's *Political Treatise*, 2.15.
7 Aristotle, *Politics*, 1.2, 1253a.
8 *The Farther Reaches of Human Nature*, p. 309.

invariably requires interaction with other people—ideally in a non-exploitative manner, whence cooperativeness and community-mindedness.

To this point I have been talking mainly about what S-order is and why it comes into being. With respect to *what* it is, all of the general characteristics of order are present—composition in the form of grouping, plus coherence, integration and wholeness. With respect to *why*, S-order is crucial to the survival of for all life-forms to which it is relevant; but S-order also facilitates diverse behaviours such as play and ritual for some species, and a sense of wanting to belong; or, more strongly, of *needing* to belong. The last is obviously applicable to *Homo sapiens*—as Spinoza pointed out, we fear isolation. *How*, then, does S-order come into being? Division of labour would be part of the answer, because of its role in the production and acquisition of the necessities of life. Communication would be another factor.

In the same section of the *Politics* quoted from a moment ago, Aristotle maintains that human beings are uniquely furnished with the 'gift' of speech. Although Aristotle's claim of uniqueness could be questionable because of the communicativeness of creatures such as birds, cats, dolphins and chimpanzees, it can be fairly said that human language has reached a much higher degree of complexity than that of any other living beings we know about. Moreover, if language in its written form (a relatively recent development) is included under the rubric 'speech', then the gift would certainly belong exclusively to us (confining our perspective to Earth: intelligent beings in possession of written language conceivably exist elsewhere in the universe). Aristotle would have known from simple observation that speech could not have come in the form of fully-developed mature language. Rather, it had to be of the nature of a capability coextensive with the species of which it is characteristic; in other words, a capacity for what he was hearing and seeing from people around him, including those whose native tongues differed from his own. A capacity, perhaps, along the lines of that proposed more than two millennia later by the linguist Noam Chomsky, one that enables human beings to use linguistic inputs from their environs to build on a deeply embedded grammatical substructure that everyone shares. Aristotle would also have realised that the capacity was there from the beginning of a person's life, and that it is therefore instinctual, as Steven Pinker in our own time has argued. The capacity for language is not something we have to learn; we are born with it. Learning comes later, culminating in mature speech. Although there are undoubtedly some things that are new under the sun (contrary to *Ecclesiastes* 1:9), certain elements of modern linguistic theory might not be among them, at least from the perspective of recorded history. From the perspective of geological or evolutionary time, all such elements and a great deal else besides would be new.

Staying with recorded history, something else that is not new are the many truths about human nature that were discerned by the ancients. Returning for a moment to Aristotle, we find that as well as the gift of speech, another thing said to be uniquely human is a sense of good and evil. When combined with speech, the 'sense' is said by him to enable us to talk about justice and injustice.[9] I think the seeds of morality and politics are perceptible there, in so far as the gift and the sense together contribute to the articulation of principles of justice, and their encoding in laws that facilitate the formation of states. I will revisit the subject of justice in the discussion of normative order, but the point at issue for present purposes is that communication serves as a means of conveying information that is critical to the cohesiveness of social groups (analogous to the genetically encoded flows of information within organisms that are fundamental to living P-order). In simple terms, communication is essential to community. Even the verbal similarity is suggestive of a relationship, one in which the complexity of communication might both reflect and be reflected in social complexity—in other words, where complexity in one is proportionate to complexity in the other.

Human society requires S-order; in other words, S-order is necessary to human social life, which is to say human life *per se*, for we are assuredly social beings. Our social nature may be reflected in sociability, i.e. in friendliness, and it commonly extends to love. Potential sources of cultural enrichment such as play and work would be severely diminished if S-order were non-existent. S-order is also necessary to the P-orderliness of human life. Much if not all of the nourishment and nurture that

---

9 Aristotle, *Politics*, 1253a.

human beings require would be impossible in the absence of efficient social organisation. S-order serves many purposes, and is therefore a general good. Everyone needs S-order, a Machiavellian prince as much as his most benevolent subject. Non-attainment or destruction of S-order would be catastrophic for human beings; harm in the form of personal isolation and Hobbesian warfare (where each is the enemy of everyone else) would be among the consequences.

E-Order

'E' = Eudaimonic. The term 'eudaimonic' derives from the Aristotelian notion of human flourishing, i.e. to arrangements of things, ideas and activities that contribute to individual fulfilment through, for example, intellectual achievement and aesthetic experience. Unlike P-order and S-order, E-order is exclusively human.

E-order consists in the kind of wholeness and integrity that David Bohm described as being 'an absolute necessity to make life worth living.'[10] Personal integrity is reflected in acts by people who are being true to themselves, i.e. people who act with sincerity and in accordance with their own self-understanding. Each of us has a personal history that reflects what we can be and can do, what we are and what we in fact do, and what we believe we should be and should do. 'Can', 'are' and 'should' are all variable with time and circumstances, and the fit at any one time between them is indicative of the degree to which we are flourishing. It is the whole self that finds expression in the actions of a person with integrity. Flourishing by means of wholeness entails a sense of healthiness of body and soul. As Bohm notes, *whole* in English derives from the old Anglo-Saxon word *hale*, which means health; *holy* has the same etymological origin.

Since the prefix *eu* denotes good and *daimon* signifies spirit, *eudaimonic* can be understood to mean good spiritedness, though not necessarily in any religious sense (Maslow's reference to religious states in so far as they are naturalistic might be recalled here; see p. 10.) The term is admittedly esoteric, but it encapsulates the sense of personal excellence that I

---

10 See Bohm, pp. 3-4.

want to convey—excellence in terms of Platonic orderliness of the soul, attainable, perhaps, through the development of imagination, wit, beauty and grace. According to John Rawls, these latter are 'excellences' that are goods for the person who possesses them and for others as well; they are 'a condition of human flourishing.'[11] A description of saintliness from William James is also apposite: 'All of the mind's objects and occupations [are] ordered with reference to the special spiritual excitement which is now its keynote.'[12] Religious conviction may not be necessary to eudaimonic order, but conviction *per se* almost certainly would be.

Maslow's views on what he called the 'value-life' are also worth noting. The value-life as he describes it has many dimensions, including spiritual, religious, philosophical, and ethical. It is, Maslow maintains, 'an aspect of human biology,' and therefore continuous with the 'lower' animal life. Because of that continuousness, the value-life is said 'probably' to be species-wide, i.e. probably 'supracultural,' although culture is required to bring it into existence.[13] Human flourishing is clearly at stake in all of this. S-order and E-order can also be seen to be connected in Maslow's idea, in the dependence of the value-life on the existence of culture. Culture is a product of socialisation; it consists in the combination of traits that serves to distinguish groups from one another. Food, dress and religious practices are just some of the ways in which cultural traits find expression. Of course, what Maslow had in mind here are not points of difference between human beings, but rather something that he considered common to all of us; namely, a 'supracultural' thing that he called the value-life, and the need for same. Nevertheless, that which is common can only be realised as an aspect (or core) of the phenomenon that is the bearer of the distinguishing traits. If social grouping among human beings had not evolved, culture would not have evolved, and the value-life envisaged by Maslow would consequently have been still-born.

When Maslow described the value-life as an aspect of human biology, he was in effect saying that it contributes to the human essence.[14] To

---

11 John Rawls, *A Theory of Justice*, p. 389.
12 James, *The Varieties of Religious Experience*, p. 247.
13 *The Farther Reaches of Human Nature*, p. 313.
14 *The Farther Reaches of Human Nature*, p. 314.

apply his terminology, the value-life is 'instinctoid' rather than 'learned'. Without it, human nature would not be full human nature.[15] Aristotle would have concurred—as well as having so-called 'vegetative' and 'appetitive' faculties in common with other life-forms, human beings were said by him to be uniquely possessed of the faculty of reason, which may be either practical or theoretical. Practical reason is the source of ethics, while theoretical reason is called 'the divine element of the soul.'[16] Without going into what 'divine' meant for Aristotle, it is clear that it was held by him to be of very high value. I will have more to say about values in the discussion of normative order, in the next section. In the meantime, some ideas on the cognitive ordering that is involved in reasoning of all kinds will help flesh out the specification of E-order.

One of the definitions of order comes from biology: 'the usual major subdivision of a class or subclass in the classification of organisms.' *Order* constitutes one of the taxonomic elements of the modernised Linnaean system; it sits between *class* and *family*. For present purposes, however, the important thing about this is the ordering process that gives rise to the taxonomy in the first place. Biological taxonomies (or any kind of taxonomy for that matter) are human constructions that are fundamental to our cognitive ordering of the world. But they are constructions that are based on, or seek to reflect, what Stephen Jay Gould referred to as 'firm' and 'testable patterns' that are susceptible to the kind of taxonomising that human beings are capable of. Taxonomies may be regarded as metaphors, as in the case of the 'tree' of life.[17] Reminiscent of Plato in the *Phaedo*, Gould was making the point that taxonomies are things that thinking beings like us impose on nature; in this case, an imposition that culminates in conceptions of divisions of life such as species, genera, families and phyla, all of which go towards constituting the metaphorical tree and its branches (which themselves could be regarded as metaphors; like all language, perhaps). However, unlike Plato, Gould was saying that there are things that actually exist in nature that can appropriately be described as 'orderly', albeit metaphorically. I believe that to be correct.

15 *The Farther Reaches of Human Nature*, p. 314.
16 http://www-philosophy.ucdavis.edu/mattey/phi001/platelec.htm (accessed 17 March 2011).
17 Stephen Jay Gould, *The Flamingo's Smile: Reflections in Natural History* (Harmondsworth: Penguin Books, 1986), p. 210.

Taxonomies are not necessary to life, but order is: if it were non-existent, there would simply be no life.

There are other means of cognitive ordering besides taxonomising; including poetry, if the literary critic I. A. Richards (1893-1979) was correct. According to Richards, poetry is capable of bringing order and coherence to a body of experience, and from that comes freedom.[18] That order and coherence may be involved is easy enough to see, but freedom from what? one may ask. I am not sure how that should be answered, but 'confusion' could be a candidate. If we are confused, our thinking is a messy tangle, where ideas are *fused* with one another, becoming indistinguishable, leading nowhere except perhaps in circles. Order and coherence counteract that tendency by unravelling and straightening out our thoughts, thereby enabling their individuality to shine through; in sum, by bringing cognitive order into effect. Each of the categories found by Kant to be involved in the workings of human understanding serve the same ultimate purpose. Regardless of how it is achieved, cognitive ordering facilitates understanding of our place in the scheme of things, and contributes to the attainment of E-order.

One of the groups of Kantian categories of the understanding is called 'quantitative', and is therefore concerned with mathematics (see p. 191 for an outline of the complete package). As a form of symbolism, and as one of the highest intellectual pursuits that human beings can engage in, mathematics properly belongs in the realm of human accomplishment. Mathematics is widely used in scientific work, especially the physical sciences. Discoveries in physics and other sciences often culminate in mathematical portrayal of pieces of reality, and are commonly spoken of in terms of beauty. Beauty evinces order, so the quest for such portrayals (which typically take the form of mathematical equations) is at least partly motivated by the need for order. The need is satisfied when a piece of mathematics is found to tie bits of reality together in a coherent and comprehensive manner. Whether all of nature is susceptible to that kind of treatment could be questionable, or perhaps altogether beyond human powers of understanding. But what seems indisputable is that the

---

18 See I. A. Richards, 'Poetry and Belief,' in *Twentieth-Century Literary Theory: A Reader*, edited by K. M. Newton (London: Macmillan, 1988), p. 40.

effort expended in the search for patterns is symptomatic of the putative need. Mathematical theories are often praised on account of their simplicity and elegance. Indeed, the same qualities are often decisive when competing theories are evaluated; so long as it works, the simpler and more elegant the theory the better. Simplicity and elegance are cognate with order; and since they are essentially aesthetic qualities, they are also relevant to art.

Aesthetic order in works of art arises from what the philosopher Marcia Muelder Eaton (b. 1938) refers to as 'formal unity'. The same expression was encountered a short while ago in the discussion of Aristotle's explanation of unity, and Eaton's use of the term is entirely consistent with Aristotle. For Eaton, formal unity is a matter of the way in which the various features of a work of art are put together, for example in displays of repetition or symmetry.[19] The 'putting together' results in a mixing of parts, and, in so far as it is the work of a human being, it will almost always be thoughtfully done. 'Thoughtful mixing' seems to me to be an appropriate way of describing the process of artistic creation. Thoughtfulness in the mixing of parts by an artist culminates in (or aims at) formal unity and aesthetic order. Formal unity and aesthetic order are purposes that the artist seeks to fulfil in the object he or she produces. In other words, fitness for purpose as an aesthetically satisfying object is the organising principle of artistic production. Because of the close connection between thoughtful mixing and order, whenever unity is brought into being by means of thoughtful mixing, order will follow. Physical entities become mixed, but it is the thought that counts.

As a final characteristic of E-order, there is its 'goodness' to consider. Although some of the characteristics of E-order point quite strongly towards moral goodness and right, others need not. Wholeness and health, and even flourishing, could conceivably be characteristic of someone otherwise oriented. An evil genius who comes across as being witty and elegant is readily imaginable. J. K. Rowling's villain Voldemort in the *Harry Potter* books, for example, is a crafty schemer who manages to conceal his true nature by means of cleverness and politeness. Evil

---

19 Marcia Muelder Eaton, *Basic Issues in Aesthetics* (Belmont, California: Wadsworth Publishing Company, 1988), p. 48.

people may be as fully integrated within themselves as good people are; their whole selves in terms of 'can do' and 'should do' find expression in their evil actions. As was the case with P-order and S-order, E-order is a general good, but its attainment can occur through behaviour that is either morally good or morally evil.

Finally, I have claimed that P-order and S-order are necessary to human life: can the same be said for E-order? Well, based on the foregoing, it is obviously necessary to a flourishing life, but it is also necessary in another sense. The kind of society and S-order that we now need, and will continue to need, to meet our requirements for nourishment and nurture would clearly be impossible in the absence of scientific and artistic effort. Effort in either realm is often the work of individuals who achieve or approach excellence in their fields. In other words, we need E-order as much as we need P-order and S-order. Harm in the form of personal under-development, and perhaps psychological impairment, plus social dysfunction, would be among the consequences of the absence or destruction of E-order.

N–Order

'N' = Normative. In view of what I have said about human nature, any specification of homosapient order that excluded morality would obviously be incomplete. Morality figures so indelibly in the human landscape that a place for it must be found in any concept of what our fundamental needs consist in; and the concept of homosapient order is emphatically of that nature. This is where norms become relevant. Norms help set the stage on which morality is played out in human life. Norms are concerned with what ought to be and what ought not to be. N-order exists when a person's behaviour is consonant with the norms that he or she considers important, i.e. norms that that have been internalised and made the person's own. Hypocrisy, it is safe to say, is a form of disorder.

Beliefs and judgements of the kind envisaged here rest exclusively with human beings, but a primitive kind of normativity is nevertheless conceivable; perhaps even a pre-human or non-human one. Mental constructions along the lines of 'better that that were not so' are not so very distant from other mental constructions, such as 'X could hurt me', 'Y has hurt me', and 'Z is to be avoided'. Constructions like those involving X, Y and Z would seem to be widespread in the animal kingdom, and are especially prevalent among the higher animals. The constructions resolve into, or are accompanied by, feelings of fear, anger and disgust. For example, a fear of snakes seems to be instinctive among primates (including us); many creatures react angrily when hurt in an attack; and rotting organic-matter is generally found disgusting. Better that things were not so. And we only need to double the negative to get from there to what would be better.

Norms tap into value-systems. Values are among the deepest structural constituents of our characters; they take the form of beliefs about what should be done and not done. This has long been known: for instance, Michael Ruse reminds us of Plato's contention that 'purpose occurs when *values* are at stake.[20] In other words, the ends towards which we direct our efforts are conditioned by whatever we believe to be of value to us; that is to say, by that which we believe to be best for us. Ruse quotes from Plato, 'If anyone wanted to discover the cause of anything, how it came into being or perished or existed, he simply needed to discover what kind of existence was *best* for it, or what it was best that it should do or have done to it' (*Phaedo*, 97 b-c). The conjunction of 'best' and 'should' gives rise to moral values, which Isaiah Berlin described as 'ultimate ends'; i.e. ends to which people who wisely understand reality are apt to dedicate their lives.[21]

Values, we have seen, are needs by another name: what we need we value, and we value having our needs satisfied, especially our basic needs. Our values include beliefs about how we and others should be treated when all of us go about satisfying our needs. Such beliefs are concerned with fairness, and therefore, ultimately, with justice. Beliefs with regard to fairness and justice obviously vary greatly between people, and across the ages and within different cultures, but a conception of justice remains a human universal. It is a species-wide trait to have some idea about what

---

20 Ruse, p. 264.
21 Isaiah Berlin, *Against the Current: Essays in the History of Ideas*, edited by Henry Hardy, introduced by Roger Hausheer (London: Pimlico, 1997 [first published 1979]), p. 45.

should be done and should not be done. It is also in our nature to strive for harmony, or balance, between our actions and those ideas, at least most of the time. In other words, N-order is necessary, like the other components of homosapient order.

That completes the exposition of N-order, but to leave matters there would result in a very unstable basis on which to ground morality. Conceptions of the kinds of behaviour required to secure N-order would vary just as much as our beliefs about justice, or anything else for that matter. And since N-order is a component of homosapient order, homosapient order would be similarly variable; the ground I am proposing appears to be shifting under our feet. However, before trying to find something more solid I need to explain why 'homosapient order' can be spoken of as a unified whole; in other words, why it is something more than a loose agglomeration of parts (more than a 'heap', to use Aristotle's term).

Homosapient Order

P-order, S-order, E-order, and N-order are all needed by us, and they share the same general characteristics, pointing towards a relationship of similarity between them. Since wholeness, coherence, integrity and composition are all concerned with structure (the shape of things and the way their parts are interrelated), P-, S-, E-, and N-order are all like one another in terms of basic structure. The question now is, how do the four kinds of order come together to form homosapient order? Precisely what is homosapient order?

The answer to the last question is that homosapient order is a compound formed from P-order, S-order, E-order and N-order. In it, all four kinds of order are brought together in some kind of relationship with one another—primarily, a relationship of dependency. P-order is historically prior to the other components of homosapient order; it is the basis of life, non-human as well as human. S-order, E-order and N-order are properties of various kinds of entities, which depend for their existence on P-order. In that very fundamental sense, S-order, E-order and N-order can be said to be dependent on P-order. P-order can exist independently of the others; therefore, as well as being historically prior, P-order is ontologically prior to them.

As well as dependency, there is interdependency. In Figure 3 each of the components is shown as being connected to all of the other components. The diagram reads in the usual way, from left to right. P-order is shown on the left in recognition of its temporal and biological priority—temporal because P-order existed in the universe long before human beings evolved; biological because it existed in life-forms that pre-dated *Homo sapiens*.

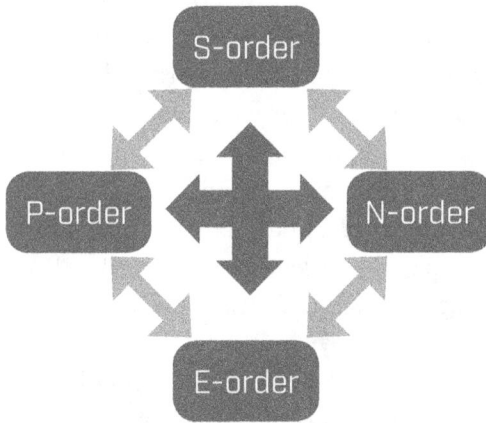

Figure 3: Homosapient Order

The arrows pointing from P-order to S-order, E-order and N-order are indicative of its priority; P-order is the keystone of homosapient order. But the arrows also point in the opposite direction. The one from S-order to P-order signifies the cooperative effort required for the production of means to satisfy our material needs (nutritious food, clean drinking water, shelter, etc.). Similarly for E-order and P-order, where the attainment of a balanced soul may culminate in a temperate and thoughtfully considered life-style; a life-style, perhaps, characterised by physiological harmony and environmental awareness. S-order and

E-order are also connected by a two-way arrow. They are interrelated by means of the influence of social and cultural products (such as science and art) on eudaimonic fulfilment—and the influence that the latter may have on social order, for example from having found one's proper place in the world and perhaps peace of mind. Finally, N-order is connected to each of the other components. N-order and S-order are reciprocally dependent, because of the relevance of justice to each of them. Justice, we have seen, has an individual dimension and a social dimension. Flourishing individuals are fully integrated and are therefore E-orderly individuals; they could not be regarded as such without some kind of moral sense; hence the arrow connecting N-order to E-order. From the other direction, N-order is shown as drawing upon E-order, on the assumption that self-fulfilment is likely to influence one's values, and therefore one's N-orderliness. P-order is necessary to N-order because of its historical and ontological priority, and because of the influence that personal physiology can have on an individual's values, beliefs and moral judgement (for example, brain damage may affect a person's ability to feel and to think). N-order flows back into P-order due to the effect that moral judgements and consequent actions have on the physical facts of life.

If the connection between P-order and N-order has you hearing alarm bells, you would be in the company of some very fine philosophers. For what we have in view here is an instance of the widely despised 'naturalistic fallacy'. Both Hume and the philosopher G. E. Moore (1873-1958) denounced the fallacy, by insisting on a strict separation of fact from value, of natural phenomena from moral phenomena. Since P-order is plainly concerned with the natural while N-order is very much of a moral nature, any suggestion of a connection between them could be frowned upon. The matter needs to be taken seriously, and I defend my position in the Appendix.

Because of the interconnectedness of its components, homosapient order can reasonably be spoken of as if it were a unity. P-, S-, E-, and N-order have each been shown to be necessary to human life, so it follows from their interrelatedness that homosapient order is also necessary. Amongst other things, it is necessary to our survival. But human behaviour is not solely concerned with survival. As well as endeavouring to maintain physical order, our behaviour is often directed towards social order, eudaimonic order, and normative order.

We can now return to the impasse that was encountered in the discussion of N-order. Is the possibility of grounding morality in homosapient order undermined by the variability of values among people and across cultures and times? Or might there be a way of settling N-order down around a particular value, thereby stabilising homosapient order? I believe the latter to be the case, and the value concerned is humaneness.

Humaneness and Homosapient Order

We have it on good authority that there is something good about order. Intellectual giants like Malebranche, Hume, Rousseau and James all clearly thought that to be the case. And there have been others, including the polymath G. W. Leibniz (1646-1716) and the cybernetics mastermind Norbert Wiener (1894-1964).

In his philosophical treatise *The Monadology* (1714) Leibniz speaks of the interconnection of all created things. Because of their interconnections, he maintains, 'each simple substance has relations that express all the others,' and each simple substance is therefore 'a perpetual, living mirror of the universe.' This is the way of obtaining, he continues, 'as much variety as possible, but with the greatest order possible, that is, it is the way of obtaining as much perfection as possible' (*The Monadology*, 56 – 58).[22] Since perfection is cognate with goodness, anyone looking for a connection between order and goodness would surely be encouraged by Leibniz's assertions.

The picture painted by Wiener is somewhat bleaker than Leibniz s, but the goodness of order is never in doubt. Taking his cue from the philosopher Søren Kierkegaard (1813-1855), Wiener considered the moral universe in which we live to be chaotic , analogous to the thermodynamic equilibrium that is the destiny of closed physical systems. In these circumstances, he saw our main obligation as the establishment

---

22 Quoted by Lee Smolin, *The Life of the Cosmos* (New York: Oxford University Press, 1998), p. 2.

of 'arbitrary enclaves of order and system.'[23] That is, enclaves of moral order, as well as physical order. Now because of our fundamental reliance on order—both moral and physical—simply to exist, all of us could be regarded as enclaves of a kind; but in Wiener's view, we have to work hard, by 'running as fast as we can,' to maintain the order that has been brought to them. Perhaps something similar could be said for other living beings, but by couching the work that must be done in terms of obligation, Wiener was obviously talking about human beings. The concept of obligation is inapplicable to non-human organisms. So the maintenance of order is our responsibility. It is something that we should do, and presumably can do. An account of how well we meet that obligation will be etched onto our personal histories.

Each of us has a personal history that reflects and determines what we believe should be done and can be done. But our personal histories are merely sub-sets of the universal history of humankind. The history of humankind reveals what we as a species believe should and can be done. The question is whether we as individuals and we as a species are fundamentally oriented towards doing good, that we believe this is the right thing to strive for; or are we at bottom evil, or something in between? To put it another way, is humaneness embedded as a value (and therefore as a need) in homosapient order; or is inhumaneness so embedded; or neither of them? My short answer is that, individually, one may be good, or one may be bad, or one may occupy some sort of middle ground. As a species, however, I think both authority and argument can show that we tend more towards goodness than its extreme alternative; that is, humaneness is more natural to us than inhumaneness is.

Authority first. We have seen that Kant considered human nature to be inclined towards moral goodness. Many others have also believed goodness to be the norm ('norm' in the sense of 'normal' or 'natural'). Plato, for instance, attributed bad behaviour to disorders of the soul, which, in turn, were said to arise from a 'want of intelligence' and to consist either in madness or in ignorance. Pathologies like these were regarded by Plato as bodily malfunctions rather than willed wrong-doing. 'No man is voluntarily bad,' he asserts in the *Timaeus*. Instead of that,

---

23 Quoted by James Gleick, *The Information* (London: Fourth Estate, 2012), p. 237.

'the bad become bad by reason of an ill disposition of the body and bad education.'[24] For Plato, then, physiological healthiness and good education are both necessary to orderliness of soul. Hume similarly: according to him, moral sense is natural, and a nature inconsistent with moral sense is a perverted nature.

Modern neuroscience offers tentative support for the positions taken by Plato, Hume, and Kant. For instance, social emotions such as compassion and empathy have been found to be associable with particular parts of the nervous system. Damage to those parts would conceivably affect an individual's capacity to respond compassionately or empathically towards the predicaments of others. If confirming evidence were available, one would be able to say, with Plato, that such a person is suffering from a bodily ill; or, with Hume, that the person's capacity for moral sense has been impaired. Further to that, studies have shown that emotional responses may be influenced by learning, which was Plato's other point. All in all, since compassion and empathy are associable with particular parts of our body, fundamental goodness would appear to be the norm. Of course, the possibility of countervailing anti-social emotions becoming associable with other (perhaps even more powerful) parts cannot be ruled out. At the present time, however, the existence of contrary emotions such as inconsiderateness and indifference seem to be due to impairment of the 'good' parts.

So much for authority; now the argument. It too revolves around an idea of Kant's, and begins by looking at whether order qualifies as a 'natural good', in the sense ascribed to the term by Philippa Foot. For Foot, living things attain natural goodness to the extent of their conformity with the life form of the species to which they belong.[25] The life form of a species consists fundamentally in what is considered to be normal for the species. For an oak tree, there would be norms of sturdiness and life span; for a cat, norms of speed, agility and playfulness would usually be thought to apply. For a human being, norms would seem to be applicable to each of the elements of homosapient order, and therefore to homosapient order in total. Amongst other things, a measure of

---

24 *Timaeus*, 86e.
25 See Foot, pp. 26-27.

healthiness would be associable with P-order, a measure of cooperative-ness with S-order, a measure of personal fulfilment with E-order, and a measure of values-matching behaviour with N-order. The sum of such norms (there would be many more besides those mentioned) constitutes the human life form. Note that by talking about 'the human life form' we are adopting a species-wide perspective, rather than focusing on individual human beings. For individuals, homosapient order is always good, regardless of how it is attained. From the perspective of the species, matters could be different.

Matters would be different if moral normativity of a particular kind, i.e. either positive or negative, were a constituent of the life form of our species. And I think we can be certain that it is. We are moral beings, endowed with a sense of good and evil; morality is integral to human nature. From the perspective of the species, the issue boils down to this. Is it the case that a homosapient order formed from a positive moral orientation of character is a natural good? Or would homosapient order formed from a negative moral orientation of character constitute a natural good? How the questions should be answered seems clear, yes and no respectively; but a few words in response follow.

Positively oriented moral character carries us in the direction of humaneness, and a negative one towards inhumaneness. As has been explained, humaneness consists in principled consideration of the needs of others. Someone who is humane will assiduously strive to ensure that harm is minimised, by acting in accordance with the PHM. Although inhumaneness could conceivably be thought of as beneficial by a wicked individual like Voldemort, it fails the Kantian test of being a species-wide desideratum for rational beings like us. If inhumaneness were adopted as a universally desirable principle of action, then all who accede to it would have to consent to being treated inhumanely, which seems implausible. As well as wanting (and needing) to be fairly dealt with, most people would understand that species-wide inhumanity would probably lead to our extinction. Species-wide inhumaneness would be a death form of *Homo sapiens*, not a life form.

We saw a short while ago how the anthropic principle is used in physics and cosmology to explain the state of the universe, i.e. its existence as we understand it. Humaneness could be regarded as an application of the principle, specifically within the sphere of human existence. Without the kind of moral order that is brought into being by humaneness, our existence even in the short term could be rendered precarious. While that might not trouble some people, I think most of us would be disturbed by the idea. Believers in the fundamental goodness of humankind such as Plato, Hume and Kant would almost certainly be appalled by it—if one thinks something is good then one would be inclined to want it to last as long as possible. Homosapient order formed from a positively oriented moral character is a Footian natural good; homosapient order formed from a negatively oriented moral character would not be. In other words, morally good humaneness is integral to the natural good that is homosapient order. Action that accords with the PHM is the means of attaining the good that is homosapient order. Violation of the PHM is contrary to homosapient order. Humaneness, then, can be regarded as an aspect of species-wide homosapient order.

Homosapient order and the PHM are bound inextricably together by the concepts (and phenomena) of harm and humaneness. Harm is always consequential upon violation of the PHM, and harm consists in the exacerbation of need, ultimately the need for order (for human beings, the need for homosapient order). Humaneness is embedded in homosapient order, and reveals itself in behaviour that accords with the PHM. In the next chapter we will see how satisfaction of the various needs delineated by Maslow contributes to the maintenance of homosapient order, thereby helping to ground morality in the phenomenon that we call 'order'.

Chapter 12: The Need for Order

Knowing harmony is constancy. Knowing constancy is enlightenment. (Tao Te Ching, Chapter 55).

To say that living entities have a need for subsistence (in the form of food and shelter) is the same as saying they need P-order. P-order is a product of entropy-avoidance and is reflected in the ways in which composite living things are structured, i.e. in the forms they take. P-order arises from the satisfaction of subsistence needs. The social needs for belongingness and esteem and the need for S-order also map onto each other with very little overlap. Social organisation is largely concerned with ranks and roles, including roles involved in cooperative relationships and organisation for care and welfare. It focuses on social structures that provide an environment in which social needs can be addressed. The mapping from E-order onto the realm of being needs is also quite precise. 'E-order' is shorthand for beauty and understanding, and denotes a form of psychological balance. E-order is one aspect of self-actualising order; N-order is another aspect of it.

The primary purpose of this chapter is to secure the connection between morally significant harm and the need for order. Need is that in respect of which living beings can be harmed, and immorality always involves harm. Therefore, if morality is to be successfully grounded in the phenomenon of order, the basic needs of living beings must be shown to be related in some way to order. The proposition on which the chapter rests is that all of our basic human needs are expressions of the need for homosapient order. This will be shown to be the case by demonstrating that satisfaction of the various human needs brings homosapient order into effect. From that, it would seem reasonable to conclude that what is true of human beings and homosapient order in particular, is also true of all living beings and order in general. Each of the Maslovian needs will now be examined to test the soundness of the proposition.

Homeostasis

As with all endeavours of the kind I am pursuing it is important to be clear about how words are being used. 'Homeostasis' is a case in point, for it means different things to different people. All of its various connotations are important in the present context. As one dictionary defines it, homeostasis consists in 'physiological equilibrium within living creatures involving a balance of functions and chemical composition.'[1] Maslow used the term in this sense, when he referred to homeostasis as the body's unconscious efforts to control the state of the blood stream.[2]

But the term has also been applied much more broadly. For example, the philosopher Roger Scruton (b. 1944) uses it in connection with political and other kinds of non-physiological systems, including markets, traditions, customs, law, and practical reasoning.[3] Almost as broadly, homeostasis is defined by the neuroscientist Antonio Damasio (b. 1944) as 'life regulation'. Damasio distinguishes between basic homeostasis and sociocultural homeostasis, the objective of both being 'the survival of living organisms.'[4] Homeostatic systems are self-stabilising systems; in other words, they are systems that have means of detecting and redressing disruptions to their orderliness. The Maslovian homeostatic (lower basic) needs correspond to Damasio's basic homeostasis, while the needs further up the Maslovian hierarchy correspond to sociocultural homeostasis. As Damasio explains it, the latter is concerned with such things as justice systems, economic and political organisation, the arts, education, medicine and technology.[5] Homeostatic impairment in Damasio's sense of 'homeostasis' would result in across-the-board homosapient disorder. But I am getting ahead of myself—let me stay for the moment with Maslow's physiological sense of the term.

Physiological needs are homeostatic needs, which, when satisfied, serve to sustain life. Such needs are the most basic and most potent of all needs;

---

1 *The Macquarrie Dictionary*.
2 A Theory of Human Motivation, p. 372.
3 Roger Scruton, *Green Philosophy: How to Think Seriously About the Planet* (London: Atlantic Books, 2012), pp. 11, 135.
4 Antonio Damasio, *Self Comes to Mind: Constructing the Conscious Brain* (London: Vintage Books, 2012), p. 27.
5 Damasio, p. 26.

basic and potent in the sense that they usually have to be satisfied before other needs can obtain motivational force. As Maslow remarked, hungry people are likely to direct all of their capacities to finding food,[6] although exceptions may occur, such as hunger-strikers who starve themselves for political purposes. Procreation by sexual means would belong at this most basic level of needs; unsatisfied desire on the part of anyone who experienced it could disturb personal equilibrium.

The terminology itself—'stasis', 'constant', 'equilibrium'—is probably enough to confirm that P-order is deeply implicated in needs of this kind. That being so, since P-order is a constituent of homosapient order, homeostatic needs can be regarded as expressions of the need for homosapient order. Physical and mental disorder would soon arise if food and water were to become unavailable, or sexual needs went unrequited. Should these most basic needs go unmet, higher needs may also be affected. For example, mental disorder would almost certainly impact adversely on E-order and N-order. S-order would also come under threat if a hungry person were to use violence against others in the pursuit of food; especially so in a famine, when large numbers of people experience starvation. P-disorder, therefore, can detract from homosapient order in its entirety. Conversely, satisfaction of the homeostatic needs, and therefore satisfaction of the need for P-order, opens the way to satisfaction of the need for homosapient order.

Safety

The need for safety occupies one rung up from the bottom of Maslow's hierarchy. Since physical survival would be at risk in the absence of safety, for example due to inadequate shelter, the need for safety can serve as a very powerful motivator. Danger may also take more subtle forms than direct threats of physical harm. According to Maslow, injustice, unfairness and inconsistency on the part of parents are among the things that make children feel unsafe. An indication of children's need for safety, Maslow observed, is their preference for a settled routine or rhythm; in other

---

6 A Theory of Human Motivation, p. 373.

words, their desire for 'a predictable, orderly world.'[7] Adults also generally prefer familiar rather than unfamiliar things, and commonly seek the
safety of predictability and orderliness in religious or world-philosophies
that organise the world and its denizens into 'some sort of satisfactorily
coherent, meaningful whole.'[8]

The tendency towards attainment of some kind of world-organising
philosophy would have a lot to do with higher-order needs, including esteem, intellectual achievement and self-actualisation: I will come
to those shortly, but here we might recall that stability, organisation,
coherence and wholeness are all properties of both order in general and
homosapient order in particular. In so far as satisfaction of the need for
safety contributes to any of these, the need for safety can reasonably be
regarded as an expression of the need for homosapient order. From that
it follows that satisfaction of the need for safety helps to bring homosapient order into effect.

Before moving on to the next of the needs, the notion of 'stability',
which has featured under both this heading and elsewhere, warrants
a moment's reflection. Is stability a reasonable desideratum? If it were
understood to mean something like *always the same*, or *unchanging*, and
these are common connotations of the term, there would immediately
be trouble. Ongoing change is a fundamental characteristic of the world,
in which case any purported description of the world that is inconsistent
with change would have to be dismissed as unrealistic. Are the notions of
stability and homosapient order inconsistent with that of change? Fairly
clearly, they need not be. Parts can be added to or removed from composite objects without disturbing their orderliness—a truism, almost,
since any object in the world, including beautiful artefacts, harmonious families and sublime natural settings, would always be undergoing
some kind of change, at levels ranging from the microscopic to the
macroscopic, all the while leaving their orderliness unaffected (or, more
accurately, moving from one orderly state-of-being to another orderly state-of-being). Change and order are not necessarily at odds with
one another. Furthermore, homosapient order itself may be inherently

---

7 A Theory of Human Motivation, p. 377.
8 A Theory of Human Motivation, p. 379.

dynamic, exemplified by processes required for homeostasis such as respiration and metabolism. Environmental stability can be seen in the same light, i.e. as orderliness within a context of inexorable change. A natural environment could hardly be otherwise, because of the influence of evolution and other processes such as solar activity and continental drift. Stability can be understood as maintenance of structure by means of either orderly succession or orderly replacement.

Belongingness

Little difficulty has been encountered in showing how homosapient order depends on the satisfaction of our homeostatic and safety needs, but the task becomes more intricate as we move up the hierarchy. As described by Maslow, the need for belongingness involves the need for affection and the need for a place in the groups one belongs to. Most people participate in many groups, in a structure that can be thought of as a series of concentric circles of ever-increasing radii. For example, from innermost to outermost: self; family; friends; social, cultural and sporting societies and clubs; political parties; municipality; state and nation; humanity; and, ultimately, nature at large. The image is akin to the philosopher Peter Singer's (b. 1946) representation of moral inclusiveness in the form of an expanding circle; a single circle but one of variable radius. As Singer's circle grows, increasing numbers of different kinds of entities are accepted as respondents to the morally relevant agency of the person concerned. Contractions in the size of the circle are also conceivable, representing dismissal from respondency.

Bonding factors that promote belongingness include affection and duty. There are others, such as legal ties, club membership, political allegiances, and so on; but affection and duty could be regarded as the emotional and rational glue that enables all of these to maintain their viscosity. Affective bonds would probably be strongest within the smaller inner circles that I have mentioned, while duty would tend to keep denizens of the outer ones together. We love our children, other close family members and close friends, but our obligations to strangers are usually couched in terms of duty. The proposition is based on the cliché that like attracts like, where likeness consists in shared bodily and mental properties; kinship would be an example of the first, while like-mindedness is common within alliances. I hasten to add that the suggested orientations towards affection and duty should be regarded as no more than tendencies, since duty would also be applicable to family, and some people appear to be capable of loving everyone and everything. Indeed, I will soon suggest that duty may be subsumable under affection—that it grows out of the feelings we have for someone or something. Nevertheless, I will use the difference between affect and duty as a point of entry into the investigation of the relationship between belongingness and homosapient order.

The nature of affective bonding can be summed up in a single word—love. In the 1943 paper in which Maslow introduced his hierarchy of needs, belongingness went under that title. Love occupied the median position in the original five-member hierarchy (the same as the seven-member table shown earlier minus the cognitive and aesthetic needs, which were originally subsidiary to self-actualisation). Its centrality may have some significance, for the need for love would seem to bear strongly on all of the other needs, those below it and those above it.

Below love in the hierarchy there are the needs for safety and homeostasis. Its connection with safety is clear from Maslow's comments on the child's need for a predictable and orderly world, something that is more likely to be satisfied where parental love exists than where it does not. Some thinkers have regarded all love as sexual (for example the philosopher Arthur Schopenhauer (1788-1860), who exerted a strong influence on the young Nietzsche)—but I believe that to be wrong. Many kinds of love, including the parental love just mentioned, plus friendship and patriotism, have little or nothing to do with sex, notwithstanding Schopenhauer. However, to the extent that it is sexual, the need for love would tend to mesh with the lower basic need for homeostasis, and therefore play a part in the attainment of P-order. But the need for love can also extend all the way up to the top of Maslow's hierarchy, perhaps best instantiated by Spinoza's conception of love, where the object of love is 'the eternal and infinite thing'. In other words, where love is directed towards the whole, or 'nature', or 'God'. Love of that kind,

Spinoza maintained, 'feeds the mind with a joy entirely exempt from sadness.'[9] The philosopher Amélie Rorty (b. 1932) has claimed that the love of which Spinoza spoke 'carries the greatest possible self-realisation.'[10] Perhaps it does, but why, or how? Here is a chain of ideas that might afford an explanation.

Joy that is so pure that admits of no sadness will likely be accompanied by inrush of magnanimity, in the latter's literal sense of greatness of soul; and that in turn will, in all probability, be attended by a feeling of benevolence, whereupon justice becomes an imperative—whence 'the greatest possible self-realisation,' or self-actualisation, in both of the senses that we will find later in this chapter ascribed to the notion, senses that may for the moment be labelled 'best-fit' and 'moral accomplishment'. The joyfully loving individual 'fits' by finding his or her proper place within the whole, i.e. within nature; and the individual is an exemplar of justice. Cognitive achievement and self-actualisation are both involved in Spinozistic love, and with them E-order.

Affective bonding is the subject of one of the great works of philosophical literature, Plato's *Symposium*. It tells the story of a drinking party, where the meaning of love is discussed. Socrates is one of the revellers, and he relates how love was explained to him in his youth by the prophetess Diotima. According to Diotima's teaching, love comes in different forms, each of which is represented by a rung on a ladder. The bottom rung is occupied by love of a particular person, which is said to begin with the perception by the lover of the beloved's beauty. The top of the ladder is reached when love of a particular person is transformed into love of the universal Platonic Forms, as represented by goodness, truth and beauty. The transformation occurs when the beauty of the particular is seen to be identical to universal beauty, not simply a manifestation thereof. For Plato, beauty consists in good measure and proportion,[11] while soberness is extolled as 'a kind of beautiful order.'[12]

---

9 Benedict de Spinoza, 'Portrait of the Philosopher as a Young Man', in Edwin Curley (editor and translator), *A Spinoza Reader*, pp. 4-5.

10 Amélie Rorty, Spinoza on the Pathos of Idolatrous Love', in Robert C. Solomon and Kathleen M. Higgins (editors): *The Philosophy of (Erotic) Love* (Lawrence, Kansas: University Press of Kansas, 1991), p. 370.

11 Plato, *Philebus*, translated by R. Hackforth in Hamilton and Cairns (editors): *Plato: The Collected Dialogues*, 64e.

12 *Republic* IV, 430e.

Beautiful order can be understood to consist in harmony of the soul—as Socrates remarks in the *Republic*, 'the man who has the spirit of harmony will be the most in love with the loveliest.'[13] So understood, harmony of the soul would amount to E-order.

In classical terms, love is usually regarded as being one of three kinds. It can be either sexual love, or friendship, or charity. In the original Greek, the three are *eros, philia, agape*; and in Latin, *amor, amacitia* or *dilectio, caritas*. According to Plato, all love is essentially erotic, in a particular sense of the term erotic. In his *Cratylus*, eros is found to have derived from the word *esron*, which means 'flowing in'. There is a 'stream' that is said to be 'an influence introduced through the eyes.'[14] 'Inflowing' is clearly met-aphorical, but I suspect that all descriptions of love are bound to be of that nature; Diotima's ladder is a prime example. 'Inflowing' might occa-sionally result in some sort of 'indwelling', when whatever it is that flows settles in the receptacle into which it flows. Quoting scripture, Thomas Aquinas spoke of *caritas* in terms of mutual indwelling: 'he who dwells in love is dwelling in God, and God in him' (1 John 5.16-17). The equiv-alent of the Greek *agape, caritas* is described in Wikipedia as love that is absolutely unconditional and self-sacrificing,[15] but the same qualities are surely characteristic of all forms of love, at least to some extent. 'Love' that says to its object 'I will love you on condition that . . .' would not be love as we know it; nor would 'love' that selfishly rides roughshod over the interests of the 'beloved'. In love of all kinds, the lover assimilates the needs and interests of the beloved, and acts in such a way as to satisfy the beloved's needs and promote his or her interests; or, more generally, the lover acts for the beloved's sake.

The notion of *sake* is highly significant, and for present purposes can be understood in either of two senses. First, in the sense of loving the beloved simply because the beloved is who (or what) he or she (or it) is. The parenthetical 'what' and 'it' are meant to cover non-human beloveds, including abstractions like the patriot's flag and the bibliophile's books. What would generally be regarded as perversions such as the miser's

---

13 *Republic* III, 402d (Jowett translation).

14 Plato, *Cratylus*, in *Plato*, translated by Benjamin Jowett (Chicago: The University of Chicago, Great Books of the Western World, 1952), Vol. 7, 420a.

15 See http://en.wikipedia.com (accessed 28 March 2011).

money and the narcissist's mirror-image might also be included—perversions they may be, but they can still serve as objects of love. This first sense of the term *sake* is captured in the idiom 'art for art's sake', and in Kant's call for us to act 'for the sake of duty'. The second sense of *sake* involves the notion of purpose, or end; for example, again idiomatically, doing something 'for the sake of her well-being'. The second sense of *sake* is Aristotelian in tenor; unlike the first, it necessarily involves action, with the agent acting solely out of concern for the being in whose interest action is undertaken.

Since mutual inflowing is accompanied by the notion of 'for the sake of', sake (in both of its senses) enables us to grasp what it is that inflows in various kinds of loving relationships. It is the delight taken by the lover in the beloved's being, and the interests of the beloved that are joyfully served by the lover. The first (the delight) could be understood as an influence taken in by the 'eyes', as maintained by Plato, again metaphorically. The lover would be interested in the beloved's flourishing, and would experience gratification from helping to bring it about. In other words, flourishing would be reciprocal. As Spinoza wrote, 'he who has done something which he imagines affects others with joy will be affected by joy, together with a consciousness of himself as the cause . . . .'[16]

Flourishing, we may assume, would be accompanied by joy, possibly even where the lover's love is not reciprocated. One-sided love is common enough; ungrateful children, for example, are usually still loved by their parents. A lover whose love remains unrequited may nevertheless strive to do whatever is believed to be best for the beloved, and obtain a sense of accomplishment from the beloved's joy. Reciprocation would be impossible in the case of non-human beloveds—flags, books, money and mirror-images have no passion to return. Even so, a feeling of accomplishment could eventuate for a lover who advances the beloved's cause to a significant extent. All of this might be expected of anyone who associates, as Spinoza did, the idea of external cause with the elation that attends love.[17] Because of its connection with personal flourishing

---

16 *The Ethics*, 3p30d.
17 *The Ethics*, 3p13s, 3def6.

and harmony of the soul, as well as its relevance to the satisfaction of lower-order (for example, sexual) needs, I leave the discussion of affective bonding with the conclusion that the need for belongingness in the form of love is itself a form of the need for homosapient order. Satisfaction of the need for love may therefore be expected to bring homosapient order into effect. What, then, of dutiful bonding?

One of the tenets of Kantian ethics is that 'the highest good possible through our agency should be realised.'[18] Such is said to be our duty, and actions that are performed for the sake of duty are the mark of what is called 'a good will,'[19] even to the extent of holiness.[20] Kant distinguished duty from inclination, defining it as 'the necessity of acting from respect for the law,'[21] where 'law' refers to the moral law in the form of the Categorical Imperative. The moral law is a law of one's own making, and is internalised as a set of maxims, which Kant described as subjective principles of volition.[22] If we are dutiful we fulfil our obligations; if we do not do that to which we are duty-bound, we fail in our obligations. So much is uncontroversial. Where disagreement with Kant may arise is in respect of the source of obligation. He derives it from reason alone, to the exclusion of the senses, or feelings.

In the *Fundamental Principles of the Metaphysic of Morals* (1790) the moral law is held by Kant to be entirely rational in nature.[23] It is entirely rational, he argues, because it can only be known *a priori*; in other words, it cannot be derived from experience.[24] We can think it, but we cannot see it or hear it or otherwise sense it. Nor, according to Kant, can it be deduced from the attributes of human nature, because that would be to confine its application to human beings, to the exclusion of all other rational beings.[25] The law and its associated maxims issue in autonomous action, as distinct from heteronymous action. Heteronymous actions are actions that are motivated by external influences rather than duty, and

---

18 Kant, *Religion*, p. 5.
19 Kant, *Morals*, pp. 257-8.
20 Kant, *Religion*, p. 42.
21 Kant, *Morals*, p. 259.
22 Kant, *Morals*, p. 259.
23 Kant, *Morals*, p. 271.
24 See Kant, *Religion,* p. liv.
25 Kant, *Morals*, p. 270.

include actions performed from inclination. While actions performed from inclination may be honourable and praiseworthy, they are not, Kant maintained, deserving of esteem—esteem was reserved by him for dutiful action. Further, 'the firmly grounded disposition strictly to fulfil our duty' was regarded by him as the essence of virtue.[26] 'To be beneficent when we can,' Kant asserted, 'is a duty,'[27] and beneficent behaviour devoid of inclination would have nothing other than the moral law in view.

Dutiful bonding based on reason alone could be seen to be more egalitarian than affective bonding. Superficially at least, there is nothing in the various formulations of the Kantian moral law to show why one human being should be preferred to another; for example, why family members should be preferred to total strangers. But even a diehard Kantian would surely have to regard absolute impartiality as an unattainable ideal. The overwhelming majority of human beings would be guided, at least in part, by affection as well as by duty, and affection would arguably decide such cases. Besides, there might even be rational reasons for giving preference to one's family, thereby giving rise to a duty to prefer them. If we are caught in a burning hospital where our child is a patient, it would be reasonable to try to rescue the child in preference, say, to the stranger in the next bed, whoever it happened to be. Why reasonable? Our love for our child would suffice as an answer, even if the other person were a magnate capable of lavishing riches on his rescuer. Why would that suffice? Because it is the way most people are made. Universalisation of preference for one's children as a maxim of moral law is more consistent with our nature, and therefore makes more sense to us than universalisation of preference for strangers.

Besides doubts stemming from the impartiality demanded by Kant's theory, there are other questions that might be asked of it. For instance, is it reasonable to leave human nature out of the picture? To suggest as Kant does that other rational beings (occupants of planets other than Earth) would be similarly inclined towards formulating reason-based moral laws appears to me to be overly speculative. Why not just stick

---

26 Kant, *Religion*, note to p. 19.
27 Kant, *Morals*, p. 258.

with what we do know—that there is something about human nature that gives rise to morality (and immorality)? Rationality is undeniably characteristic of human nature, but I would further question whether rationality alone is sufficient (or even necessary) to ground the disposition to fulfil our duty. We commonly speak of having a 'sense' of duty, and such speech could be indicative of a deep truth about the nature of obligation—and perhaps points to the involvement of a moral sense of the kind promoted by Hume (and others).

One might also observe that parents and children, and other beloveds, are commonly the objects of our strongest feelings of duty. That raises the question of whether we need to feel a sense of belongingness towards someone before we can feel obligated in any way towards them. My suspicion is that we do, although I won't try to argue the matter in any depth. But another piece of ordinary language can show how an argument might go. When we talk about duty it is normal for us to couch it in terms of 'duty to *do*', where *do* stands for some kind of action. Most generally the action would be along the lines of protecting or attending to the interests of whoever or whatever it is we feel duty-bound. And by bringing in interests, we invoke the kind of belongingness that involves affection, or love—and with that, the need for homosapient order. We might then come to the view that the sense of obligation tends to vary directly with the degree of belongingness that is felt—the closer the relation the stronger the sense of duty. If affection were totally absent, a feeling of duty towards the persons or things concerned would seem unlikely. And if affection were replaced by antipathy, then there would probably be no chance of its arising. But it need not follow that we would go out of our way to harm those for whom we feel indifference or hatred. For many people (perhaps most people), to do so would be to act out of character. In effect, a sense of duty would still exist, but it would be inwardly directed—our obligation would be to follow the dictates of our (hopefully good) character. Benevolence, therefore, is important.

Where does this leave Kantian reason-based duty? Without much of a leg to stand on, I believe. Duty as Kant propounds it might be part of the story of moral law, but it is not all of it. Reason serves to clarify whatever is going on when we talk about duty (or indeed anything else)—for one thing, it enabled Kant to formulate maxims that gel with the putative sense of duty that he no doubt felt towards certain entities. Reason could also help entrench the sense of duty—but the sense, or feeling, comes first. In spite of all that, the esteem that Kant found to be consequent upon dutiful action and bonding would be real, and would help to cement social order. It would therefore be productive of homosapient order, irrespective of how obligation is grounded.

Summing up, the need for belongingness is equivalent to a need for bonding of either an affective or a dutiful nature, but most likely a mixture of the two. Both kinds of bonding evidently result in homosapient order—in other words, satisfaction of the need for belongingness brings homosapient order into effect, either in the form of personal fulfilment, or by finding our place in the world, within family and society. In either form, a feeling of personal worthiness, or self-esteem, could accompany satisfaction of the need for belongingness. This brings me to the next of Maslow's needs.

Esteem

It was Maslow's view that people generally have a need for self-esteem, and for the esteem of others.[28] Few would disagree, but Spinoza can help deepen our understanding of what self-esteem and the esteem of others involve. All of the emotions are said by Spinoza to have their origin in three primary emotions: joy, sadness, and desire. In particular, he refers to our 'love of esteem,' defining it as 'joy accompanied by the idea of an internal cause'—this is also given as the definition of self-esteem. The joy that we feel arises from the belief that one is praised.[29] Conversely, should sadness accompany the idea of internal cause, repentance comes to pass; and shame is felt when sadness arises from the blame of others.[30] Spinoza's definitions are obviously concerned with the need *for* respect, but there is another aspect of esteem that also deserves consideration, namely the need *to* respect. Most of the ensuing discussion is concerned

---

28 A Theory of Human Motivation, p. 381.
29 *The Ethics*, 3p30s.
30 *The Ethics*, 3p30s.

with the *need for*, but I will have something to say about the *need to* towards the end of the section.

Spinoza's definition of self-esteem is succinct, but there is a deep truth embedded in it, or something that would generally be recognised as a deep truth. For what Spinoza is in effect saying is that self-esteem is a product of freedom, or autonomy. How one gets from freedom to self-esteem is derivable from the terms used in his definition. Joy, for Spinoza, is the product of a person's 'passage from a lesser to a greater perfection,'[31] where the passage consists in an increase in one's power of acting.[32] Now the power of acting putatively resides in one's ability to cause things, which is held to be the hallmark of freedom;[33] from which it follows that the joy experienced in self-esteem derives from freedom. The other part of the definition—'accompanied by the idea of an internal cause'—tells us that self-esteem requires that we be aware of our ability to cause things to happen. Cause in this context can be understood to be of an internal nature: if it were external, it would be contrary to the kind of causation that is implicit in the joy obtained from the power of acting. All of this makes perfectly good sense—most of us tend to feel better about ourselves when we feel that we are in control of things.

More recently, we find the philosopher Owen Flanagan (b. 1949) in company with Amélie Rorty conjecturing that the key to self-respect consists in consonance and consistency between a person's ideals, character and mode of life.[34] It is not hard to see how homosapient order might be involved in that. Similarly John Rawls, for whom self-respect has two aspects: positive self-evaluation, and confidence that one will be capable of fulfilling one's intentions.[35] The confidence of which Rawls speaks would conceivably contribute to one's positive self-evaluation.

With these remarks in mind, the issues attending the need for esteem can be structured in the form of a chiasmus, as shown in Figure 4. One axis of the chiasmus represents the individual's self-evaluation, its poles

---

31 *The Ethics*, 3def2.
32 *The Ethics*, 4pref.
33 Michael Della Rocca, *Spinoza* (London: Routledge, 2008), p. 188.
34 Flanagan and Rorty, *Identity, Character, and Morality: Essays in Moral Psychology*, p. 4.
35 Rawls, *A Theory of Justice*, p. 386.

consisting of self-esteem and self-disesteem; the other axis represents the public's evaluation of the individual, its poles being esteem and disesteem. Consideration of the four quadrants will help clarify the relationship between the need for esteem and homosapient order.

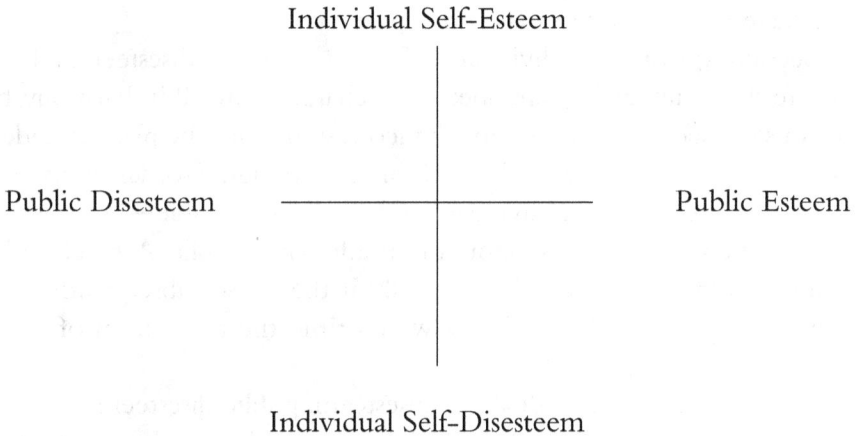

Individual Self-Esteem

Public Disesteem ———————————————————— Public Esteem

Individual Self-Disesteem

Figure 4: Public and Private Evaluation in Esteem and Self-Esteem

First quadrant: individual self-esteem, public esteem. Here the individual is pleased to have achieved consistency between his or her actions and ideals; the actions are also in reasonable accord with the public's ideals, thereby eliciting external approval. S-order would be facilitated by the latter, E-order by the former. With regard to S-order, this is where the Kantian 'dutiful bonding' that was discussed in the previous section might be expected to occur. As we have seen, Kant believed that actions performed for the sake of duty (as distinct from those performed from inclination) are deserving of esteem. Dutiful bonding as a form of belongingness on that account would facilitate esteem. Since belongingness and homosapient order have been found to be positively related, esteem would be similarly related to homosapient order. With regard to E-order, constancy and consistency between one's ideals, action and character are aspects of human flourishing. Rawls maintained that self-respect could be our foremost primary good, ahead of other primary goods such as rights, liberties, opportunities, income and wealth.[36] On that basis, one's sense of self-worth would depend on one's assessment (and the assessment of others) of the justness of one's characteristic actions, so setting the stage for N-order to make an appearance.

Second quadrant: individual self-esteem, public disesteem. This is where the individual's plans, ideals and character are all in harmony, but actions consequent upon them are inconsistent with the plans and ideals of the public. S-order would be inhibited, although E-order on the part of the self-respecting individual might still be possible—he or she is joyful, but without the support of an admiring public. A rebel with a cause would be an example, especially if the cause subsequently turns out to be generally tolerable; by which time the admiration of others might have been secured.

Third quadrant: individual self-disesteem, public disesteem. Here the individual is burdened by shame, in the knowledge of his or her culpability in respect of what may be presumed to have been serious misdeeds, compounded by an awareness of others' knowledge of them. Sadness and disapproval prevail. From the perspective of the individual, S- and E-order would both be out of the question.

Fourth quadrant: individual self-disesteem, public esteem. This is the domain of the guilty secret, where Spinoza's 'repentance' becomes manifest. Other people are largely unaware of the individual's lapses, and still consider his or her actions to be consistent with their own plans and ideals; their respect remains undiminished. Now the mere fact of respecting another may contribute to S-order, possibly by reinforcing social stability: it is a question of whether the need *to* respect can contribute to homosapient order, and I will come to that in a moment. However, E-order on the part of the respected individual would be highly unlikely: pervading repentance is not conducive to flourishing.

The analysis suggests that satisfaction of the need for respect results in homosapient order, in which case the need for esteem may reasonably be viewed as an expression of the need for homosapient order. I turn now

---

36 Rawls, *A Theory of Justice*, pp. 54, 386.

to the *need to* respect. The relevant issues are (1) whether such a need exists, (2) if it does exist, how might it be characterised? and (3) whether satisfaction of the need culminates in homosapient order.

It would be a very strange world if everyone went around wrapped in cloaks of self-respect without anyone else respecting them. Could self-respect survive in such circumstances? Except perhaps for solipsists and extreme egotists, it seems unlikely. Moreover, as the analysis of the need for respect has shown, self-respect often occurs in conjunction with the respect of others. Presumably, then, those who are doing the respecting feel some kind of impulsion to respect the self-respecter; i.e. they feel a need *to* respect. The need must be congruent with their personal character, for why else would they do it? Respect for people cannot be coerced or compelled. The need would also seem to be very common. The existence of the Universal Declaration of Human Rights is indicative of a fairly widespread belief in the equality of basic rights—and to respect the rights of a person is tantamount to respecting the person. All in all, the need to respect and the need for respect are complementary sides of the same coin.

Accepting that there is a *need to* respect, what can be said about its nature? Spinoza's definition of esteem is inappropriate, because of its orientation towards the one who is respected rather than those doing the respecting. But love as he describes it could fit the bill, i.e. love as a sense of joy in company with belief in an external cause of the joy. The joy felt by one who respects (or loves) derives from having witnessed the joy felt by the respected person upon fulfilment of his or her proper purposes. The other person's joy upon fulfilment constitutes an external cause, but the notion of internal cause should not be totally dismissed. The joy experienced upon witnessing fulfilment of the respected person's purposes would be augmented if the one who respects were to believe that he or she had contributed to their fulfilment. Should that be the case, Spinoza would have a ready explanation for any joy that is felt by the person who respects: as we have seen, joy for him consists in being the cause of things—in making things happen, thereby achieving autonomy.

Can the act of respecting bring something into effect? Perhaps it can. The actions of anyone who respects could contribute directly to the fulfilment of the respected entity's purposes. Such would be the case with regard to the environment, where a contribution is made to ecological balance (a form of P-order) by means of respectful action—S-order as well, through the cooperativeness that is implicit in the notion. In his writings on the environment Aldo Leopold maintained that 'a land ethic changes the role of Homo sapiens from conqueror of the land-community to plain member and citizen of it. It implies respect for his fellow-members, and also respect for the community as such.'[37] The community referred to by Leopold is the biotic community; i.e., the interdependent collection of flora and fauna resident in a region at a particular time. Leopold had a very clear idea of what the world should be like, and the ethics required for the realisation of the ideal, as he envisaged it, revolved around the principle of respect. The act of respecting and any attendant action would provide a pathway to Spinozistic self-respect; and with it, the possibility of E-order.

In sum, both the need for respect and the need to respect can reasonably be regarded as expressions of the need for homosapient order. Accordingly, satisfaction of both kinds of need would contribute to the realisation of homosapient order. The discussion of this highly complex subject has been all too brief, but the next step up Maslow's hierarchy awaits us.

Intellectual Achievement

Most if not all human beings need to apply their minds to problems and issues that confront them. The need arises from other needs—from, say, 'where is my next meal going to come from?' to 'what would be the best way of combatting global warming?' Playfulness would also often be involved—crosswords, cribbage, chess, and so forth. Besides having sometimes to use our wits merely to survive, we generally like to use them. Satisfaction from having solved a puzzle is sufficiently common to warrant believing that the need for intellectual achievement is universal. We need to explain and justify things. My aim in this section is to show

---

37 Leopold, p. 240.

that satisfaction of the need for intellectual achievement contributes to homosapient order.

Solving problems and coming to terms with issues involves the use of reason, judgement, understanding and imagination, all of which are forms of cognition. Cognition involves thinking, which I take to be necessary to intellectual achievement, but not sufficient for it: intellectual achievement consists in a relatively high level of thinking. I will endeavour to explain what it is that raises cognition to the required level in a moment. First, though, a few words on the ordering nature of basic cognition will help explain how homosapient order and intellectual achievement are related. The proposition is this: If cognition is essentially an ordering process, then, on the assumption that intellectual achievement stems from cognition, intellectual achievement would also involve ordering.

I begin, therefore, with the ordering that occurs with basic cognition. Kant can help point the way. Ideas were regarded by Kant as being dependent on what he called 'categories of cognition', which pretty well encompass the various ways we think about things. The categories are employed in the faculty of understanding of a perceiving and knowing subject to produce objective judgements from sense-perceptions. The faculty of reason, in which the power of inference resides, is used to relate judgements to one another. The categories that bring order to our intuitions fall under four main headings—relation, quantity, quality and mode. Relational concepts and judgements are concerned with the sub-categories substance-accident, cause-effect and reciprocity; quantitative ones with unity, plurality and totality; qualitative ones with reality, negation and limitation; and modal ones with possibility-impossibility, existence-nonexistence and necessity-contingency. Although Kant's is by no means the only theory of cognition that we might consult, it seems clear that something like what he was talking about does indeed happen—the transformation of raw sense-data into usable, orderly information. In so far as the terms 'transformation' and 'information' both involve the root 'form', we can see that ordering is implicit in both steps of the process. Kant's categories cover a very broad spectrum of our means of cognition (he would have said the complete spectrum), but their order-creating function is especially relevant here.

A few ideas from some thinkers closer to our own time are also worth noting. The philosopher W.V. Quine (1908-2000) observed that we and other animals share a capacity for detecting similarities and contrasts between things. The capacity appears to be innate, and prior to language. Indeed, it is a prerequisite for learning language;[38] it works by identifying uniformities in things. The capacity therefore involves categorisation, i.e. putting like with like (or what are perceived as such—perhaps wrongly); it is a matter of sorting, of situating things in space and time, in the manner of Aristotelian prioritisation and Kantian categorisation. It is therefore concerned with ordering.

Ordering can also be seen to be involved at a fundamental level of cognition in a theory of understanding advanced by the mathematical physicist Roger Penrose (b. 1931).[39] Based on some insights of two famous twentieth century mathematicians, Kurt Gödel (1906-78) and Alan Turing (1912-54), Penrose argues that mathematical judgement and understanding are necessarily formed (that word again!) from a position that is independent of computational (i.e. algorithmic) processes. Such processes, he maintains, if they are sound, can never be complete (this is what Gödel proved in relation to axiomatic systems). Most tellingly, in so far as judgements of consistency are non-computational, the processes themselves are incapable of determining whether they are consistent (another of Gödel s conclusions). The ideas are obviously very complicated, but the desideratum of consistency is simple enough, and is what is important for our purposes. If consistency is what is wanted, and we along with Penrose most certainly do want it, then we will also want order. Cognition without consistency, i.e. without order, would hardly count as cognition at all. Having mentioned Penrose's non-computational approach, I should mention that his theory has attracted some fairly severe criticism, for example from Steven Pinker. Pinker is an advocate of a computational theory of the mind, and is therefore

---

38 W.V. Quine, *Quintessence: Basic Readings from the Philosophy of W. V. Quine*, edited by Roger F. Gibson, Jr. (USA: The Belknap Press of Harvard University Press, 2004), p. 196.
39 Roger Penrose, *Shadows of the Mind: A Search for the Missing Science of Consciousness* (Reading: Vintage, 1995).

diametrically opposed to Penrose. Even so, I don't think Pinker would deny the underlying importance of order to cognition. He maintains, for instance, that human intelligence is largely explained by the way in which neural networks are structured, in the form of 'programs for manipulation.'[40] Structure is a feature of organisation, and organisation is characteristic of order.

That will suffice for the ordering nature of basic cognition. I now want to examine how intellectual achievement differs from basic cognition, and, in so doing, tie it in with homosapient order. Spinoza, Maslow and Midgley will be the main contributors to the discussion.

Spinoza described cognition in terms of three faculties—imagination, reason and intuition.[41] Knowledge acquired through the imagination was adjudged by him inferior to the products of reason, which in turn stood below those of intuition. For Spinoza, inferiority consisted in a comparative lack of clarity and distinctiveness, in accordance with criteria proposed by his illustrious near-contemporary René Descartes (1596-1650). Intuition was considered paramount, because, in Spinoza's estimation, it is the only means of accessing the limited stock of things that might be known of God. 'Knowledge of God,' he declared, 'is the mind's greatest good; its greatest virtue is to know God.'[42] (Remember that Spinoza's 'God' is equivalent to 'nature'.) Where reason was thought to come into its own is in the development of adequate ideas of the properties of things; truth was said to consist in such ideas. While an adequate idea of the properties of God (i.e. nature) would be impossible, reason was believed by Spinoza to be capable of construing order between things. Spinoza's low opinion of the imagination is obvious from the terms in which he couched his rejection of the belief that order exists independently of human cognition. Such beliefs were held by him to have their origin in the mistaken impression that the imagination is the intellect, thereby giving rise to false apprehensions with regard to the nature of things.

Intuition was also lauded by Gödel. For him, mathematical intuition counted as a form of perception, one that is just as important as sense

---

40 Pinker, p. 112.
41 *The Ethics*, 2p40s2.
42 *The Ethics*, 4p28.

perception in the construction of physical theories.[43] Whether intuition meant the same thing for Gödel as it did for Spinoza is probably open to question, not to be settled here; but both men seem to have regarded it as some kind of immediate grasping of an object by the 'mind's eye'. Also, whether Spinoza would have endorsed Gödel s mathematical Platonism is doubtful, although Spinoza's proposition 'Singular thoughts, *or* this or that thought, are modes which express God's nature in a certain and determinate way' (*The Ethics*, 2p1d) could be understood as a move towards the objectification of ideas, including mathematical concepts. As expressions of God's nature, ideas could perhaps be accorded independent status. Then again, since the ideas are ours (though caused by God—*The Ethics*, 2pp6-8), they presumably reside in us. I will not try to resolve the problem (if it is indeed a problem); I simply wish to highlight the importance attributed to intuition by two of history's foremost thinkers.

The proposition that intellectual achievement is a heightened form of cognition can obviously be accommodated within Spinoza's theory. Intuition is purported to be superior to the other forms of cognition, and it is superior precisely because of the understanding it affords of the infinite being, without which 'nothing can either be or be conceived.'[44] Intuitive knowledge, Spinoza wrote, 'proceeds from an adequate idea of the formal essence of certain attributes of God to the knowledge of the . . . essence of things.'[45] Adequate ideas for Spinoza are true ideas,[46] and true ideas are those that agree with their objects.[47] In a Spinozistic world, such understanding would constitute the highest degree of human flourishing, and therefore contribute to E-order.

Turning now to Maslow, we find that his conception of what might be called maximal cognition is very similar to that of Spinoza. Maslow drew a distinction between D-cognition and B-cognition, where, to repeat, 'D' stands for 'deficiency' and 'B' for 'being'. The denotations obviously place B-Cognition above D-Cognition. As Maslow explained

---

43 See Palle Yourgrau in *A World Without Time: The Forgotten Legacy of Gödel and Einstein* (New York: Basic Books, 2005), p. 101 (where Gödel is quoted).
44 *The Ethics*, 4p28.
45 *The Ethics*, 2p40s2.
46 *The Ethics*, 2def4.
47 *The Ethics*, 1a6.

it, D-cognition consists fundamentally of basic cognition; it could also be seen as a combination of Spinozistic imagination and reason. D-cognition is cognition that we use in our everyday interactions with the world; it actively shapes percepts, organises and selects them; it compares, judges and evaluates; it is concerned with need-satisfaction; it dissects, differentiates, and it employs a form of reason that Maslow refers to as 'Aristotelian logic.' B-cognition is said to endeavour to achieve a higher unity or integration within 'a superordinate whole;' and, unlike D-cognition, it is non-instrumental, in so far as its object is 'permitted to be itself,' i.e. the object suffers minimal distortion from attempts to assimilate it to existing beliefs (my gloss).[48]

Maslow's B-cognition and Spinoza's intuition are very similar in nature. Their ultimate objects are the same—intuition for Spinoza affords a measure of knowledge of God (= nature), while B-cognition for Maslow is fundamentally concerned with 'Cosmic Consciousness.'[49] B-cognition might appear somewhat other-worldly, and perhaps even discontinuous with D-cognition, but that was not Maslow's view. Given the fact that there is only one world, he held that both 'D' and 'B' attitudes should be retained towards it.[50] For a Maslovian, to achieve B-cognition would be of the highest intellectual order, and help bring E-order into effect.

Cognition as concept-formation and judgement is essential to rationality, the latter being a term that stems etymologically from 'ratio'. The concept of ratio in turn involves the notions of reason, reckoning and relation, all of which feature in rationality, and it is rationality that provides a further link between cognition and homosapient order. The link derives from an observation from Mary Midgley, to the effect that rationality means more than cleverness. As well as cleverness, rationality, is said to include 'a definite structure of preferences, a priority system based on feeling.'[51] The priority system sorts out and adjudicates with regard to desires, wants and needs that conflict with one another. In so far as it is 'based on feeling', the priority system brings reason into conjunction

---

48 *The Farther Reaches of Human Nature*, pp. 249-253.
49 *The Farther Reaches of Human Nature*, p. 249.
50 *The Farther Reaches of Human Nature*, p. 247.
51 Midgley, *Beast and Man*, p. 246.

with the emotions, and therefore entails a sense of wholeness—and with that, conditions ripe for the emergence of homosapient order. The germ of an order-based morality is discernible in Midgley's views on the matter, for we again have before us the Aristotelian relationship between order and prioritisation, supplemented by conflict resolution.

Rationality can obviously be of very broad application. Rather than merely solving puzzles, through the exercise of 'cleverness', it is central to the realisation of our deepest wishes and desires, many of which have their origin in our basic needs, fundamentally our need for homosapient order. By applying our minds to things that concern us, a measure of orderliness is imposed upon the world—and upon us as part of the world. Through cognitive order, other forms of order may also arise, including P-, S-, E- and N-order—and, as part of E-order, aesthetic order as well. Again, therefore, it can be concluded that cognition is involved in homosapient order, and that cognitive needs (including the need for intellectual achievement) are expressions of the need for homosapient order.

The mention of aesthetic order brings me to the need for aesthetic experience, which occupies the penultimate rung of Maslow's hierarchy.

Aesthetic Experience

The aim of this section is to demonstrate that satisfaction of the need for aesthetic experience contributes to the realisation of homosapient order. If that indeed is what it does, we could correctly conclude that the need for aesthetic experience is a form of the need for homosapient order. 'Aesthetic' is used here in the sense attributed to the related term 'aesthetics' by the philosopher Alexander Baumgarten (1714-1762). Amongst other things, the philosophical aesthetics Baumgarten inaugurated sought to examine questions concerning the nature of art and of beauty. Until then, 'aesthetics' referred to the philosophical theory of sense perception, derived from the Greek *aesthesis* ('perception'). I will start with a discussion of the nature of the need in question, and then try to explain how its satisfaction gives rise to homosapient order.

What is 'aesthetic experience'? It would be a truism to say that it consists in experiencing something in terms of either beauty or the sublime.
Beyond that, however, a universally acceptable answer would be hard to
find. My supposed truism could even be questionable, in view of the
dismissal of beauty by the twentieth century modernist and postmod-
ernist movements. Nevertheless, I will stick with beauty, for it still seems
to be a widely-held desideratum amongst artists and their audiences.
Aesthetic beauty was held by Plato to be dependent upon due measure:
in the *Statesman*, the 'Stranger' (Plato's spokesman) maintains that the arts
would not exist were it not for due measure,[52] but neither would due
measure exist without the arts; to deny either would be to deny both.[53]
Due measure is described in terms of the realisation of a norm, where
neither excess nor deficiency is present. Therefore, aesthetic beauty for
Plato entailed a sense of balance, and with that, order. Since the concept
of balance also underwrites his notion of justice, aesthetic experience
and moral experience were associated at a very fundamental level in the
Platonic scheme of things.

In Chapter 5 we saw how Kant differentiated between aesthetic
judgements of beauty and aesthetic judgements of the sublime. Aesthetic
judgement would obviously involve aesthetic experience. We also saw in
that chapter how the sublime connects up with the notion of respect,
due to the sense of grandeur and awe that it can inspire in us. In view of
the link established in the present chapter between respect and homosapient order, I will leave matters there with regard to the sublime. Suffice
to say that an aesthetic experience of the sublime is conducive to the
production of homosapient order, because of the respect that is paid to
the sublime object. In this section I will focus on beauty.

Kant considered beauty to be one of three possible sources of pleasure,
the others being agreeableness and goodness. The agreeable gives rise to
gratification, the good evokes esteem, while the beautiful is that which
simply pleases.[54] The pleasure associated with beauty derives from a faculty of judgement Kant referred to as 'taste'. Aesthetic judgements of
taste for Kant are not cognitive in the sense of relying on concepts of

---

52 Plato, *Statesman*, translated by J. B. Skemp, in *Plato: The Collected Dialogues*, s. 284.
53 Plato, *Statesman*, s. 284.
54 Kant, *Judgement*, s. 5.

utility and purpose in respect of the object under consideration, but they appear to be cognitive in another sense, for they are said to require 'the harmonious accordance of two powers of representation,' namely the imagination and the understanding.[55] Harmonious here is said to mean 'subjectively final,' which in turn is equated with delight in the object.[56] The judgements that issue from the process are such that 'universal assent' is called for.[57] Even though judgements of beauty or otherwise are intensely personal matters ('in our general estimate of beauty we seek its standard *a priori* in ourselves')[58] the beautiful, according to Kant, is that which pleases universally.[59]

Further light can be shed on the nature of beauty by revisiting some territory that was traversed a short while ago. In the discussion of belongingness we saw that beauty and love were considered by Plato to be related. Similarly his pupil Aristotle, who maintained that the 'pleasure of the eye is the beginning of love,' and 'no one loves if he has not first been delighted by the form of the beloved.'[60] Aristotle diverged from his teacher on many issues, but the relationship between beauty and love was not one of them. Delight in the form of the beloved would contribute to the erotic inflow that is characteristic of love; and by virtue of the inflow, the lover would arguably partake of the being of the beloved—in Plato's *Phaedrus* it is said that 'he who loves the beautiful is called a lover because he partakes of it.'[61] Either or both of the usual connotations of 'partake' would make sense in this context—'participate in' and 'consume' would both fit. The statesman and philosopher Edmund Burke (1729-97) also believed beauty and love to be inseparable, so much so that he defined them in a rather circular fashion. According to Burke, beauty is 'that quality or those qualities in bodies by which they cause love, or some passion similar to it,' while love is 'that satisfaction which arises to the mind upon contemplating the beautiful, of whatsoever nature it may

55 Kant, *Judgement*, s. 35.
56 Kant, *Judgement*, s. 39.
57 Kant, *Judgement*, Introduction s.VII. See also s. 22.
58 Kant, *Judgement*, s. 58.
59 Kant, *Judgement*, s. 9.
60 Aristotle, *Nicomachean Ethics*, IX.5, 1167a.
61 *Phaedrus*, Jowett translation, 249d-e.

be.'[62] If there had been any doubts about the universality of the need for aesthetic experience (of beauty), then its connection with love should have dispelled them—for the need for love is assuredly universal.

Having seen how love contributes to E-order, S-order, and P-order, the relationship between love and beauty could be looked upon as a bridge that connects aesthetic experience to homosapient order. Kant's harmonisation of the imagination with the understanding provides another means of linking them. Fundamentally, however, the creation or perception of beauty may actually be capable of bringing order into effect. Order was considered by Aristotle to be one of three constituents of beauty; another was symmetry,[63] which was found earlier to be commonly regarded as a form of order. (I will have something to say about the third constituent—definiteness—in a moment.) In a strong sense, therefore, beauty for Aristotle derives from some kind of order: if beauty exists then order also exists. Disagreement with that would surely be minimal, for it is hard to imagine how a disorderly (unbalanced, incoherent, unintegrated, etc.) object could be considered beautiful. The idea is captured in the poem *Nightfall* by Gwen Harwood (1920-95), especially where reference is made to 'earth's beauty mending the miseries of time.' Miseries such as suffering and death are inescapable accompaniments of time; beauty provides us with a way of dealing with them. Earth's beauty 'mends' the miseries, by putting the pieces of our world back the way we believe they belong, thus restoring their proper function. Beauty on that account enhances the orderliness of one's world.

Harwood's words constitute a very nice way of expressing a famous idea of Nietzsche's. In Section 5 of his book *The Birth of Tragedy*, Nietzsche proclaims that the world's existence is justified only as an aesthetic phenomenon. One often comes across the proposition, especially in works of literary and aesthetic theory. Now to justify something is to show its appropriateness in the light of some set of human values. When one justifies an action or phenomenon, one explains what is right and proper about it, i.e. how it fits in relation to whatever we believe should obtain. Beauty, then, is something that bestows fittingness upon the world—the

---

62 See David Wolmersley (editor), *Edmund Burke: A Philosophical Enquiry into the Origin of our Ideas of the Sublime and the Beautiful and Other pre-Revolutionary Writings* (London: Penguin Books, 2004), III.i.
63 See *Metaphysics*, XIII.3.

only thing according to Nietzsche. On that account, Nietzschean beauty entails order, and to experience beauty brings orderliness (a thing of value in itself) into the world, including that part of the world represented by the person doing the experiencing. For Nietzsche, a world without beauty would always be out of kilter. Or, as Harwood would say, a world in need of mending.

Creative activity that gives rise to philosophy like Nietzsche's and poems such as Harwood's may itself be informed by a sense of natural order. In an essay dealing with the sculpture of Henry Moore, the art historian and critic Bernard Smith (1916-2011) suggests that formal order in works of art 'springs ultimately from the order of the natural world,' and that apprehension thereof is where aesthetic pleasure comes from. Should that be the case, he continues, knowledge of the methods of 'nature's sculpture'—for example wind and water erosion—could be a key to good artistic practice.[64] Smith's suggestion regarding the source of formal artistic order is especially pertinent in the present context. From natural order to formal order to aesthetic pleasure—if the sequence holds, then artistic creation can be understood to involve insight into the orderliness of nature. Elucidation of the relationship would require a full-length study in its own right, and I will only add here that the earlier discussion of the role of 'thoughtful mixing' in the creation of aesthetic order points in the same direction, as does the application of aesthetic criteria in mathematical theory.

The connection between aesthetic experience and homosapient order would be strengthened if the need for aesthetic experience could be shown to be a form of the need for homosapient order. That would be so if the following four premises were valid. (1) Human beings have a need to experience aesthetic beauty. (2) Experience of aesthetic beauty contributes to E-order in people who experience it. (3) E-order contributes to homosapient order. (4) The experience of homosapient order implies that people who experience it have a need for homosapient order. The steps in the argument will now be discussed.

---

64 Bernard Smith, *The Antipodean Manifesto: Essays in Art and History* (Melbourne: Oxford University Press, 1976), p. 19.

The first premise has already been dealt with. The need to experience beauty is a universal human trait, especially in view of its connection with love.

The second premise—that aesthetic experience contributes to E-order—could be more contentious. I will offer two sets of ideas in support of it. First, the parts of which a beautiful object is composed fit together in such a way as to exhibit balance and harmony. On that account, an experience of aesthetic beauty necessarily involves order, as Aristotle said it does. An object whose parts fit together will evoke a sense of wholeness, a quality that we have seen Aquinas associating with perfection; and perfection was identified by him as one of three ingredients of beauty, the others being due proportion and clarity. Since wholeness and due proportion are integral to orderliness, the connection between order and beauty is further reinforced. It follows, therefore, that the second premise would be valid if some or all of these conditions or ingredients of an object's beauty could be linked to the E-orderliness of the person who experiences it. Aristotle and Aquinas can help with that as well, specifically by deploying the third member of their respective taxonomies: definiteness and clarity. Definiteness in an object and the attendant absence of confusion would help satisfy Aquinas's criterion of clarity—with clarity of perception culminating in clarity of thought; that is to say, culminating in clear and distinct ideas, as urged upon us by Descartes. Clarity, in turn, opens the way to enlightenment; the latter, perhaps, of the kind envisaged by Lao Tzu when he pinpointed its source in harmony and constancy (see the epigraph to this chapter). Lao Tzu's utterances are often rather gnomic, but I think what he had in mind here was the possibility of insight by means of grasping the ways of nature and abiding by them.

The other set of ideas in support of the second premise revolves around an assertion made by the philosopher Ernst Cassirer (1874-1945). According to Cassirer the forms of art 'are not empty forms;' such forms, he maintained, 'perform a definite task in the constitution and organisation of human experience.' He continues, 'To live in the realm of forms does not signify an evasion of the issue of life; it repre-sents, on the contrary, the realization of one of the highest energies of life itself.'[65] The notion 'highest energies of life' is consistent with that of human flourishing, and the involvement of energy points to the fact that aesthetic experience entails activity. Etymologically, energy and activity imply one another—the root idea derives from the Greek and Latin terms *enérgei* and *energia*, both of which signify activity. As Cassirer said, one of the fundamental features of art is 'its constructive power in the framing of our human universe.'[66] Activity, or energy, would be involved in the framing process.

References to energy are common in critiques of stage-plays, art exhibitions, musical performances and films. For example, from the Melbourne newspaper *The Age*: a performance by John Bell in Hamlet is described as 'an unforgettably etched study, dripping with frenetic energy;'[67] some paintings by the German Brucke group are said to have displayed 'vibrant, pulsating colours and deliberately crude forms,' which 'unleashed a new and spontaneous energy in art;'[68] a concert given by the jazz musician Don Burrows is lauded for its 'extraordinary energy and authority;'[69] and Meryl Streep is said to have had 'all the energy' in her performance in *Julie and Julia*.'[70] It seems that an appropriate level of energy, along the lines of Plato's 'due measure', or 'norm', is needed in a work of art before it can communicate with us; and communication, should it occur, brings into being a community consisting of the artwork and its audience.

Kant delineated three modes of communication, and associated each of them with particular kinds of art. Communication can be by word, as in rhetoric and poetry; it can be by gesture, as reflected in formalistic arts such as painting and sculpture; and we may communicate by tone, or modulation, which find expression in music and the art of colour.[71] Energy is clearly required for each of the modes, but again, only at an appropriate level. Too little energy, and the message is lost; too much energy, and garishness, or simply noise, eventuates. Either extreme results

65 Ernst Cassirer, *An Essay on Man* (Toronto: Bantam Books, 1970 [first published 1944]), p. 185.
66 Cassirer, p. 185.
67 Peter Craven, *The Age*, 22 May 2010.
68 Gabriella Coslovich, *The Age*, 12 June 2010.
69 Jessica Nicholas, *The Age*, 19 May 2010.
70 Philippa Hawker, *The Age*, 15 January 2010.
71 See Kant, *Judgement*, s. 51.

in a failure to communicate; subtlety together with strength are needed. Energy in an artwork contributes to its vitality, which in turn enlivens the imagination of its audience. As we have seen, Kant considered imagination to be a 'power of representation;' strengthening the power may enable the audience to see the world or some aspects of it in a different light. Should that happen, insight into the Aristotelian interconnectedness of ostensibly disparate things could become clearer. In short, heightened imagination through aesthetic experience opens the way to enlightenment, thereby contributing to human flourishing. In the words of the second premise, aesthetic experience contributes to E-order.

The third premise claims that E-order contributes to homosapient order. This follows straightforwardly from the definition of homosapient order.

The fourth premise states that the experience of homosapient order implies that people who experience it have a need for homosapient order. Now it must be acknowledged that there are things we experience that we have no need of experiencing, for example disease and war; or, more generally, everything contrary to satisfaction of the Maslovian needs. But there are also things that we experience that we need to experience, and my argument all along has been that homosapient order belongs in that category—we need it in order to survive and to flourish.

This completes the argument. If the premises are deemed valid, as I believe them to be, then the need for aesthetic experience may reasonably be claimed to be an expression of the need for homosapient order.

Self-Actualisation

We have reached the top of the hierarchy. According to Maslow, even if all of the other needs are satisfied, we may still experience 'a new discontent and restlessness' unless we are doing what we are fitted for.[72] By doing what one is fitted for, one attains self-actualisation. Self-actualisation amounts to self-fulfilment, and bears a strong resemblance to the ideal of self-realisation propounded by the eighteenth-century Romantic movement. As the philosopher Frederick Beiser (b. 1949) describes it,

---

72 A Theory of Human Motivation, p. 382.

self-realisation for the Romantics was achievable first through the development of all of one's human powers, second by forming those powers into a unity, and third by securing one's individuality, or uniqueness.[73] Flourishing, and therefore homosapient order, would clearly be involved in the process.

Self-actualisation for Maslow is Janus-faced. Unlike the other needs, which he describes solely in terms of *what is*, self-actualisation is also couched in terms of *what ought to be*: besides its factual aspect, it has a normative one. In Maslow's opinion, the description of what a person ought to be is almost the same as the description of what the person deeply is.[74] 'Almost' could be the operative word here, because it allows for a divergence of 'ought' from 'is'. And, as we will see, Maslow had strong views on what 'ought to be' consists in. The attainment by an individual of the mode of life best suited to his or her character can be regarded as the primary focus or objective of self-actualisation. This might be called pre-moral or best-fit self-actualisation. Its secondary focus would then be its normative aspect; and this, I will argue, gives rise to two kinds of self-actualisation: Maslow's kind, and a different kind. The first will be called *Maslovian self-actualisation*, and the second *malignant self-actualisation*. Discussion of the primary focus of self-actualisation follows; its secondary, normative focus will be examined after that.

Best-Fit Self-Actualisation
Maslow was of the view that the self is 'partly constructed and invented.'[75] We might also say, one part learned and another part consisting of that which is deep, or instinctoid, and perhaps unalterable except through the slow workings of natural selection. The 'partly constructed' comment is made by Maslow in a footnote to one of his texts without elaboration, but I believe my interpretation to be consistent with his general approach. Construction of the self involves assimilation of inputs received from others, within a community of selves. Connections are formed from encounters, fleeting or otherwise, between people and other entities. The effects that others have on us include attitudes of

73 Beiser, p. 39.
74 *The Farther Reaches of Human Nature*, p. 108.
75 *The Farther Reaches of Human Nature*, p. 108.

mind such as gratitude and antipathy, depending on whether we have been helped or hindered, or possibly even harmed. In so far as they motivate present behaviour, attitudes that can be traced to events in the relatively distant past would involve what Elizabeth Anscombe referred to as 'backward-looking motivation' (see p. 37). Like the encounters from which they are formed, attitudes of mind are constantly taking shape; sometimes solidifying, other times undergoing modification, and occasionally being erased. All in all, the self is a dynamic, evolving entity; for most of us, it would continue to evolve as long as encounters last, until death renders them impossible.

Self-construction, or self-invention, can also be understood in terms of self-creation. According to the philosopher Richard Rorty (1931-2007), self-creation comes about when 'the blind impress' that is stamped upon us by the contingencies of life is internalised and made our own, by redescribing it in terms of our own.[76] 'Blind impress' is from the poem *Continuing to Live* by Philip Larkin (1922-85), and refers to the impressions made on a person by his or her unique set of experiences. Externalities are a factor, but the experiences are made one's own. The process is inescapable, and the need to come to terms with it is described by Rorty as being 'universal.' Nietzsche's influence is discernible here; perhaps unsurprisingly, since, in Rorty's view, Nietzsche was one of the very few 'edifying' philosophers ever to have lived. (Rorty considered most philosophy down through the ages to have been of an inferior 'systematising' nature.) For Nietzsche, creativity and art were so important that the artist-philosopher became, for him, the nearest thing on Earth to a deity—a creator who forms human beings;[77] a true *Übermensch* (superman), one might say. Beauty issues from art that consummates the artist's will to power. Beauty is life-affirming, and art is the highest expression of freedom—'how liberating is Dostoevsky,' Nietzsche exclaimed.[78]

It is probably fair to say that few of us would be capable of becoming a Nietzschean artist-philosopher, but Rorty may nevertheless have

---

76 Richard Rorty, *Contingency, irony, and solidarity* (USA: Cambridge University Press, 1999 [first published 1989]), p. 43.

77 Friedrich Nietzsche, *The Will to Power*, translated by Walter Kaufmann and R. J. Hollingdale, edited by Walter Kaufmann (New York: Vintage Books, 1968), s. 795.

78 *The Will to Power*, s. 821.

been correct in his belief that the need for self-creativity is universal. The vast majority of people can both create and think to some extent, and it may be the case that the more we create and think the greater the need becomes for us to do so. If we were to follow John Dewey, a kind of self-enriching, compounding process could be seen to be involved. According to Dewey, activity is creative 'in so far as it moves to its own enrichment,' by bringing with it a release of further activities—activities such as scientific inquiry, artistic production, and social companionship. Indeed, it was Dewey's view that some amount of creativity is 'a normal accompaniment of all *successfully coordinated action*.'[79] Successfully coordinated action on those grounds would encompass acts of self-creation.

The notion of self-creativity is a close relative of Maslow's concept of self-actualisation. Self-actualisation entails realisation of one's potentialities, making choices conducive to growth rather than regression, taking responsibility, and listening to and being one's own self[80]—all of which would serve well as acts of self-creation. Intellectual achievement and aesthetic experience are also kinds of creativity; as we have seen, both contribute to E-order, and to the sense of wholeness that comes with it. They are therefore also likely to be involved in self-actualisation, for some people at least. And for some of those people, satisfaction of the need for either intellectual achievement or aesthetic experience could in fact suffice for self-actualisation to occur—people, for instance, like Stephen Jay Gould, whenever laborious scientific fieldwork such as that in which he was engaged (researching snails) is punctuated by a flash of excitement, when a new discovery is made; when one's understanding is enlivened by a glimpse of the order that lies beneath nature's apparent confusion. What is more, as Gould says, 'this pleasure can be savoured every day if one loves the little things as well.' He doubts that any reward could be greater.[81] Self-actualisation is clearly at issue here.

Although intellectual achievement and aesthetic experience are necessary to self-actualisation for some people, matters could be different for others. For someone like Gould, or Nietzsche, or Spinoza, or indeed

---

79 John Dewey, *Human Nature and Conduct* (New York: Dover Publications, Inc., 2002 [first published 1922]), p. 143 (my italics).
80 *The Farther Reaches of Human Nature*, pp. 43–47.
81 Stephen Jay Gould, *The Flamingo's Smile*, p. 184.

any of the other thinkers and doers we have met in these pages, satisfaction of the need for either or both kinds of creativity would have been necessary—their lives would otherwise have been incomplete. But there are many people who have lived perfectly satisfying lives without ever having scaled the intellectual and aesthetic heights that these men did. As I have said, what suffices for self-actualisation, more particularly its primary focus, is finding out what one is best fitted to do, and doing it. For Maslow there was something else that is necessary to self-actualisation, namely moral goodness; which brings us to the concept's secondary focus.

Self-Actualisation: Its Moral Content

Maslow regarded self-actualisation as an altogether salutary state-of-being—so much so that the 'B' in his formulations could reasonably be understood to signify 'beneficence' instead of 'being'. According to him, delight in bringing justice into effect, in preventing cruelty and exploitation, are among the motivations and gratifications that attend self-actualisation.[82] Action that is consistent with the PHM would come easily to a Maslovian self-actualiser. In Chapter 7 I suggested that the moral aspect of self-actualisation could reasonably be conceived of as a separate need, namely the need for humaneness. If that were to occur, satisfaction of the need for best-fit self-actualisation could then be seen as pre-requisite for the assumption of motivational force by the separately conceived need. However, in what follows I will stay with Maslow, and treat humaneness as an aspect of self-actualisation. Nothing of what I will say will conflict with the conjectured splitting-off.

Maslow declares self-actualisers to be psychologically healthy people, better able than others to cognise and to perceive.[83] Cognition and intellectual achievement have already been paid considerable attention in these pages, but an idea from Rawls will help confirm their relevance to self-actualisation, and strengthen the connection between the latter and justice. The idea is called the 'Aristotelian principle', according to which, other things being equal, people enjoy exercising their capacities, whether innate or learned, and their enjoyment increases the more

---

82 *The Farther Reaches of Human Nature*, p. 298.
83 *The Farther Reaches of Human Nature*, p. 5.

the capacities becomes manifest, or the greater their complexity. The principle is described as Aristotelian because of the prominence of intellectual achievement in Aristotle's doctrine of virtue. For Rawls, the idea is indicative of a basic principle of motivation.[84] It ties in with self-respect; it contributes to judgements of value; its realisation is tantamount to self-realisation; and it is central to the moral psychology that underlies Rawls's primary notion of 'justice as fairness.'[85] 'Compassionate' could be an apt description of the practitioner of the Aristotelian principle, who would also qualify as a Maslovian self-actualiser, especially if compassion is understood to be akin to the Confucian 'strenuous attention to conduct.' Recalling that the B-needs were regarded by Maslow as instinctoid (i.e., innate rather than learned), self-actualisation accompanied by beneficence in general and compassion in particular would arise from innate processes. Strong grounds for optimism, one might conclude.

Maslow's optimism is consistent with the views expressed a short while ago regarding species-wide humaneness. The world would be quite a different place from the way most people find it if evil did in fact outweigh goodness. Instead of the everyday kindnesses, helpfulness and sympathy that generally characterise civil society, there would be cruelty, uncooperativeness and indifference. Certainly the latter malignancies are common enough, but it seems to me that civil society as it presently exists could not have evolved if they were predominant. Human beings have, as an aspect of the need for self-actualisation, a need for humaneness—a need to be humane and a need to be treated humanely.

Self-actualisation on the foregoing grounds would seem to be indisputably good; and, moreover, good in a morally relevant way. That is how Maslovian self-actualisation should be understood. Satisfaction of the need for Maslovian self-actualisation would contribute to homosapient order, and the need for it may therefore be understood as an expression of the need for homosapient order. But there are also grounds for pessimism, in the form of evil.

There is no escaping the fact that some people are decidedly evil. Adolf Hitler and Pol Pot are common examples; their actions included

---

84 Rawls, *A Theory of Justice*, p. 374.
85 See Rawls, *A Theory of Justice*, s. 65.

some that were grievously harmful, and intentionally so. However, in terms of self-actualisation, utterly evil people would nevertheless seem capable of attaining what they are best fitted to be and do, in accordance with the primary sense of the notion. I now wish to explore the problem of evil from a Maslovian perspective. Evil as a type of moral wrong will be shown to be a feature of what I will refer to as 'malignant self-actualisation'.

Malignancy is to be understood here in its usual sense of maliciousness—of being disposed towards harming others, and making that disposition manifest by actually harming them. As well as being malevolent, malignant self-actualisers are maleficent. People motivated by a need for malignant self-actualisation tend to act in morally reprehensible ways. Might we all be afflicted with a need for malignant self-actualisation, at least some of the time? Perhaps we are, each to a varying extent. What matters are the degree to which we are and the frequency with which the need is expressed. Degree and frequency of expression are big topics, and will not be pursued at any length here; but I will touch on them in the course of the discussion.

Contrary to Maslovian self-actualisation, malignant self-actualisation is destructive rather than constructive, maleficent rather than beneficent. Given an opportunity to do harm, malignantly self-actualising individuals will likely avail themselves of it. Neither Hitler nor Pol Pot could be said to have had much concern for justice (especially in the Rawlsian sense of fairness), nor with harm-minimisation in general. Rather, in them, traits such as cynicism, vulgarity, and selfishness reached very high levels of expression. Both men were responsible for mass murder, displacement of populations, and untold misery. Their remorselessness suggests that their deeds were consistent with their true selves. Adolf Eichmann similarly: 'The death of five million Jews on my conscience gives me extraordinary satisfaction,' the Nazi overseer is said to have exclaimed.[86] Since his conscience was clear, Eichmann was presumably acting in full accord with his true self when he arranged the mass killings. Perhaps Hitler could be regarded as having occupied the opposite

---

86 Quoted in http://sprott.physics.wisc.edu/pickover/good.html (accessed 1 April 2011).

extreme of Eichmann's coldly efficient discipline; he seems to have been driven by a violent, raging hatred of non-Aryans, especially Jews.

Malignant self-actualisation can be viewed from the perspective of the Tennyson principle (see p. 84). To illustrate, I might have had the misfortune of having met predominantly with evil people and iniquitous circumstances throughout the course of my life. Evil may have become part of me, i.e. constitutive of my self—in which case, I might have proceeded to actualise that self by committing evil deeds, with the deeds themselves also contributing to my selfhood. Such a scenario is contrary to the association of self-actualisation with health, beauty, justice and goodness—if self-actualisation were only that, then the evil person that I have become would have to be regarded as not the real me. But 'the real me' is the person I now am; to say otherwise would surely be fallacious. In general, the actions of evil people such as those mentioned would be in pursuit of goals consistent with their characters, and therefore serve as steps towards their own kind of self-fulfilment. Evil characters would no doubt be regarded by many as ill-formed, due wholly or partly to circumstances beyond their control, for example poverty, poor parenting, lack of education, and so on. They might also be described as sociopaths, or psychopaths, or otherwise impaired; but the harm they inflict would generally be considered morally intolerable.

Support for the notion that malignantly inclined individuals can be self-actualisers is available from William James, a psychologist like Maslow but also a significant figure in philosophy. James described the healthy soul as 'harmonious and well balanced,' which gives rise to a consistency of impulse, a will that follows without trouble the guidance of intellect, passions that are not excessive, and few continuing regrets.[87] But the description can also be applied to malignant self-actualisers. James observed that the transition from dividedness of self to unity 'may be from moral scrupulosity into freedom and licence; or it may be produced by the irruption into the individual's life of some new stimulus or passion, such as love, ambition, cupidity, revenge, or patriotic devotion. In all these instances,' James concluded, 'we have precisely the same psychological form of event—a firmness, stability, and equilibrium succeeding a

---

87 James, *The Varieties of Religious Experience*, p. 142.

storm and stress and inconsistency.'[88] On that principle, if the self were to become unified under the aegis, say, of cupidity or revenge, then harmful (as opposed to salutary) outcomes might be expected. Patriotism likewise, should it find expression in xenophobia, while ambition might also become unhealthy, especially for those who stand in the ambitious person's way. Unification of the self on such a basis would be characterised by malignancy, and actualisation of such a self would be malignant self-actualisation.

Maslow's own writings occasionally point towards the possibility of malignancy in self-actualisation, at least some features thereof. In one of his essays he observes that self-honesty and self-knowledge are prerequisite to all 'authentic moral decisions.'[89] The same qualities could also be counted among the indispensable characteristics of self-actualisation. Now there would seem to be nothing to preclude 'authentic moral decisions' from being morally bad decisions; their results may be either good or bad, that is to say, either harmless or harmful. Therefore, some of the essential characteristics of self-actualisation may be associable with moral badness. From which we may infer, for Maslovian self-actualisation to eventuate, self-honesty and self-knowledge must be augmented by moral goodness itself; without it, malignancy remains possible.

But now the question arises, is malignant self-actualisation capable of engendering homosapient order? The short answer is no, but that would seem to undermine the proposition on which the present chapter rests, that all of our basic needs derive from the need for homosapient order. If malignant self-actualisation is indeed a basic need, then homosapient order must somehow be implicated in it. But there really is no problem. Like other human beings, evil-doers come equipped with all of the basic needs, from surviving through to thriving: they need P-order, S-order and E-order, but the N-order that they also need is devoid of humaneness; instead, inhumaneness would be the motivating force. This is not the homosapient order that constitutes a natural good for our species; at most it is quasi homosapient order, or, more strongly, a corruption thereof.

---

88 James, *The Varieties of Religious Experience*, p. 149.
89 *The Farther Reaches of Human Nature*, p. 107, note 4.

Self-actualisation by inhumane individuals would likely encompass satisfaction of the various homeostatic and social needs, to whatever extent they might be felt. Malignant self-actualising behaviour would also satisfy the agent's need to fulfil his evil self, i.e. to do what he is best fitted to do. From the perspective of the malignant self-actualiser, self-actualisation would be fulfilling, regardless of its effects on other people. As shocking as it may be, Hitler by his own lights would probably have felt that he had achieved his goal in life, especially after having implemented the Final Solution. Similarly for malignantly self-actualising intellectual and artistic high-achievers, such as the Nazi doctor Josef Mengele and the Marquis de Sade, and the earlier examples of the Machiavellian prince and J. K. Rowling's Voldemort. Someone is adversely affected by malignantly self-actualising behaviour, since, by definition, satisfaction of the need results in harm. Those harmed would suffer an insult to their need for homosapient order. In considerations of moral right and wrong, the effect that morally relevant behaviour has on respondents must be taken into account.

Conclusion

Each of the kinds of order of which homosapient order is composed involves a relationship between parts. Physical order exists for a person when there is healthy cooperation between various parts of the body. Social order is experienced by a person who fits in with the social groups and organisations of which he or she is a part. Eudaimonic and normative order are enjoyed to the extent that a person's actual and ideal selves are in harmony, where the ideal is consonant with the dictates of humaneness and the PHM. Each of the components of homosapient order is concerned with proper functioning: physiologically, socially, psychologically and normatively. The four kinds of order are interdependent, as are the related functions. Satisfaction of our basic needs gives rise to the kind of order to which they are related, and, ultimately, to homosapient order.

Order has been found in this chapter to be implicated in human needs. 'Implicate order'— the term is David Bohm's, for whom it appears to have referred to some kind of noumenal order that exists implicitly in every region of space and time, and which becomes manifest (or explicit) to us in the form of orderly phenomena. This Kantian interpretation of the notion would probably have been rejected by Bohm, but it serves to situate it in the realm of metaphysics, where I think it belongs. If, contrary to Bohm, *implicate order* is understood in the simpler sense in which I have used it, as 'that which underpins and informs all of our human needs', then we are left with our feet firmly planted in the realm of nature. And that is where we must remain if a naturalistic foundation of morality is to be found in the concepts of order and needs. The search for a foundation continues in the next chapter.

Chapter 13: Foundationalist Credentials

A person's ontology is basic to the conceptual scheme by which he or she inter-prets all experiences, even the most commonplace ones (pace W. V. Quine).[1]

To Ground or Not to Ground?

In this chapter I will attempt to demonstrate that homosapient order provides sufficient grounds on which to base a secular morality, and that it therefore serves to satisfy the philosophical need that I have spoken of. To that end, I will argue for the reality of homosapient order. A prelim-inary argument for the reality of order was advanced earlier, based on the pervasiveness of natural law (see p. 132). Here we will be taking a different tack, and go into a bit more detail.

The reality of homosapient order will be established in a roundabout way: it will be shown to be the conceptual counterpart of something that is integral to our living experience, namely homosapient disorder. By virtue of its form as a concept, I will maintain that homosapient order constitutes the basis of a viable ontological commitment. The 'commonplace experiences' referred to by Quine in the epigraph would assuredly include moral experiences, from which it follows that clarifi-cation of one's ontology (or, more generally, one's metaphysics) would help one understand what morality is about. At least, I believe that it follows. By being the subject of an ontological commitment, homosa-pient order assumes the mantle of an operative reality; or, perhaps, of an 'as if' reality. Before getting started, I can imagine someone asking, Why should anyone try to find a ground for morality? Not that everyone would agree, but from the perspective of the present book, an appro-priate answer to that question would be—because it answers to the

---

1 See W.V. Quine, 'On What There Is', in Gibson (editor): *Quintessence: Basic Readings from the Philosophy of W. V. Quine*, p. 185.

philosophical need of metaphysically inclined secularists such as me, and perhaps the reader also.

Metaphysics is concerned with things of which no direct experiential knowledge is attainable by us. In other words, metaphysical pursuit is an *a priori* endeavour, but not necessarily *a priori* to the exclusion of *a posteriori*. Indeed, since *a priori* is a term used to describe knowledge that is attained by thought alone, without input from experience, one may well wonder whether such a thing is even possible. Human beings unavoidably experience things, and consequently acquire knowledge in an *a posteriori* manner. Our first thoughts are likely to have been acquired in that manner, including those concerned with such esoteric topics as space and time. We learn about space and time by becoming acquainted with our position in them, the position of other entities in them, and the changes that occur in them. Because of its priority, knowledge derived experientially would conceivably influence the way we think about things that are inaccessible to direct experience, such as 'first causes', and the 'true nature' of things. We might never be troubled by such matters, but speculation with regard to first causes could be prompted by questions along the lines of 'how did the universe and life within it originate?' and may lead to such notions as 'God as uncaused cause', as promulgated by Aristotle. With regard to the nature of things, Kant argued that the cognitive equipment possessed by human beings necessarily conditions the way in which we perceive and think about things, and that the true nature of the objects of perception will therefore always elude us—hence his insistence on the distinction between unknowable-unknown *noumena* and knowable-and-sometimes-known *phenomena*. Clearly, if metaphysics were solely concerned with *noumena*, then, on Kant's thesis, it would be a futile exercise—as indeed Kant maintained it is, in his *Critique of Pure Reason* (1781). Nevertheless, notwithstanding his disavowal of metaphysical inquiry into *noumena*, Kant himself persisted with metaphysical inquiry of the kind I am interested in; i.e., in discovering and understanding the foundations of morality.

I will lead into the argument for moral foundations with some ideas from Spinoza, especially those opposing what I am advocating. You will by now have gathered that Spinoza is one of my main guiding lights, so

I must take his opposition seriously. Spinoza endeavoured to locate the grounds of an ethics of benevolence in something other than the will of a benign deity. But the 'something other' for him was certainly not order.

Spinoza on the Foundation of Ethics and the Reality of Order

Spinoza's metaphysics centres on substance monism, according to which all things are one, and things that are perceived to be separate and distinct entities are in fact modes of the single substance. Human beings are one kind of mode of substance, a kind specially equipped with a capacity for reason. Reason enables us to attain some understanding of reality. Such understanding would include coming to grips with the principle of *conatus*: as noted earlier, *conatus* signifies that everyone and everything strives for survival and an increase in power. Power, Spinoza maintained, derives from the possession of adequate ideas with regard to the causes of things. Thence comes the crucial step to an ethics. Having attained an understanding of our true nature as modes of the single substance, it becomes impossible for the rational beings that we are to wish to harm other modes. To harm others would, in effect, amount to self-harm, which would be contrary to the principle of *conatus*.

Although Spinoza's ethics is specifically concerned with interpersonal relationships, it might be seen to encompass entities other than other human beings, since all things are modes of the single substance— grounds, perhaps, for extending the range of ethics to objects other than human beings (cf. Peter Singer's 'circle'). There are also consequences for education: since reason provides the basis of benevolence, it would be to everyone's benefit if the overall level of reason were increased as far as possible. All in all, Spinoza's is a profoundly naturalistic solution to the problem of how ethics might be grounded metaphysically. In Spinoza's system, there is no omnipotent, omniscient creator from whom an ethics has been received. Rather, his ethics derives from the oneness of things, and human understanding of their oneness. The upshot is a plausible and ethically attractive vision of the world.

But it is my belief that a similarly plausible and attractive ethics can be obtained from a different starting point. Instead of substance monism, which could be considered too high a price to pay for a link between metaphysics and ethics (for reasons that will soon be spelt out), let us remain with the view that each and every human being along with everything else that exists are individuals in their own right. That view gives rise to an ethics based on interconnectedness rather than one-ness. Interconnectedness, we have seen, constitutes the essence of order; and order in the form of homosapient order, I maintain, provides the required link. Spinoza would certainly have rejected any such connec-tion, because, in his view, order is not real; and if order is not real, in some sense of the term 'real', then it is hard to see how homosapient order could perform any kind of ontological service.

According to Spinoza, order is imagined when we project our pre-dilection for it onto external phenomena. Justice, fairness and honour, and order itself, are all said by Spinoza to be human constructions, and derived from human nature. In response to that, I would suggest that the very existence (i.e. reality) of things–plural could be called into question by Spinoza's substance monism. If the singular substance is the only thing to which thingness may legitimately be attributed, then there would be no other things in respect of which prioritisation (i.e. ordering) could occur. In a rather convoluted way, Spinoza's ontology could be held to be consistent with his denial of the reality of order: a Spinozist might even derive the denial from the ontology. However, I will soon argue for an ontology that is inconsistent with substance monism, and must reject the argument from Spinoza's ontology.

Whether Spinoza was entirely consistent with regard to the unre-ality of order might also be questioned. For instance, he can be found maintaining that 'the order and connection of ideas is the same as the order and connection of things.'[2] According to him, thought always runs in parallel with physical objects. The theory is known as 'parallelism', and Spinoza promoted a very strict version of it: neither thought nor extended beings were believed by him to be explainable in terms of the other. In other words, the causal chains that give rise either to thought

---

2 The Ethics, 2p7.

or to physical objects are totally independent of one other. Now, if reality were accorded to the modes of the all-encompassing substance, instead of confining it to substance as I did a moment ago, and if the things that Spinoza speaks of here are regarded as modes, then the 'order and connection' between the things (as distinct from our ideas about order) would also be real: his parallelism would demand as much.

Further, among the infinite modes of substance proposed by Spinoza were the laws of nature. Laws of nature can be thought of in two senses: on the one hand, as human constructions; on the other hand, as real relationships (probably causal) between real things. In either sense, they are indicative of order. Laws of nature as we formulate them are generalisations with respect to real things and the relations between them. Albert Einstein's $E = mc^2$ will no longer have anyone to reflect on it after the human species and any other sufficiently cognisant beings that might happen to have evolved have become extinct, but energy and matter will continue to behave in the manner described by the equation (or perhaps in accordance with a later and better account of the physics involved). By referring to laws of nature as modes of substance, Spinoza was presumably thinking of them in an objectively real sense, rather than human constructions. If that is so, then his ascription of unreality to order would be questionable.

Laws of nature might amount in the first instance to beliefs or conceptions distilled from perceptions of physical orderliness: planetary movements, seasonal variations in the climate, patterns of generation and degeneration, and so forth. Whether there are things in nature that correspond to the beliefs is the point at issue. Spinozists would say there are not, but I will now argue otherwise.

What is Real?

What does reality consist of? Many answers have been proposed, and the issues are certainly complex. The following sketch begins with an account of the opposition between two principal streams of ontology, *stuff-based* versus *thing-based*.[3]

---

3 The discussion is based on Theodore Sider's *Four Dimensionalism: An Ontology of Persistence and Time* (New York: Clarendon Press, 2003 [first published 2001]).

The dispute between the stated ontologies centres on the question of when fundamental reality is thought to become individuated, i.e., it is a dispute about wholes and parts. An extreme stuff-based ontologist would insist that only one individual exists: namely, the stuff of which reality is composed. Spinoza's metaphysics of substance monism is of this kind—to repeat, all things were believed by him to be one, while things that are commonly perceived to be separate and distinct entities were seen as modes of the single substance. Extreme thing-based ontologists would conversely hold that reality resides in the multitude of bits (for example sub-atomic particles) of which aggregates are composed: such ontologists deny that aggregates of any kind are real, even though we talk (mistakenly) about them as if they were. A less extreme stuff-based ontologist would grant that stuff can credibly be thought of as being divided into assemblages that can be referred to as 'things'. A moderate thing-based ontologist would acknowledge that fundamental bits invariably merge to form composites: any one 'bit' can be a part of an array of wholes. The less extreme versions of the two ontologies therefore converge on one another.

My commitment is to the point of convergence; in other words, to the view that there is more than one thing in the world, where 'thing' consists of a portion of 'stuff'. The phrase 'portion of stuff' comes from Quine, and my commitment is based on Quine's ontology.[4] Why Quine's?—basically because of its austerity. In Quine's opinion, the only kinds of things that exist are physical objects (as distinguished by science) and sets (as used in the construction of mathematics). Equal in rank to physical objects in the Quinean ontology are the 'states-of-being' in which physical objects may be found to exist. If something as austere as this is sufficient to generate a basis on which morality can be found to rest, then it seems to me that the basis would be relatively sound. Each part comprising the basis of a theory will have its own set of challenges to confront, and failure of any one of them could bring down the entire structure. So the fewer the parts the better.

---

4 W.V. Quine, 'Things and Their Places in Theories', in Gibson, Jr. (editor): *Quintessence: Basic Readings from the Philosophy of W. V. Quine*, p. 239.

Science, Quine maintained, is concerned with a domain of four-dimensional physical objects. Such objects would in 'ancient' times have been referred to as substances, and modes of substances. Now they are seen as things that extend in space-time along each of its four dimensions—height, length, width and time. Each spatio-temporal part of an object counts as another four-dimensional object. 'Parts' might also be termed 'states-of-being'. Quine gives two examples. First, that of a president-elect; i.e. an object that is a person for as long as the condition of president-electedness lasts. Second, a fit of ague, in respect of which, for 'ontological clarity,' the illness is identified with the sufferer, again for as long as the condition lasts.[5]

A state-of-being on this basis is equivalent to an 'ancient' mode of substance, and contributes to the identity of the physical object of which it is a state for as long as the state lasts. Quine's ontology has an attractive simplicity about it. I nevertheless propose to focus predominantly on physical objects: sets are of no significance to moral theory, whereas physical objects such as human beings are of utmost significance. Also significant are what I will refer to as 'social entities', which will be included in the ontology alongside physical objects.

Most physical objects are composites of other physical objects, so non-composite things presumably form the basis of composite things. What might the non-composite entities be? Science is currently divided between the sub-atomic particles of quantum physics and so-called 'strings'. Whether particles or strings, the most fundamental things go under the rubric 'matter', which, according to Einstein's $E = mc^2$, is equivalent to energy.[6] Perhaps the formation of physical entities could be regarded as an act of order-imposition, whereby inchoate, seething, disorderly accumulations of energy waves (i.e. electromagnetic waves) are converted into the things that, for us, represent physical objects. We might even see in this a basis for effecting a merger between stuff-based

---

5 W.V. Quine, 'The Scope and Language of Science', in Gibson, Jr. (editor): *Quintessence: Basic Readings from the Philosophy of W. V. Quine*, p. 206.

6 Strictly speaking, 'm' in Einstein's equation stands for mass, not matter. However, since mass is the exclusive property of matter (and things composed of matter), the stated equivalence is valid. As well as equivalence, what the equation tells us is that mass (and therefore matter) and energy are transformable into one another. Huge amounts of energy (E) are locked up in each unit of mass (m), since the latter must be multiplied by the square of the speed of light (c^2) in order to obtain the former.

ontology and thing-based ontology, with energy waves as stuff and physical objects as things, each being transformable into the other. Above
the level of the most fundamental things, things combine to form other
things. Lower level things become parts of other wholes, for example
when atoms combine to form molecules, and molecules are mould-
ed into cells. A composite entity arising from an act of combination
is a whole in its own right. Composite entities can also decompose.
Composition and decomposition through aggregation and disaggrega-
tion pervade nature. States-of-being of physical objects can be thought
of in terms of the location within space-time of both the entity concerned and the parts of which the entity is composed. If they were
otherwise located, then the entity would be something other than it is.
If I have ague, then, because of the presence of the virus in my cells, my
physical constitution is not the same as when I do not have ague—nor
would the way I feel be the same.

I come now to social entities, which I wish to add to the Quinean
ontology. The term refers to organisations that have living physical objects
at the lowest level of membership. Ant colonies, bird flocks, whale pods,
chimpanzee tribes, human families, corporations, and nations are just a
few of the many kinds of social entities. Individual ants, birds, persons
and so forth are the parts that come together to form their respective
social entities. The concept of social entity is fundamental to many fields
of inquiry: amongst others, it is indispensable to economics, sociolo-
gy, anthropology, and social psychology. Quine's inclusion of sets in his
ontology was based on the fact that sets are fundamental to mathematical
science, and therefore all 'science as currently constituted.'[7] Social entities
could be admissible on similar grounds.

Social entities may themselves be constituents of other social entities.
Student unions and sporting associations within a university are examples of the latter, but there are always individual people at the base level
of the over-arching entity. Social entities are wholes whose parts are held
together by some kind of unifying principle. Physical objects are subject
to unifying principles that are generally explainable in terms of physics, chemistry and biology—variously for objects ranging from atoms

---

7 W.V. Quine, 'The Scope and Language of Science', p. 207.

to organisms. The unifying principles applicable to social entities are of a different nature. They include cooperation, custom, love, norms, laws, and like-mindedness—some of which would be permeated by values, and none of which would be satisfactorily explainable in the same terms as those appropriate for physical objects.

Like physical objects, social entities are subject to various states-of-being. They may be functional or dysfunctional, at war or not at war, authoritarian or democratic, orderly or disorderly, and so on. Quine's inclusion of the office of president-elect as an example of a state-of-being could help confirm the reality that I am attributing to social entities. The office depends for its existence on the laws of the nation, so the state-of-being in question has a social aspect as well as an individual (physically objective) one. In the terms of this argument, the social entity (nation) is in a particular state-of-being (of having a president-elect). Moreover, the social entity and state-of-being are identical for as long as the state-of-being lasts—the nation with a president-elect is different from the nation without one.

The ontology resulting from these deliberations is fundamentally Quinean, but, because of the inclusion of social entities, 'Q-R' ('R' for revised) could be a suitable label for it. In summary, my ontological commitment with respect to things centres on physical objects and social entities, in conjunction with their various states-of-being—Peter with ague is not the same as Peter without ague; a nation with a president-elect is not the same as the nation without a president-elect. For some physical objects, states-of-being may include states-of-mind, or brain-states. States-of-mind correspond to thought, and in this sense, all thoughts are real, i.e. they exist. Whether the things that are thought of are also real is another (epistemological) matter. The question that must now be asked is whether homosapient order is real. The tack I will be taking is based on the Q-R ontology, and the proposition I wish initially to defend is that disorder in general and homosapient disorder in particular are experiential realities for us.

The Experiential Reality of Homosapient Disorder

By 'experiential reality' I mean something that is empirically observable and verifiable. Disorder is experienced by us in the form of a need, specifically as a need to ameliorate the disorderly state. There seems little reason to doubt the reality of the various Maslovian needs, and all of these were shown in Chapter 12 to be symptomatic of the need for homosapient order—or, as it might otherwise be expressed, of the need to avoid homosapient disorder. On the basis of Q-R, homosapient disorder would be real if it were either a physical object or a social entity, or a state-of-being of either a physical object or social entity. The possibility of homosapient disorder being a physical object or a social entity can be dismissed, but it could plausibly be regarded as a state-of-being of a particular kind of physical object, namely a human being. But its precise ontological specification doesn't matter all that much. Its reality is the point at issue, and the fact that it is experienced by all human beings would seem to be sufficient confirmation of its existence. For the purposes of exposition, I will continue to speak of homosapient disorder as a Q-R state-of-being.

Since physical objects and social entities are all in some kind of state-of-being for the duration of their existence, and since homosapient disorder applies to human beings, my proposition is that homosapient disorder consists in states-of-being of human beings either in their own right or as members of social entities, and is therefore Q-R real. The discussion that follows is based on Table 1.

The question is whether the characteristics of homosapient disorder can plausibly be said to be states-of-being of human beings either in their own right or as members of social entities. On the first row of the table, P-disorderly objects would be in a state of disunity and dysfunctionality, the latter in the sense of 'poor working order'. The converse P-orderly states-of-being are those shown in column 4; they are some the general characteristics of order discussed in Chapter 10. Ague was one of Quine's examples of a state-of-being: as a state of ill-health, the condition could reasonably be regarded as a state of disorder, specifically here as a state of P-disorder that may be suffered by human beings (and some other kinds of organisms as well). The disorderliness of P-disorderly objects arguably consists in states-of-being such as those described.

Social order was seen earlier to be characteristic of many creatures besides human beings; for example honeybees and chimpanzees. However, since moral agency is confined to human beings, I will focus here on human S-disorder. From the perspective of our species, disrespectful-ness would often be a sign of S-disorder, and lawlessness is specifically mentioned by Aristotle and Maslow; lawlessness might well culminate in riotousness. Insecurity and cynicism are metapathologies that Maslow associates with injustice, and they suitably describe what could happen if confidence in the nation-state were lacking. Community-mindedness has been included as a state-of-being associable with S-order to coun-terpoint isolation, which was considered by Aristotle to be contrary to the notion of 'social animal,' or 'sociability' as the general state-of-being might be called. Justness is the last of the states-of-being included under S-order. The term is intended to describe the state-of-being of a just person, i.e. one who is concerned with justice, but it is also associable with E-order: it has both a social dimension and a eudaimonic one, plus a normative one. Its social aspect might be summed up as 'respect for and observance of the law'; its S-disorderly counterpart consists in rejection of the law.

Category of Homosapient Order/Disorder	Relevant Object	Associated State-of-Being: Homosapient Disorder	Contrary Homosapient Orderly Conception
1	2	3	4
Physical (P)	Human Beings	Disunity Dysfunctional	Wholeness Functional integrity
Physical (P)	Human Beings	Ague	Freedom from ague
Social (S)	Human Beings	Disrespectfulness Rejection of law, riotousness Insecurity, cynicism Isolation Lawlessness	Respectfulness Obedience to law Confidence in state Community-mindedness Justness
Social (S)	Human Beings within Social Entities	Riotous Unjust Arbitrary, unlawful	Peaceful Just Lawful
Eudaimonic (E)	Human Beings	Disunity Disbelief, mistrust, cynicism Vulgarity, tastelessness	Wholeness Truth seeking Aesthetically vibrant
Normative (N)	Human Beings	Selfishness Hopelessness, meaninglessness	Other-directedness Justness, Humaneness Self-respect

Table 1: Homosapient Order as States-of Being of Physical Objects and Social Entities

To this point I have been discussing S-disorder from the perspective of individual members of a social entity, but the notion of S-disorder is also applicable to social entities themselves. Expressions such as 'just society', or, to use an expression from Rawls, 'fair society', are common enough— as are their opposites. Similarly for some of the other S-disorderly states-of-being that have been mentioned: for example lawlessness, arbitrariness and riotousness, which have obvious S-orderly counterparts in lawfulness and peacefulness. All of the S-disorderly and S-orderly states of being that have been mentioned would both derive from and influence the people that comprise the social entities in question.

E-disorder and N-disorder will be discussed together; their effects overlap. The first state-of-being listed in the table is disintegration, where the world is felt to be falling apart.[8] Its converse manifests as wholeness, which is one of Maslow's B-Values. A feeling is a state-of-being, just like ague is. I have suggested that E-order is attainable by means of intellectual achievement. In the table, intellectual achievement is reflected in 'truth-seeking', which is another of Maslow's B-Values— disbelief, mistrust and cynicism are the corresponding metapathologies, and are states-of-being associable with E-disorder. Next we have aesthetic vibrancy, which is another means of attaining E-order. Vulgarity and tastelessness are the corresponding E-disorderly states-of-being. N-disorderliness is characterised by selfishness, which is contrary to other-directedness. Other-directedness is described by Finnis as an element of justice, and is an apt cognomen for generosity of spirit, or good-spiritedness, the latter being a literal rendering of 'eudaimonia'. The ideas are based on those of Aristotle and Maslow. Similarly, justness as a state of personal character, as distinct from justness in an S-orderly (juridical) sense, is also opposed to selfishness, which can be understood as the hallmark of the Aristotelian self-sufficient 'god or beast'; i.e., a person who feels no need for anyone else's involvement in his or her life. Finally, there are the contraries 'hopelessness' and 'self-respect'. Self-*dis*respect may arise from thwarted expectations, the upshot of which could be a sense of hopelessness, or meaninglessness, and a feeling that there is

---

8 *The Farther Reaches of Human Nature*, p. 308.

nothing to work or live for.[9] All of the E-disorderly and N-disorderly
conditions that have been mentioned point towards a need for homosapient order, and are clearly states-of-being that can be experienced by
individual human beings.

This completes the argument for the reality of homosapient disorder.
P-, S-, E, and N-disorder have all been found to consist in states-of-
being of human beings and social entities composed of human beings,
in which case each of them may reasonably be claimed to be Q-R real.
While an exhaustive list of states-of-being would be very hard (if not
impossible) to compile, the one presented may be enough to justify the
claim. Since the four kinds of disorder combine to form homosapient
disorder, homosapient disorder can also be considered real.

Homosapient Order and Ontological Commitment

The reality of homosapient disorder is an unpleasant aspect of the
human condition. Homosapient disorder is a state-of-being that we
attempt to ameliorate, by means of behaviour designed to satisfy the various Maslovian needs. The purpose of such behaviour is to get as close
as possible to a state of homosapient order. States of perfect homosapient
order are probably unattainable, but that need not prevent us from believing in homosapient order *per se*, even to the extent of being ontologically
committed to it, i.e. committed to its existence. An ontological commitment in respect of an object is formed within a cluster of beliefs that is
such that the existence of the object makes good sense—it 'fits' so nicely
that one is prepared to become rationally committed to it.[10] Whether
the ideas on needs, harm, order and morality that have been presented in this book are sufficient to justify an ontological commitment to
homosapient order, I leave to you to determine. My own position on the
matter should be clear enough.

By virtue of the ontological commitment, homosapient order
becomes an operative reality. By 'operative reality' I mean something

9 The idea is Maslow's. See *The Farther Reaches of Human Nature*, p. 309.
10 Based on Thomas Hofweber, 'Logic and Ontology', *The Stanford Encyclopedia of Philosophy* (*Summer
2012 Edition*), Edward N. Zalta (ed.), URL=http://plato.stanford.edu/archives/sum2012/entries/logic-on-
tology/, p. 9 (accessed 12 November 2012).

that is unified and real in the sense that it operates within nature so as to cause certain things to happen (because of our commitment to it). That it is operative in the indicated manner was the subject of Chapter 12, where homosapient order was linked to the basic needs of human beings (basic needs cause us to behave in certain ways, including ways that are the subject of moral judgement). Even Spinoza might have conceded as much: a few pages ago there was mention of his having spoken about the human predilection for order, and about order as something fabricated by our imagination. On that basis, the reality of the concept of order would at least have to be acknowledged, as would the fact that it causes us to do certain things—in Spinoza's case, the reality of the concept of order causes us to imagine orderly states of affairs that are external to us.

Something that is operatively real may be thought of *as if* it were real, even while its precise ontological status remains unresolved. More strongly, the philosopher J. J. C. Smart (1920-2012) held that if things happen in the world *as if* a particular object exists, then the best explanation of those happenings is that the object does in fact exist.[11] Human beings are of the world, and we behave as if it were possible to bring order into existence, by counteracting disorder. Disorder gives rise to the need for order, and the need for order (including homosapient order) finds expression in the various Maslovian needs. On the one hand, needs, and therefore disorder, are experientially real; on the other hand, order (including homosapient order) is an operative *as if* reality, something to which an ontological commitment may be made.

It is hard to imagine how there ever could be a world totally free of disorder. Physically, we know, this is impossible, because of the operation of the Second Law of thermodynamics. The phenomenal world will always be characterised by degrees of disorder, including homosapient disorder for as long as we are around. A continuum of homosapient disorder is conceivable, with homosapient order as one of the extremes and maximum homosapient disorder as the other. Neither extreme would be attainable by a living being: maximum homosapient disorder would entail death; maximum order would be prevented by the Second Law.

---

11 See Ellis, p. 25.

Disorder avoidance (including avoidance of homosapient disorder) is foundational in so far as human existence depends on it. Since order follows upon disorder avoidance, order (including homosapient order) may also be considered foundational. Disorder avoidance (and therefore order-attainment) is necessary to human existence, and therefore also to the existence of morality. Whether it is also sufficient for morality is the point at issue. The present argument can be regarded as an attempt to show that it is.

The Need for Homosapient Order as Ground for Morality

What I am proposing is this: as something that is real, homosapient disorder constitutes philosophical ground on which a secular morality can be based. But now it might be asked: in what sense could a state-of-being be said to be the ground of anything? The being itself would appear to be ontologically prior to its state—the being always comes first. The objection has force, but I think it can be met by looking behind the state, with a view to discovering its cause—for example, the ague virus, and the electoral laws and processes that bring a president-elect into being. So we now have a 'cause-of-state' to consider—whereupon another question would probably arise: what was the cause of the cause-of-state? An infinite regress looms.

The regress can be brought to a halt in the *need* for homosapient order. The need for homosapient order is generated by the experienced reality of homosapient disorder in conjunction with the operative, *as if* reality of homosapient order. The fact of the disorder and the idea that the disorder might be ameliorated give rise to the need to move from the disorderly state-of-being to a more orderly state-of-being. We need homosapient order in order to survive and to flourish. If homosapient order is deficient in any way (for example, due to insufficient food), then we would in normal circumstances seek to redress the deficit—i.e., satisfy the need. But now the objector would most likely ask: how, in principle, does the need for homosapient order differ from homosapient order itself? Aren't both of them states-of-being in which people might

find themselves? Furthermore, the objector might warn us against looking behind the need to find its cause, since that would only give rise to
the same kind of regress. Again, the objection has force. What is the cause
of the need? How might this new regress be terminated?

It can be terminated by distinguishing between two senses of the term
'need'. On the one hand, need in the sense of requiring something to
redress a deficit ('lack' for short); on the other hand, need in the sense of
being necessarily so, or 'could not have been otherwise' ('necessary' for
short). A person trapped in a desert might lack the water that would keep
him alive. Metaphysically-speaking, this would be regarded as a contingent event, and his thirsty state-of-being a contingent phenomenon.
Matters could have been different; for example, if he had decided on a
skiing holiday on Mount Kosciusko instead of trekking through central
Australia. However, for the same person, or any person for that matter, an
adequate supply of water would always be a necessity, regardless of his or
her circumstances. Metaphysically, this would be considered a physically
necessary phenomenon: it is a permanent state-of-being, one that is fully
coincident with each and every individual. Metaphysically, each individual is a contingent being, since there is no compulsion for anyone to be
born; but as soon as birth occurs, an adequate supply of water becomes
necessary; it could not be otherwise. Need as lack may be transitory, but
that which is necessary persists as long as life lasts.

Viewed as a necessary need, the need for homosapient order is an
essential property of humanness; in other words, it is a permanent state-
of-being for each and every human being. Need as lack derives from
need as necessary. If something is necessary, then it would be lacked if it
were not obtained; but the reverse does not apply. Just because we lack
something (immense wealth, beautiful body, Einsteinian intellect, etc.)
does not mean that it is necessary. Homosapient order has been shown to
be 'necessarily' needed by human beings; it is an ineradicable feature of
the human condition. In which case, the problem of priority dissolves. In
virtue of being coincident with *Homo sapiens*, the need for homosapient
order is neither prior nor posterior. The need for homosapient order is a
fundamental state-of-being that is uniquely human. It therefore satisfies
the requirements of the philosophical ground I am looking for.

Chapter 14: Concluding Remarks

What if I do not care to abide by the norms that are usually associable with goodness?

Scepticism and Rules of Moral Conduct

Philippa Foot was seen a while back contemplating the possibility of scepticism with regard to morality. The doubter's question was the one posed in the epigraph, where goodness itself appears to be under attack. The question is a form of what Philip Kitcher refers to as the 'sceptical challenge.'[1] Now, if the question, or challenge, reflects indifference to the pain and suffering of others, then I would say that we would probably be dealing with something bordering on cynicism rather than scepticism; and the cynic would probably remain cynical, regardless of how one responded. If, on the other hand, the question reflects a sincere quest for understanding of what morality is about, then addressing it may well help clarify one's own position at the same time as (possibly) assuaging the sceptic's doubts. In dealing with the challenge, we would probably have to explain, or try to explain, what moral rules are about, including how they become established.

Moral rule-setting is concerned with promoting certain kinds of behaviour and proscribing other kinds of behaviour. It is a matter of that which is permissible and that which is impermissible. But where should we start—with the permissible, or with the impermissible? Although permissibility would simply seem to be the obverse of impermissibility—opposite sides of the same coin—problems arise if it is understood to mean 'that which is best done'. How might we decide that the best way of doing right has been found, if that in fact is what we are looking for? Must we always search for the optimal course of action? Perhaps we should instead try to find one that precludes harm from being done to others, or if harm seems unavoidable, of identifying a way of mitigating it.

---

1 Kitcher, p. 279.

Having decided on a tolerable (i.e., not intolerable) course of action, we should go ahead and do it. The search for the best could prove endless. To circumvent the difficulties and enable us to bring the search to an end, we could try a negative approach, in the same way that good was defined by Aquinas (and endorsed by Foot) as that which is not evil. Negatively, then, we could say that anything that is not impermissible is permissible. But specification of the impermissible (and therefore permissible) might not be easy. Even something seemingly as straightforward as 'I must not kill' is fraught with difficulties, as we will now see.

Most of us generally prefer that things not be killed. We try not to think about where our ham and veal come from, and we chase the cat away if we see it stalking a bird. Some people carry the tendency to extremes, for example Jain monks in India, who wear face-masks to avoid destroying microbes through inhalation. But there is a deep irony in our reluctance to kill, because all animal life, ours included, depends on death. We rely for our existence on the death of organisms below us on the food chain—similarly for every other link in the chain apart from most kinds of flora. To require the death of at least some organisms is natural to us. Why, then, do we shoo the cat away? After all, it is only acting in accordance with its nature. I suspect the answer might have something to do with the fact that we may be the only kinds of creatures with an awareness of the death that awaits us. The philosopher Susanne K. Langer (1895-1985) observed that such knowledge constitutes a major difference between us and other animals. Although non–human animals certainly seek to avoid death, they seem to be unaware of its inevitability.[2] Knowledge along those lines could reinforce the repugnance that the thought of death usually evokes in us, and avoidance of being reminded of it by witnessing acts of killing. It might even prompt us to prevent the destruction of other beings, wherever practicable. As well as that, we could set about frustrating the cat in its endeavours because of a feeling or belief that pain-prevention is more important than pleasure-attainment. That would be consistent with the Aquinas/ Foot position on the negative definition of good—the bird's potential pain carries more weight for us than the cat's pleasure.

---

2 Susanne K. Langer, *Philosophical Sketches* (Baltimore: The Johns Hopkins Press, 1962), p. 115.

Notwithstanding the difficulties involved in rule-setting, a humane person will understand that some things are wrong and will avoid doing them. Humane prescriptions typically serve as rules of conduct, as formulated by people of good character. Humane rules recognise the rights of others, such as those specified in the Universal Declaration of Human Rights (UDHR); they are grounded in our basic needs, the need for homosapient order being the most basic of all. Whence the call for the minimisation of harm that is encapsulated in the PHM. Humaneness of character answers the question of virtue ethics, 'what kind of person should I be?' Humane rules issuing from a humane character answer the deontologist question, 'what ought to be done?' The two questions, and the responses to them, are clearly interdependent.

Ideally, moral rules and an ethos of care will find themselves enshrined in law. But the relationship between morality and law is by no means straightforward. A few words on that vexed issue bring the book to an end.

Morality and Law

We saw earlier that many countries have enacted bills of rights based on the UDHR. Since rights are closely associable with moral prescriptions, law and morality would be similarly associable, at least in principle. Laws come with reasons for acting (or not acting) in certain ways. 'That is what the law stipulates', we might say—we understand that transgressions, if detected, will be punished. Morality is also concerned with understanding reasons for acting (or not acting) in certain ways; but moral transgressions will always be detectable—by agents themselves (provided they are competent), even if no-one else learns of them. Therefore, for competent agents, moral transgressions will always be subject to 'punishment', perhaps in the form of guilt, shame, or remorse. If others become aware of a transgression, then repugnance, repudiation and denouncement may also follow. Moral transgressions would be understood to consist in the violation of the needs of others, culminating in harm.

Understanding that that is the case would provide humane people with rational justification for acting in a morally tolerable manner.

Most people would probably agree that blind obedience to an unjust law would rarely if ever constitute an adequate excuse for inhumane behaviour. If the dictates of law are inconsistent with PHM-based moral prescriptions, then principled consideration would weigh in favour of the latter. In other words, for a moral person, moral law would always trump juridical law, in the determination of right and wrong. Those who engage in behaviour that is sanctioned by statute but condemnable under moral law would typically invoke the 'I was only following orders' line of argument, a variety of which might be called 'the executioner's excuse'. In jurisdictions that sanction capital punishment, executioners practise their unpleasant trade within the full ambit of the law. But 'I was only following orders' would not wash where the laws concerned are patently unjust.

We saw earlier some instances of the close fit between morality and juridical law in respect of conspiracy and attempted crime. But morality and law don't always coincide. Divergences are common, especially where discriminatory practices are unconstrained by law. History is replete with examples, including recent history. To outline just a few, the confiscatory rules that targeted Jewish property in Weimar Germany; property and educational criteria resulting in widespread disenfranchisement in virtually every country, in the early stages of democracy; and, most glaringly, Apartheid in South Africa. Discriminatory laws play favourites by excluding some groups of people from the full range of rights enjoyed by other groups. Discriminatory grouping commonly occurs along ethnic, property, or religious lines.

Spinoza's life offers an example of religious discrimination. The philosopher's pantheistic views eventually brought the wrath of the Jewish establishment down on him. He was excommunicated, thereby cutting him off from family and friends. Was the punishment justifiable? Jewish law would answer in the affirmative, but the terms and consequences of the sentence (isolation, impoverishment) were arguably extreme, and perhaps not warranted by the 'crime' of propounding an unorthodox theory. If similar circumstances were to occur today, reference could be made to UDHR Article nos. 18 and 19, which entitle people to freedom of thought and opinion, and to expression thereof. Orthodoxy could argue that excommunication denies neither of these freedoms, but it would be hard pressed to demonstrate that banishment from kin and kith was consistent with Article no. 16, where the family is set down as 'the natural and fundamental group unit of society.'

A more contentious case of divergence of morality from law concerns the 'custom of the sea'. According to the custom, shipwrecked sailors faced with starvation choose to offer themselves as food for their crewmates, and the person to be killed and eaten is selected by drawing lots (as is the person who must do the killing). Perhaps the most famous instance is one that involved the ship *Essex*, which sank after being rammed by a whale early in the nineteenth century. The incident served as inspiration for Herman Melville's novel *Moby-Dick* (1851). The *Essex's* crew took to whaleboats in an attempt to reach land, many thousands of kilometres away. After several weeks and in dire straits, the men in one of the boats chose to exercise the custom of the sea. A young man was consequently killed and eaten. (Another who later died of natural causes also served as food for the survivors.) By choosing to abide by the custom, at the risk of their lives and the possibility of having to do something they would normally find abhorrent, sailors effectively forfeit their own needs for the sake of others. The willingness shown by some people to make the supreme sacrifice suggests that the need for humane assimilation of others' needs can run very deep indeed. Nevertheless, the killing would fail the PHM's non-vindicated harm test, which asks whether the action is harmful without being intended to prevent the person being harmed from doing or suffering harm. Only a contorted (and unacceptable) line of reasoning could hold that the person who is killed would have being doing harm were he to remain alive. But the *Essex* incident passed without legal prosecution, let alone condemnation.

Matters were different for the men involved in another nineteenth century shipwreck, that of the *Mignonette*. The crew of one of its lifeboats chose to kill man who, after falling ill, had lapsed into unconsciousness. Whereas the actions of the *Essex* men were based on the acquiescence of all involved, those of the *Mignonette* were not. After they were rescued, the *Mignonette* perpetrators were found guilty of murder and received life sentences. The dire circumstances were deemed insufficient justification for what they did. Interestingly, however, the sentences were subsequently commuted to six months imprisonment. The legal outcome therefore ended up being very similar to that of the *Essex*. Whether the ultimate leniency was justified would depend on a full review of the circumstances, and will not be pursued here. While the custom of the sea is admittedly fraught, that of the executioner is straightforward. Capital punishment conflicts with the tenets of humaneness, as encoded in UDHR Articles, no. 3 and no. 5; these, we have seen, proclaim the right to life and denounce inhumane and degrading punishment.

Conclusion

All species of living things are characterised by a particular set of basic needs, and what they need are the things that by nature they must have in order to survive, to replicate, and, for some species, to live well. Such things comprise the basic goods pertaining to the species, and organisms suffer harm when their need for the relevant basic goods goes unsatisfied. The basic goods of humankind correspond to the suite of basic human needs delineated by Abraham Maslow, all of which converge in our underlying need for homosapient order. Any morally significant harm that we suffer will be in respect of our need for homosapient order. Since that is the same need in which morality can be grounded, matters might be generalised as follows:

That in respect of which we can be harmed is that in which morality can be grounded.

Which brings us pretty much back to where we began—with Socrates' identification of harm with wrong (see epigraph to Chapter 1). The scope of the generalisation could be broadened to accommodate other living beings, simply by expanding the locus of harm from 'the need for homosapient order' to 'the need for living order'.

The need for self-actualisation is one of the components of the need for homosapient order. And, as part of the need for self-actualisation, there will be the need to express our particular moral proclivities. Broadly speaking, one's moral proclivities will tend towards either benignancy or malignancy; that is to say, towards either humaneness or inhumaneness. Humane human beings generally strive to avoid doing harm: they would likely be willing adopters of the PHM. Inhumane persons have no qualms about doing harm. Arguably, there are more humane people on Earth than inhumane ones, perhaps by a significant margin: some of our most profound thinkers have believed that to be the case. We might take heart from that. But it does not follow from the majority in numbers that there must be more goodness in the world than there is evil; i.e. good in the form of harmlessness, evil in the form of harm-doing that is contrary to the PHM. For it is clear from simple observation of what goes on around us that immense harm can be inflicted by very small numbers of persons. Only time will tell whether the cumulative good stemming from countless everyday humane interactions will suffice to overwhelm evil. Nevertheless, if humane (i.e. Maslovian) self-actualisation is indeed the norm, as has been argued in this book, then there could be hope for us.

Appendix: The Naturalistic Fallacy

In the discussion of homosapient order in Chapter 11, I mentioned that any possibility of a connection between physical order and normative order would almost certainly be dismissed by some people on the grounds of naturalistic fallaciousness. The order-based theory of morality could stand or fall depending on whether it is capable of fending off the challenge, so let's see whether it can. At least two versions of the naturalistic fallacy are discernible. One stems from Hume's ideas and the other from those of G. E. Moore. Respectively, the two kinds may be described as *logical* and *metaphysical*.

Hume was troubled by what he saw as slippage between factual premises and ethical conclusions in some philosophical arguments, i.e., slippage between *is* and *ought*.[1] Philip Kitcher refers to this as 'Hume's Challenge'.[2] Example (mine): Cruelty is painful; therefore one ought not to be cruel. One way of solving the problem (if it is indeed a problem) would be to begin with an ethical premise. Example: People ought to be able to live their lives without being subjected to cruelty; therefore .... The inference becomes logically satisfactory, and the problem is shifted to justification of the premise—why shouldn't people be subjected to cruelty? Kant would have an answer to that. For someone to say that cruelty is acceptable, he or she would have to accept that they might rightfully be subjected to cruelty. Since that would be unlikely, the principle would be contrary to universalisation in the form of a Categorical Imperative. The order-based theory also has an answer. Cruelty is contrary to some of our most basic needs, including homeostasis, safety and respect; in short, it is harmful.

Another way of dealing with Hume's challenge would be to break down the distinction between fact and value. Needs are factual—they are real by virtue of the contribution they make to states-of-being of those who have them. While right and wrong are incontestably value-terms, morally relevant values are based on morally relevant needs,

---

1 See Hume, *Treatise* 3.1.1.
2 Kitcher, §40.

from which it follows that such values are also facts. Order consists in bodily and psychological states that are described in terms of orderliness and disorderliness. Such descriptions have objective reference, and they carry with them ascriptions of value. Order and legality are right, i.e. good in a morally relevant sense of right; conversely for disorder and dirtiness—whereupon ought and is become reciprocally influential with respect to one another. Bias or prejudice would almost inevitably infiltrate the ascriptions, so it could not be said that they are objective in the sense of 'free from bias'; but they could nevertheless attain objectivity in another sense, i.e., as things accessible to cognition—as such, they become capable of contributing to the content of our consciousness. By so doing, the values themselves become facts, and are inextricably entwined with other facts. The logical problem perceived by Hume is thereby dissolved.

Turning now to Moore's challenge, which I have labelled 'metaphysical', a naturalistic fallacy is said to occur when an ethical concept (right, wrong, good, etc.) is directly derived from a natural concept (for example order). Even if morality can be shown to be related in some way, perhaps analogically, to order, would it follow that a biological and psychological phenomenon such as our need for (homosapient) order helps form the basis of a universal moral principle? That would require a very big leap—an unnecessary if not impossible one in Moore's view. As he saw matters, ethics is primarily concerned with giving reasons for believing that certain things are good.[3] Moore's fundamental position was that good is a 'simple' concept that is impervious to reduction to non-moral concepts. By seeking to explain morality in terms of order and needs, my project is clearly at odds with Moore. How might the objection be met?

The first thing to note is that 'good' for Moore is something that is entirely natural. It occurs within the ambit of nature, and is attached as an epithet to things that are considered or felt to be good—things such as food, love and music. It is the task of philosophy, Moore says, to explain why such things are good. This seems to conflict quite strongly with the order-based theory, according to which moral right derives from (is

---

3 G. E. Moore, 'Principia Ethica, chapter 1', in David E. Cooper (editor): *Ethics: The Classic Readings* (Oxford: Blackwell Publishing Ltd., 2003 [first published 1998]), p. 234.

caused by, and therefore explained by) the non-deleterious effect that morally classifiable behaviour has on our need for homosapient order. But the conflict may be only superficial. For it is clear that homosapient order is a consequence of such things as food, love and music; or, more precisely, consequential upon satisfaction of our need for them. In other words, homosapient order is good because it encompasses all of the things that are likely to be regarded as good, for the simple reason that it is consequential upon satisfaction of our basic needs, which is of fundamental value to us. Finally, homosapient order is a good that is natural to the same extent that human beings are natural, which is to say fully natural.

By their very nature, accounts of morality such as the order-based theory are destined to fall foul of Moore's idea. But a theory that satisfactorily explains the origins and nature of morality could lead one to wonder whether the naturalistic fallacy might itself be fallacious. As well as dealing with origins, any such theory would also have to provide rational justification for engaging in moral behaviour, and for a theory to be satisfactory in all of these respects it would at least have to be coherent. I think the order-based theory measures up satisfactorily in that regard. As well as coherence, however, the theory would have to be based on sound principles and formed from valid propositions. To my mind the principle of homosapient order is patently sound—we would simply not exist without some degree of homosapient order. The propositions that I have put forward are also reasonably defensible. Human beings have been shown to have a need for homosapient order, that the need for homosapient order finds expression in the various human needs identified by Maslow, and moral right and wrong can be explained in terms of homosapient order. The foregoing propositions constitute the basis of the explanatory or descriptive part of the theory. In addition, I have shown that the need for Maslovian self-actualisation is characterised by the need for humaneness (defined as 'principled consideration'), and that it is rationally justifiable for us to seek satisfaction of our needs. I believe that the order-based theory has the resources to combat accusations of naturalistic fallaciousness.

Implicitly or otherwise, Stephen Jay Gould took up the cudgels on both Hume's and Moore's behalves in his advocacy of the separation of morality from nature. In Gould's view, religion (from which ethics is said by him to derive) and science must be regarded as non-overlapping magisteria (NOMA, for short—magisteria are domains of teaching, based on the Latin word for master, *magister*). NOMA would most likely have been endorsed by Moore. If the two domains are forever kept at arm's length from one another, then moral good could never be held to derive from natural good. Of course I disagree, and Gould himself might not have been entirely consistent on the matter. In his essay 'A Humongous Fungus Amongst Us', in the book *Dinosaur in a Haystack* (1995), he observes that incestuous marriage is commonly subject to legal prohibition and taboos because of the reduction in genetic variability amongst offspring that attends close interbreeding.[4] Since laws and taboos are cultural products and therefore cognate with ethics, Gould's observation would seem to be a very clear instance of *is* giving rise to *ought*, in violation of Hume's injunction.

---

4 Gould, 1997 p. 338.

BIBLIOGRAPHY

Alder, Ken. *The Measure of All Things: The Seven-Year Odyssey that Transformed the World* (London: Abacus, 2004 [first published 2002])

Angier, Natalie. *The Canon* (New York: Houghton Mifflin Company, 2007)

Anscombe G. E. M. *Intention* (Cambridge, Massachusetts: Harvard University Press, 2000 [first published 1957])

Aquinas, Thomas. *The Summa Theologica*, translated by Fathers of the English Dominican Province, revised by Daniel J. Sullivan (Chicago: The University of Chicago, Great Books of the Western World, 1952), Vols. 19-20

Aristotle. *Aristotle: 1* and *Aristotle: 2* (Chicago: The University of Chicago, Great Books of the Western World, 1952), Vols. 8-9

Baier, Kurt. 'Egoism', in Singer (editor): *A Companion to Ethics*

Bate, Jonathan. *The Song of the Earth* (London: Picador, 2000)

Beiser, Frederick. *Hegel* (London: Routledge, 2006)

Benjamin, Walter. *Illuminations: Essays and Reflections,* edited by Hannah Arendt; translated by Harry Zohn (New York: Schocken Books, 1968)

Berlin, Isaiah. *Against the Current: Essays in the History of Ideas*, edited by Henry Hardy, introduced by Roger Hausheer (London: Pimlico, 1997 [first published 1979])

Bohm, David. *Wholeness and the Implicate Order* (London: Routledge Classics, 2002 [first published 1980])

Braybrooke, David. *Meeting Needs* (Princeton: Princeton University Press, 1987)

Brock, Gillian (editor). *Necessary Goods: Our Responsibilities to Meet Others' Needs* (Lanham, Maryland: Rowman & Littlefield Publishers, Inc., 1998)

Brock, Gillian. 'Needs and Global Justice', in Reader (editor): *The Philosophy of Need*

Buckle, Stephen. 'Natural Law', in Singer (editor): *A Companion to Ethics*

Burke, Edmund. See Wolmersley (editor)

Camus, Albert. *The Rebel*, translated by Anthony Bower (Harmondsworth, Middlesex: Penguin Books, 1962 [first published 1951])

Casebeer, William D. *Natural Ethical Facts: Evolution, Connectionism, and Moral Cognition* (Cambridge, Massachusetts: The MIT Press, 2005)

Cassirer, Ernst. *An Essay on Man* (Toronto: Bantam Books, 1970 [first published 1944])

Cervantes, Miguel de. *Don Quixote*

Clark, Thomas W. *Encountering Naturalism: A worldview and its uses* (Cambridge, MA: Center for Naturalism, 2007)

Cohen, Morris R. 'The Metaphysics of Reason and Scientific Method' in Ryder (editor)

Cooper, David E. (editor). *Ethics: The Classic Readings* (Oxford: Blackwell Publishing Ltd., 2003 [first published 1998])

Curley, Edwin (editor and translator). *A Spinoza Reader: The Ethics and Other Works* (Princeton: Princeton University Press, 1994)

Damasio, Antonio. *Self Comes to Mind: Constructing the Conscious Brain* (London: Vintage Books, 2012)

Darwin (Chicago: The University of Chicago, Great Books of the Western World, 1952), Vol. 49

David, Catherine; Lenoir, Frédéric; de Tonnac, Jean-Philippe (editors); Maclean, Ian; Pearson Roger (translators), *Conversations about the End of Time* (London: Allen lane The Penguin Press, 1999)

Davis, Nancy (Ann). 'Contemporary Deontology', in Singer (editor): *A Companion to Ethics*

Dawkins, Richard (editor). *The Oxford Book of Modern Science Writing* (Oxford: Oxford University Press, 2008)

Dawkins, Richard. *The Selfish Gene* (USA: Oxford University Press, 2006 [first published 1976])

De Waal, Frans. *Good Natured: The Origins of Right and Wrong in Humans and Other Animals* (Cambridge, Massachusetts: Harvard University Press, 1996)

Della Rocca, Michael. *Spinoza* (London: Routledge, 2008)

Dennett, Daniel C. *Freedom Evolves* (New York: Viking, 2003)

Dewey, John. *Human Nature and Conduct* (New York: Dover Publications, Inc., 2002 [first published 1922])

Dobzhansky, Theodosius. In Dawkins (editor), *The Oxford Book of Modern Science Writing*

Dupré, John. *Darwin's Legacy: What Evolution Means Today* (New York: Oxford University Press, 2003)

Eco, Umberto. *Signs of the Times*, in David et. Al (editors): *Conversations About the End of Time*

Einstein, Albert. *Religion and Science*, in Dawkins (editor)

Elliot, Robert (editor). *Environmental Ethics* (USA: Oxford University Press, 2004 [first published 1995])

Ellis, Brian. *The Philosophy of Nature: A Guide to the New Essentialism* (Great Britain: Acumen, 2002)

Emmet, Dorothy. *The Nature of Metaphysical Thinking* (Great Britain: Macmillan, 1966 [first published 1945])

Festenstein, Matthew and Thompson, Simon (editors). *Richard Rorty Critical Dialogues* (Great Britain: Polity Press, 2001)

Finnis, John. *Natural Law and Natural Rights* (Oxford, Great Britain: Oxford University Press, 1980)

Flanagan, Owen and Rorty, Amélie Oksenberg (editors). *Identity, Character, and Morality: Essays in Moral Psychology* (Cambridge, Massachusetts: The MIT Press, 1993)

Flanagan, Owen. 'Identity and Strong and Weak Evaluation', in Flanagan and Rorty (editors): *Identity, Character, and Morality: Essays in Moral Psychology*

Foot, Philippa. *Natural Goodness* (Oxford: Oxford University Press, 2010 [first published 2001])

Fortey, Richard. *Life: An Unauthorised Biography* (London: Folio Society, 2008 [first published 1997])

Gaita, Raimond. *After Romulus* (Melbourne: Text Publishing, 2011)

Gibson, Roger F. Jr. (editor). *Quintessence: Basic Readings from the Philosophy of W. V. Quine* (Cambridge, Massachusetts: The Belknap Press of Harvard University Press, 2004)

Gleick, James. *The Information* (London: Fourth Estate, 2012)

Gould, Stephen Jay. *Ever Since Darwin* (New York: W. W. Norton & Company, 1979)

Gould, Stephen Jay. *Hen's Teeth and Horse's Toes* (New York: W. W. Norton & Company, 1983)

Gould, Stephen Jay. *The Flamingo's Smile* (Harmondsworth: Penguin Books, 1986)

Gould, Stephen Jay. *The Lying Stones of Marrakech* (London: Vintage, 2001)

Griffin, James. *On Human Rights* (New York: Oxford University Press, 2001 [first published 2008])

Haack, Susan (editor) with Lane, Robert (associate editor). *Pragmatism Old & New: Selected Writings* (New York: Prometheus Books, 2006)

Hamilton, Edith and Cairns, Huntington (editors). *The Collected Dialogues of Plato*, (Princeton: Princeton University Press, Bollingen Series LXXI, 1999 [first published 1961])

Hanley, Ryan Patrick. 'Rousseau's Virtue Epistemology', in *Journal of the History of Idea* vol. 50 no. 2

Harwood, Gwen. *Nightfall.*

Hilgard, Ernest R., Atkinson, Rita L., Atkinson, Richard C. *Introduction to Psychology* (New York: Harcourt Brace Jovanovich, Inc., 1979 [first published 1953])

Hobbes, Thomas. *Leviathan* (Chicago: The University of Chicago, Great Books of the Western World, 1952), Vol. 23

Hofweber, Thomas. 'Logic and Ontology', *The Stanford Encyclopedia of Philosophy* (*Summer 2012 Edition*), Edward N. Zalta (ed.), URL=http://plato.stanford.edu/archives/ sum2012/entries/logic-ontology/

Holland, John H. *Hidden Order: How Adaptation Builds Complexity* (New York: Basic Books, 1995)

http://dictionary.reference.com

http://en.wikipedia.com

http://sprott.physics.wisc.edu/pickover/good.html

http://villains.wikia.com/wiki/Category: Evil_Genius

Hume, David. *A Treatise of Human Nature* (London: Penguin Books, 1984 [first published 1739 and 1740])

http://www-philosophy.ucdavis.edu/mattey/phi001/platelec.htm

Inwood, Brad and Gerson, L. P. (translators and editors). *The Epicurus Reader* (Indianapolis: Hackett Publishing Company, Inc., 1994)

James, William. 'The Moral Philosopher and the Moral Life', in Haack (editor) and Lane (associate editor), *Pragmatism Old & New: Selected Writings*

James, William. *The Varieties of Religious Experience: A Study in Human Nature* (London: Folio Society, 2008 [first published 1902])

Journal of the History of Philosophy Vol. 50, no. 2 (Baltimore: The Johns Hopkins University Press, 2012)

Journal of the History of Philosophy Vol. 52, no. 4 (Baltimore: The Johns Hopkins University Press, 2014)

Kafka, Franz. *In the Penal Settlement: Tales and Short Prose Works*, translated by Willa and Edwin Muir (London: Secker and Warburg, 1949)

Kant (Chicago: The University of Chicago, Great Books of the Western World, 1952), Vol. 42

Kant, Immanuel. *Religion within the Limits of Reason Alone*, translated and introduced by Theodore M. Greene and Hoyt H. Hudson (New York: Harper & Row, 1960 [translation first published 1934])

Kauffman, Stuart A. *The Origins of Order: Self-Organization and Selection in Evolution* (New York: Oxford University Press, 1993)

Kenny, Anthony (editor). *The Oxford History of Western Philosophy* (Oxford: Oxford University Press, 1994)

Kitcher, Philip. *The Ethical Project* (Cambridge, Massachusetts: Harvard University Press, 2011)

Kolb, David A., Rubin, Irwin M., McIntyre, James M. (editors). *Organizational Psychology: A Book of Readings* (Edgewood Cliffs, New Jersey: Prentice-Hall, 1974)

Krieger, Martin H. *Doing Physics: How Physicists Take Hold of the World* (Indiana: Indiana University Press, Second Edition 2012)

Langer, Susanne K. *Philosophical Sketches* (Baltimore: The Johns Hopkins Press, 1962)

Lao Tzu. *Tao Te Ching*, translated by Gia-Fu Feng and Jane English (New York: Vintage Books, 1972)

Leopold, Aldo. *A Sand County Almanac: With Essays on Conservation from Round River* (New York: Ballantine Books, 1970 [*A Sand County Almanac* first published 1949, *Round River* first published 1953])

Levi, Primo. *The Periodic Table*, translated by Raymond Rosenthal (Melbourne: Penguin Books, 2010 [first published 1975])

Lin Yutang (translator and editor). *The Wisdom of Confucius* (New York: The Modern Library, 1966 [edition first published 1938])

Lind, Marcia. 'Hume and Moral Emotions', in Flanagan and Rorty (editors): *Identity, Character, and Morality: Essays in Moral Psychology*

Livio, Mario. *The Equation That Couldn't Be Solved: How Mathematical Genius Discovered the Language of Symmetry* (New York: Simon & Schuster, 2006)

Livio, Mario. *The Golden Ratio: The Story of Phi, the Extraordinary Number of Nature, Art and Beauty* (London: Review, 2003)

Mackie, J. L. *Ethics: Inventing Right and Wrong* (London: Penguin Books, 1990 [first published 1977])

Mandela, Nelson. *Conversations with Myself* (Sydney: Macmillan, 2013 [first published 2010])

Marcus Aurelius, *Meditations*, translated by George Long (Chicago: The University of Chicago, Great Books of the Western World, 1952), Vol. 12

Maslow, Abraham H. 'A Theory of Human Motivation', in *Psychological Review* Vol. 50(4), July 1943

Maslow, Abraham H. *The Farther Reaches of Human Nature* (New York: Penguin, 1993 [first published 1971])

Mayr, Ernst. *What Makes Biology Unique?* (New York: Cambridge University Press, 2004)

McClelland, David C. 'The Two Faces of Power', in Kolb, Rubin, McIntyre: *Organizational Psychology: A Book of Readings*

Midgley, Mary. *Beast and Man: The Roots of Human Nature* (London, Routledge, 2002 [first published 1979])

Midgley, Mary. 'Duties Concerning Islands', in Elliot (editor): *Environmental Ethics*

Mill, J. S. in Stillinger (editor)

Mill, John Stuart. *Utilitarianism, Liberty and Representative Government* (London: J. M. Dent & Sons, Everyman's Library, 1971)

Milton, John. *Paradise Lost*

Mitchell, Sandra D. *Biological Complexity and Integrative Pluralism* (New York: Cambridge University Press, 2003)

Moore, G. E. 'Principia Ethica, chapter 1', in Cooper (editor): *Ethics: The Classic Readings*

Muelder Eaton, Marcia. *Basic Issues in Aesthetics* (Belmont, California: Wadsworth Publishing Company, 1988)

Nadler, Stephen. *A Book Forged in Hell* (Princeton: Princeton University Press, 2011)

Nadler, Stephen. *The Best of All Possible Worlds: A Story of Philosophers, God, and Evil in the Age of Reason* (Princeton: Princeton University Press, 2010)

Nahm, Milton C. (editor). *Selections from Early Greek Philosophy* (USA: Appleton-Century-Crofts, 1947)

Newton, K. M. (editor). *Twentieth-Century Literary Theory: A Reader* (London: Macmillan, 1988)

Nietzsche, Friedrich. *The Gay Science*, translated by Walter Kaufman (New York: Vintage Books, 1974)

Nietzsche, Friedrich. *The Philosophy of Nietzsche* (New York: The Modern Library, 1927)

Nietzsche, Friedrich. *The Will to Power, translated by Walter Kaufmann and R. J. Hollingdale, edited by Walter Kaufmann* (New York: Vintage Books, 1968)

Nozick, Robert. *Philosophical Explanations* (Cambridge, Massachusetts: Harvard University Press, 1994 [first published 1981])

Nussbaum, Martha. 'Aristotelian Social Democracy', in Brock (editor): *Necessary Goods: Our Responsibilities to Meet Others' Needs*

O'Neill, Onora. 'Rights, Obligations, and Needs', in Brock (editor): *Necessary Goods: Our Responsibilities to Meet Others' Needs*

Orwell, George. *Essays* (London: Penguin Books, 2000)

Parfit, Derek. *Reasons and Persons* (Oxford: Clarendon Press, 1987 [first published 1984])

Pascal, Blaise. *Pensées*, translated by W. F. Trotter (London: J. M. Dent & Sons, 1940)

Passmore, John. 'Attitudes to Nature', in Elliot (editor)

Penrose, Roger. *Shadows of the Mind: A Search for the Missing Science of Consciousness* (Reading: Vintage, 1995)

Pinker, Steven. *How the Mind Works* (New York: W. W. Norton & Company, 1997)

Pinker, Steven. *The Blank Slate: The Modern Denial of Human Nature* (New York: Viking, 2002)

Pirsig, Robert M. *Zen and the Art of Motorcycle Maintenance: An Inquiry into Values* (Great Britain: Vintage, 1999 [first published 1974])

Plato. 'The Dialogues of Plato' translated by Benjamin Jowett and 'The Seventh Letter' translated by J. Harward (Chicago: The University of Chicago, Great Books of the Western World, 1952), Vol. 7

Pope, Alexander. *An Essay on Man*

Pope, Stephen J. *The Evolution of Altruism & The Ordering of Love* (Washington DC: Georgetown University Press, 1994)

Psychological Review, Vol. 50(4), July 1943

Putnam, Ruth Anna. 'The Moral Life of a Pragmatist', in Flanagan and Rorty (editors): *Identity, Character, and Morality: Essays in Moral Psychology*

Quine, W. V. In Gibson (editor): *Quintessence: Basic Readings from the Philosophy of W. V. Quine*

Rawls, John. *Lectures on the History of Moral Philosophy* (Cambridge, Massachusetts: Harvard University Press, 2000)

Rawls, John. *A Theory of Justice* (Cambridge, Massachusetts: Harvard University Press, revised edition 1999 [first published 1971])

Reader, Soran (editor). *The Philosophy of Need* (Cambridge: Cambridge University Press, 2005)

Richards, I. A. 'Poetry and Belief,' in Newton (editor)

Ridley, Matt. *Genome: The Autobiography of a Species in 23 Chapters* (London: Fourth Estate, 2000)

Rorty, Amélie. 'Spinoza on the Pathos of Idolatrous Love', in Solomon and Higgins (editors): *The Philosophy of (Erotic) Love*

Rorty, Richard. *Contingency, irony, and solidarity* (New York: Cambridge University Press, 1999 [first published 1989])

Rose, Steven. *Lifelines: Life Beyond the Gene* (London: Vintage, 2005 [first published 1997])

Ruse, Michael. *Darwin and Design: Does evolution have a purpose?* (Cambridge Massachusetts: Harvard University Press, 2003)

Ryder, John (editor). *American Philosophical Naturalism in the Twentieth Century* (New York: Prometheus Books, 1994)

Schrödinger, Erwin. *What is Life?* (London: The Folio Society, 2000 [first published 1944])

Scruton, Roger. *Green Philosophy: How to Think Seriously About the Planet* (London: Atlantic Books, 2012)

Setiya, Kieran. "Intention", *The Stanford Encyclopedia of Philosophy (Spring 2011 Edition)*, Edward N. Zalta (ed.), URL=<http://plato.stanford.edu/archives/spr2011/entries/intention/>

Sharp, Hasana. 'Eve's Perfection: Spinoza on Sexual (In) Equality', *Journal of the History of Philosophy* Vol. 50, no. 4

Sider, Theodore. *Four Dimensionalism: An Ontology of Persistence and Time* (New York: Clarendon Press, 2003 [first published 2001])

Singer, Peter (editor). *A Companion to Ethics* (Cornwall, United Kingdom: Blackwell, 2003 [first published 1991])

Smith, Bernard. *The Antipodean Manifesto: Essays in Art and History* (Melbourne: Oxford University Press, 1976)

Smolin, Lee. *The Life of the Cosmos* (New York: Oxford University Press, 1997)

Solomon, Robert C. and Higgins, Kathleen M. (editors). *The Philosophy of (Erotic) Love* (Lawrence, Kansas: University Press of Kansas, 1991)

Southwood, Richard. *The Story of Life* (Oxford: Oxford University Press, 2007 [first published 2003])

Spade, Paul Vincent. 'Medieval Philosophy', in Kenny (editor): *The Oxford History of Western Philosophy*

Spariosu, Mihai I. *Dionysus Reborn: Play and the Aesthetic Dimension in Modern Philosophical and Scientific Discourse* (Ithaca: Cornell University Press, 1989)

Spinoza, Benedict de. *Theological-Political Treatise*, edited by Jonathan Israel, translated by Michael Silverthorne and Jonathan Israel (Cambridge, United Kingdom: Cambridge University Press, 2014 [first published 2007])

Spinoza, Benedict de. 'The Ethics', in Curley (editor and translator): *A Spinoza Reader: The Ethics and Other Works*

Stevens, Wallace. *Thirteen Ways of Looking at a Blackbird*

Stillinger, Jack (editor). *Mill Autobiography* (London: Oxford University Press, 1971)

The Age (Melbourne), 15 January 2010, 19 May 2010, 22 May 2010, 12 June 2010

The Bhagavad-Gītā

The Macquarrie Dictionary, Revised Edition (Dee Why, NSW, Australia: Macquarrie Library, 1985)

Thompson, D'Arcy. *On Growth and Form* (Cambridge: Cambridge University Press, 1997 [first published 1961])

Williams, Bernard. *Truth and Truthfulness* (Princeton: Princeton University Press, 2002)

Wilson, Edward O. *The Social Conquest of Earth* (New York: Liveright Publishing Corporation, 2013)

Wolmersley, David (editor). *Edmund Burke: A Philosophical Enquiry into the Origin of our Ideas of the Sublime and the Beautiful and Other pre-Revolutionary Writings* (London: Penguin Books, 2004).

Wong, David. 'Relativism', in Peter Singer (editor): *A Companion to Ethics*

Wulf, Andrea. *The Invention of Nature: The Adventures of Alexander von Humboldt the Lost Hero of Science* (London: John Murray, 2015)

Yourgrau, Palle. *A World Without Time: The Forgotten Legacy of Gödel and Einstein* (New York: Basic Books, 2005)

Zalta, Edward N. (editor). *The Stanford Encyclopedia of Philosophy (Summer 2012 Edition)*

Index

www.ingramcontent.com/pod-product-compliance
Lightning Source LLC
Chambersburg PA
CBHW070801280326
41934CB00012B/3000